A Treatise On Vocal Physiology and Hygiene, with Especial Reference to the Cultivation and Preservation of the Voice - Primary Source Edition

Gordon Holmes

A TREATISE

ON

VOCAL PHYSIOLOGY AND HYGIENE

WITH ESPECIAL REFERENCE

TO THE

CULTIVATION AND PRESERVATION OF THE VOICE

BY

GORDON HOLMES, L.R.C.P. Edin.

PHYSICIAN TO THE MUNICIPAL THROAT AND EAR INFIRMARY; FORMERLY *CHEF-DE-CLINIQUE*
AT THE HOSPITAL FOR DISEASES OF THE THROAT; ETC.

SECOND EDITION, REVISED AND ENLARGED

LONDON

J. & A. CHURCHILL, NEW BURLINGTON STREET

1881

[The right of translation is reserved]

τοῦ καὶ ἀπὸ γλώσσης μέλιτος γλυκίων ῥέεν αὐδή.

———

ὄπα τε μεγάλην ἐκ στήθεος ἵει
καὶ ἔπεα νιφάδεσσιν ἐοικότα χειμερίῃσιν.

———

ἱμερόεν κιθάριζε· λίνον δ'ὑπὸ καλὸν ἄειδεν
λεπταλέῃ φωνῇ.

HOMER, *Iliad*, i. 249, iii. 221, xviii. 570.

(OF NESTOR.)

'Voice sweeter than honey flowed from his tongue."

(OF ULYSSES.)

'He sent forth a great voice from his breast and words like to the flakes of winter's snow."

(OF A YOUTH.)

"He played delightfully on the lyre, and sang to the melodious string with a clear voice."

PREFACE.

THE chief aim of this treatise is to furnish persons who make an artistic or professional use of the vocal organs with a concise, but complete, account of those scientific relations of the voice, physical and medical, which are generally only alluded to cursorily or passed over altogether in works on elocution and singing.

That physiological information is needed by, and of practical importance to, speakers and singers is, perhaps, sufficiently evident; but if any proof were required it might be found in the fact that some of the most careful researches into the action of the larynx have been made by teachers of singing—Garcia, Battaille, and Seiler, for instance.

I hope, also, as works on the physiology of voice-production and the hygienic aspects of vocal exercise are comparatively rare in English literature, and there is no recent systematic account of either subject, that some of the chapters in the present volume may be of interest to members of the medical profession.

The second edition has been carefully revised, and some additional matter and woodcuts have been introduced, tending to make the descriptions more intelligible.

G. H.

27A, FINSBURY SQUARE,
December, 1880.

CONTENTS.

———◦◦◦———

INTRODUCTION.

HISTORICAL REVIEW OF THE ORIGIN AND PROGRESS OF VOCAL CULTURE.

PAGE

ORIGIN OF LANGUAGE 2
  Mythical explanation — Various scientific theories —
  Sources of words, onomatopœia, etc.—Question as to com-
  mon origin of all languages, Leibniz and Max Müller.

ORIGIN OF SINGING 8
  Conception of Lucretius—Emotional impulses to singing
  —Its religious connections—Utility of singing in rude ages;
  evidence of Plutarch and Aristotle.

THE EGYPTIANS. 11
  Their civilization—Their knowledge of oratory, but dis-
  trust of rhetorical display—Their advance in music, but
  disregard of it as a serious pursuit—They had no drama.

THE GREEKS 15
  Their civilization chiefly derived from Egypt—Their
  oratory and voice-training: extravagancies of the Sophists:
  the *phonascus*, etc. — Their invention of the drama:
  peculiarities of vocal delivery in their theatres—Their
  devotion to music, but backwardness in its science and
  practice—Their medicine and hygiene of the voice.

PAGE

The Vocal Tube, or Resonance Apparatus 92
    The pharynx, mouth, and nasal passages—Use of the lower jaw.

The Tongue, Lips, and Teeth 94
    Great muscular mobility of the tongue and lips; they form, with the soft-palate, the active articulating organs: the teeth or fulcrum.

CHAPTER III.

PHYSICAL ACTION OF THE VOCAL ORGANS.

Action of the Air-Chamber (Respiration) 96
    Different modes of breathing; diaphragmatic, costal, and clavicular: breathing in the female—Complements of thoracic air; tidal air, vital capacity, residual air, and fixed air.

Action of the Vibrating Element (Vocal Reeds) 99
    Former confusion of ideas as to the formation of voice—Survey of principal pre-laryngoscopic theories: Hippocrates, Aristotle, Galen, Fabricius, Mersenne, Dodart, Ferrein, Cuvier, Dutrochet, Liscovius, Geoffroy St. Hilaire, Savart, Magendie, Malgaigne, Lehfeldt, Müller—The laryngoscope; Garcia and Czermak; its description—Action of the vocal reeds as observed with the laryngoscope: chest-register; falsetto-register—Action of the intrinsic laryngeal muscles in the different registers: doubtful questions: Oertel's observations: action of the extrinsic laryngeal muscles—Function of the ventricular bands.

The Resonance Apparatus (Vocal Tube) 126
    Use of the ventricles: their variations in different animals—The epiglottis: laryngoscopic observation of its movements in phonation; variability of shape and size; theories regarding its use; conclusions to be drawn from comparative anatomy—The pharynx: its alterations and influence on voice—The mouth: harmonious vocal timbre mainly due to its reinforcement of overtones—The nose: discordant tones produced in the nasal channels; their pernicious effect on voice—The soft-palate: its movements and directive functions over the laryngeal vibrations.

PAGE

COMPASS OF THE VOICE—INDIVIDUAL AND SEXUAL DIFFERENCES
—REGISTERS 136
 Bass, baritone, tenor, contralto, mezzo-soprano, soprano
—Tabular view—Conflicting theories as to registers.

ARTICULATING APPARATUS 142
 Nature of vowel-sounds and mechanism of their formation:
Kratzenstein, Kempelen, Willis, Wheatstone, Donders,
Helmholtz: difficulty of pronouncing vowels in certain
pitches of voice—Consonants: means of classifying,
acoustic and anatomical, division into breathed and voiced;
tabular view; remarks on formation of various letters.

CHAPTER IV.

PHYSIOLOGICAL PRINCIPLES OF VOCAL CULTURE.

The Subject Defined.

GENERAL CONSIDERATIONS 155
 Force, timbre, compass, execution—Mental, muscular,
and morphological influences — Proximate physiological
possibilities of voice-development—Importance of youth
and progressive adaptability of exercises to successful
training.

MANAGEMENT OF THE MOTOR ELEMENT (RESPIRATION) . . . 162
 Measure of breathing: necessity of imposing certain re-
strictions on the chest movements—Mode of breathing:
abdominal, costal, and clavicular types of respiration; their
comparative value in the artistic use of the voice—Vocal
gymnastics: principles for the elaboration of a course of
breathing-exercises.

MANAGEMENT OF THE VIBRATING ELEMENT 173
 Incompleteness of physiological data leaves much to
empiricism—Force, means of gaining an increment of—
Timbre, refinement of—Compass, practicability of extending in different registers—Execution, methods to increase
facility of.

PAGE

MANAGEMENT OF THE RESONANCE APPARATUS 181
  Faulty timbre : guttural and nasal qualities of voice—
  Enlarged tonsils and malposition of tongue—The soft-
  palate ; abnormal deficiency, incomplete action, and disuse
  of—Habitual closure of the teeth during phonation.

MANAGEMENT OF THE ARTICULATING APPARATUS 184
  Vowel timbre, means of modifying in relation to musical
  effect—Consonants : culture of executive faculty of tongue
  —Stammering and stuttering, or psellism, definition of :
  nature of stammering and mode of remedying : the
  pathology and treatment of stuttering, various theories
  advanced concerning ; Demosthenes, Itard, Leigh,
  McCormac, Serres, Arnott, Colombat, Berthold, Becquerel,
  Guillaume, Dieffenbach ; mechanical, gymnastic, and
  surgical methods : summary and conclusions : statistical
  estimate of the causes and frequency of stuttering.

CHAPTER V.

THE HYGIENE OF THE VOICE.

Scope of the Subject.

SPECIAL HYGIENE OF THE VOCAL ORGANS 202
  Direct results of local muscular activity : gains derived
  from judicious exercise : effects of over-exertion, effort, and
  strain : persistent fatigue of the voice : congestion leading
  to glandular sore-throat and laryngeal growths—Influence of aerial motion : emphysema : nasal breathing :
  oral inspiration : rules for speakers and singers while
  sustaining their part—Simple voice remedies with local
  action : sipping cold water : demulcent draughts : emollient substances : voice lozenges and nostrums for
  hoarseness.

GENERAL HYGIENE IN ITS RELATION TO THE VOICE 220
  Effects of regular vocal exercise on the animal economy :
  benefits to health by increase of thoracic capacity : degrees

of voice-production : ill-results of vocal efforts—Influences
of mode of life on the voice. Alimentation ; food, animal
and vegetable ; digestibility ; errors in diet causing
dyspepsia, resultant voice troubles ; inexpedience of vocal
exercise after eating ; corpulence ; its invariable association
with shortness of breath, physiological reasons of ; means
of combating obesity by diet : condiments, precautions to
be observed in the use of : tobacco, its effect on the
constitution and on the throat : drink ; tea, coffee, cocoa ;
alcohol, amount that may be taken habitually without
injury, deterioration of voice from excess of, harmfulness
of frequent small quantities. Exercise ; necessity of to
health, desirable daily extent of, training, etc. ; advisa-
bility of limited gesticulation in public speaking. Care of
the skin ; its functions and relations to respiration ; attention to clothing ; baths and bathing ; cosmetics. Climatic
influences : hot climates ; sea air ; miasma ; cold climates ;
cold and damp, their effects on the voice ; temperate climates,
their sudden variations ; mountain air.

APPENDIX.

I.   Galen on the Action of the Laryngeal Ventricles . 261
II.   Talking Machines 262
III.   The Vocal Powers of the Lower Animals 264

Index of Authors Referred to 269

Index of Subjects 273

LIST OF ILLUSTRATIONS.

PAGE

1. The cartilages of the larynx seen from behind . . . 84

2. Transverse vertical section of the larynx seen from behind 87

3 and 4. Diagrams of the intrinsic laryngeal muscles . . 90

5. Anatomical section, showing the relations of the organs of voice 95

6. Laryngoscopic appearance of the larynx during quiet breathing 116

7. Laryngoscopic appearance of the larynx when sounding a note about the level of the ordinary speaking voice 116

8. Laryngoscopic appearance of the larynx when emitting falsetto tones 119

9. Section of the laryngeal cartilages, showing how longitudinal tension of the vocal bands is effected 122

PLATO'S CONCEPTION OF SOUND AND AUDITION.

—◦◦◦—

Τρίτον δὲ αἰσθητικὸν ἐν ἡμῖν μέρος ἐπισκοποῦσι τὸ περὶ τὴν ακοὴν, δι' ἃς αἰτίας τὰ περὶ αὐτὸ ξυμβαίνει παθήματα λεκτέον. ὅλως μὲν οὖν φωνὴν θῶμεν τὴν δι' ὥτων ὑπ' ἀέρος ἐγκεφάλου τε καὶ αἵματος μέχρι ψυχῆς πληγὴν διαδιδομένην, τὴν δε ὑπ' αὐτῆς κίνησιν, ἀπὸ τῆς κεφαλῆς μὲν ἀρχομένην, τελευτῶσαν δὲ περὶ τὴν τοῦ ἥπατος ἔδραν, ἀκοήν· ὅση δ'αὐτῆς ταχεῖα, ὀξεῖαν, ὅση δὲ βραδυτέρα, βαρυτέραν· τὴν δὲ ὁμοίαν ὁμαλήν τε καὶ λείαν, τὴν δὲ ἐναντίαν τραχεῖαν· μεγάλην δὲ τὴν πολλήν, ὅση δὲ ἐναντία, σμικράν.—*Timæus*, c. 29 (67).

"A third department of our perceptions, that which concerns hearing and the causes in which this feeling arises, must now be spoken of to observers. We may certainly conclude that voice (sound) is a shock transmitted through the ears to the soul by the air, the brain, and the blood, and that the motion thereof, which begins in the head and ends in the region of the liver, is hearing. When this motion is swift, the sound is acute, when slow, grave. If the motion is regular, the sound is even and smooth, if the opposite, harsh. A great motion gives a loud sound, the opposite, a faint one."

See also Timæus Locri, *De Anima Mundi*, c. 12.

VOCAL PHYSIOLOGY AND HYGIENE

—◦•◦—

INTRODUCTION.

HISTORICAL REVIEW OF THE ORIGIN AND PROGRESS OF VOCAL CULTURE.

ORIGIN OF LANGUAGE — ORIGIN OF SINGING — THE
EGYPTIANS — THE GREEKS — THE ROMANS — THE
MIDDLE AGES — THE TWO FACULTIES OF VOICE:
SPEECH AND SONG.

THE importance of cultivating the vocal powers arises
from the dispensations of Nature herself, and is the
consequence, or perhaps the cause, of the physiological
constitution of mankind and the social conditions under
which they are impelled to live. Thus, it has been
observed that "man is man only by means of speech;
but in order to be able to form a language, he must
first be man."[1] One of the great, probably the
greatest of, barriers between man and the lower

---

[1] "Der Mensch ist nur Mensch durch Sprache; um aber die
Sprache zu erfinden, müsste er schon Mensch sein." W. von Humboldt's *Gesammelte Werke*, Berlin, 1841-46, Bd. iv. p. 252.

B

converse appears beyond a doubt.[1] And the power
of producing varied vocal sounds must have long
preceded even the rudest attempts at speech.   In
proportion, however, to his intellectual development,
from the use of one word man was led on to the
employment of several, and language was thus
gradually formed through the exertion of the organs
of voice under the guidance of those of hearing.[2]
By this theory, which seems to be a reversion to
the opinion long ago advanced by Lucretius[3] and
other philosophers of antiquity, language is assumed
to be a kind of a growth, which came gradually of itself
according as the continually increasing intelligence
and interdependence of mankind gave birth to the
necessity for a complex means of intercommunication.

---

[1] For instances of modern gesture language, see Lubbock, *Origin
of Civilization*, 3rd ed. ch. ix.

[2] The experiment of isolating two children from their birth in
order to see what language they would speak was made by Psam-
mitichus, King of Egypt, about 650 B.C.   After a time they articu-
lated the word *becos*, which in the Phrygian language meant
"bread."   The king concluded, therefore, that Phrygian was the
primitive language of the earth. —Herodotus, l. ii. c. 2.   Kavanagh
fancifully suggests that the first word used was O (to designate the
sun, the most striking of objects), because the mouth has somewhat
of the shape of this letter when forming the sound.   A transition
is thus obtained from a gesture to audible speech.—*Origin of Language and Myths*, 1871, vol. i. p. 4.

[3] " At varios linguæ sonitus natura subegit
        Mittere et utilitas expressit nomina rerum,
        Non alia longe ratione atque ipsa videtur
        Protrahere ad gestum pueros infantia linguæ
        Cum facit ut digito quæ sint præsentia monstrent."
                                —*De Rerum Natura*, l. v. 1028.
Further on Lucretius combats the idea that language could have been
an invention.

From this point of view the origin and development of language is an evolutionary problem to be worked out in a manner parallel with the other questions of the Darwinian hypothesis. But an intimate discussion of such transcendental propositions is beyond the scope of this treatise.

A clear exemplification of the paucity of words, as well as of ideas, in the infancy of civilization, may be discovered on examination of the languages used by savage nations at the present day. The Abipones, an aboriginal tribe of La Plata, have no word to signify God, nor such words as man, body, place, time, never, to be, etc. They are, moreover, unable to express in words any number beyond three. The Malay language is also so deficient that an attempt of the St. Petersburg Bible Society to translate the Lord's Prayer and the Ten Commandments into it resulted in an entire failure to produce intelligible sentences. Again, the Tasmanians had no general term for a tree, though they had a name for each species; nor could they express qualities, such as hard, soft, warm, cold, tall, short, round, etc. For " hard," they would say "like a stone;" for "tall," "long-legs;" and for "round," "like a ball," "like the moon," and so on.[1]

One of the difficulties with which philologists have to deal is to account for the source from which the first words uttered were drawn. Two principal explanations have been offered of this problem. The first theory, most ably advocated by Herder[2] in the last century, supposes that man's first words were

---

[1] Lubbock, *Prehistoric Times*, 3rd ed. p. 573, et seq.

[2] See Steinthal, *Der Ursprung der Sprache*. Berlin, 1858, p. 13.

formed in imitation of the sounds emitted by beasts and of the noises which everywhere strike the ear in Nature, such as the falling of water, the rushing of wind, the collision of hard bodies, etc. Many words have evidently arisen in this way, *e.g.*, cuckoo, crow, pee-wit, etc., and creak, crash, crack, splash, dash, purr, whizz, etc. The second theory affirms that the interjectional exclamations uttered by man almost involuntarily under the influence of various emotions became adopted as the first words used. In this way from Oh! Ah!, the instinctive cries of pain, we may derive such words as woe, wail, ache; from Ugh! ugly, huge; from Fie! fiend, foe, feud, foul, and so on in many other instances.[1] Although there is evidently much truth in both these methods of accounting for the origin of words, Max Müller thinks that the essential roots of language were not produced in this way, but by an instinctive and irresistible faculty of the human mind, which impelled it to give articulate expression to its conceptions.[2]

However man obtained his first stock of words, it is at least certain that he eventually to a great extent left off naming the objects which came under his notice in a strictly imitative manner. His later attempts at nomenclature were carried out by applying the words

[1] For a list of numerous words probably formed on these principles, see Lubbock, *Origin of Civilization*, 3rd ed. ch. ix.

[2] Op. cit. vol. i. p. 440. These two hypotheses as to the origin of words are called technically *onomatopœia* and the *interjectional* theory, though both may be included under the former term. In rejecting them Max Müller formerly stigmatized them as the "Bow-wow" and "Pooh-pooh" theories. Ibid. p. 407, et seq. They are now, however, more favourably received by this philologist.

he already possessed, either combined or separately, in such a manner as to describe or illustrate the most striking qualities of the things he wished to express by speech. Thus the horse might be named from its swiftness; the moon from its affording a means of measuring time by its periodic changes; wheat because it is the whitest of grain, etc.[1] But, in the lapse of ages words have been so altered by the omission of some letters and the softening or slurring of others, that they can seldom be traced back for any distance to the roots from whence they sprung. Thus in their constant passage through the vocal organs they have suffered a kind of attrition comparable to that which transforms the rough fragments of rock, after they have lain for centuries in a current of water, to the smooth, round pebbles of the river-bed or sea-shore.

For the common origin of all languages, which was believed in by Leibniz and which is still sustained by Max Müller,[2] there is considerable evidence. In various tongues, used by nations whose existences are separated by great distances of time and space, the similitude to be perceived between many of their words and forms of expression furnishes an absolute proof of their radical identity. As an example of this resemblance, the following sentence in Latin, Greek, and Sanscrit (the ancient language of the Hindus, which was dead prior to 300 B.C.) may be quoted :—

[1] Thus in Sanscrit, from the root *as*, to be sharp or swift, we have *asva*, the runner, the horse; and from a root *mâ*, to measure, *mâs*, the moon (the measurer). The relation of *wheat* to *white* is evident in our own language; see Müller, op. cit. vol. ii. p. 68, et seq., vol. i. p. 6.

[2] Op. cit. vol. i. p. 372.

Jovis mei pater genitor
Ζεὺς ἐμοῦ πατὴρ γενετήρ
Dyaús me petâ genitâ.[1]

This part of philological inquiry is intimately and apparently inseparably connected with the question as to the descent of the whole of mankind from a single pair of progenitors. But through the great number and wide diversity of races and languages these problems become so complex that no near approach to their solution has yet been made by the researches of science.

ORIGIN OF SINGING.

The pleasing poetical suggestion of Lucretius,[2] that man learned to sing by imitating the voices of birds, has a reflection in the conjectures of Herder as to the source of words. But singing must have come by an impulse as natural as that which produced speech, and as song is not necessarily connected with articulate pronunciation, it was probably the prior faculty of the two. Under the influence of joyful emotions, man, and even lower animals, are led to give vent to their feelings by the utterance of more or less varied and prolonged vocal sounds.[3] It

---

[1] Meaning "God my father (and) creator." Müller, *Comparative Mythology : Oxford Essays*, 1856, p. 14.

[2] "At liquidas avium voces imitarier ore
Ante fuit multo, quam lævia carmina cantu
Concelebrare homines possent, aureisque juvare."
—Op. cit. l. v. 1378.

[3] See Darwin, *The Expression of the Emotions in Man and Animals*, ch. iv. ; also Spencer, *The Origin and Function of Music*, in *Essays, Scientific, Political, and Speculative*, vol. i. p. 210.

seems likely therefore that the human vocal organs were first systematically exercised, and possibly to a great extent prepared for the more definite action required by spoken language, in the practice, on occasions, of crude, though not altogether meaningless, phrases of vocal melody.

At a later period, after language had come into general use, the mind would be awakened to the conception of a God, and the rationalism of endeavouring to gain his favour by some form of worship. And the propriety of addressing him in a manner more exalted than by the tones employed in ordinary converse would soon lead to the adoption of singing as an integral part of the religious ceremonial. The rudest races are led to sing as the most natural means of expressing their devotion. Thus the ancient Germans, before they had a written language, celebrated in song the praises of their gods Teuton and Mannus.[1] On the same principle, in ancient Greece, the oracles of Apollo were delivered in song and unpremeditated verse by the first priestesses at Delphi. And when they afterwards lost this improvisatory faculty, in order to render properly impressive the answers of the god, a company of prophets surrounded the Pythia to receive her inspirations and convert them into hexameter verse before they were communicated to those who had come to ask the will of Zeus.[2]

In the infancy of civilization not only is singing an emotional resource, but it sometimes becomes of practical utility. Before the invention of letters,

[1] Tacitus, *De Moribus et Populis Germaniæ*, 2, 19.
[2] Plutarch, *De Pythiæ Oraculis*, 22, 25.

without the aid of writing to register any matter of importance, memory unaided must often fail to fulfil its part with the necessary exactitude. Under these circumstances.the greatest aids are to be found in song and verse. By means of the impressive intonation and rhythmic nature of song and the measured feet of verse, sentences and even lengthy compositions may most easily be fixed on the minds of an audience and, by occasional repetition, retained with but slight alteration in the memory of successive generations. " Time was indeed," says Plutarch,[1] " when, in order to give a mark of authority to anything spoken, men made use of metre, verse, and song, setting to poetry and music all history, philosophy, and in fact any event that required to be announced in an impressive manner." For this reason primitive nations have resorted to the expedient of singing their laws, and hence kept up such a custom even after they had a written language.[2] By the same means the Homeric poems were preserved for nearly three centuries before Pisistratus collected and committed them to writing.

So far the matters dealt with have been mainly theoretical and speculative. I will now endeavour to portray briefly the state of vocal culture amongst the leading nations of antiquity—viz., the Egyptians, Greeks, and Romans—in mediæval times, and in the earlier part of the present age. In most instances, however, no definite accounts of the systems of voice-training remain to us, although there is proof that

[1] Loc. cit. 24.
[2] Aristotle, *Problemata*, s. xix. 15, 28.

the teaching and practice were elaborate. Our ideas of the subject must therefore be drawn generally from a consideration of forensic, histrionic, and musical achievements.

THE EGYPTIANS.

The monumental evidences of the valley of the Nile form the earliest series of authentic records which link our history with the civilization of the remote past. From these pictorial and hieroglyphic chronicles an intimate view is obtained into the political and private life of the Egyptians some four or five thousand years before the Christian era.[1] At that early period this nation had already attained a high degree of social refinement. They ascribed their origin to the Earth,[2] their civilization to Osiris,[3] and the beginning of their literature to Thoth, who was " Lord of the Divine Words " and the " Scribe of Truth "[4] in their religious system. The latter deity taught men to speak distinctly and articulately, invented letters, gave names to many things, and was the god of eloquence and music.[5] At a later period a second Hermes, great in the domain of letters, arose and was deified. He was surnamed Trismegistus, or the Thrice-Great, and with

---

[1] See Wilkinson, *Manners and Customs of the Ancient Egyptians*, 1847, vol. i. ch. 2; Bunsen, *Egypt's Place in Universal History*, vol. i. 1868, pp. xxx. 35; and Lepsius, *Die Chronologie der Ægypter*, Th. i. 1849, passim.

[2] Diodorus Siculus, l. i. 10.

[3] Ibid. 15, 17, 18, etc.

[4] Bunsen, op. cit. vol. i. p. 393.

[5] Diod. Sic. l. i. 16. Plato, *Philebus*, 8; *Phædrus*, 59.

him the initial character of Thoth ultimately coalesced, through a similarity in their legendary attributes. Trismegistus was the author of numerous works on science, amongst them a volume of hymns to the gods and of rules for the conduct of monarchs, which were considered sacred and always borne by a band of singers in front of the religious processions of the Egyptians.[1]

Their Ideas of Oratory.

Whether the ancient Egyptians cultivated rhetoric as an art is uncertain, but that they were acquainted with the power of oratory is shown by the manner in which trials were conducted before their judges. The arch-judge, having the image of Truth suspended from his neck and the eight books of the laws of the nation before him, took his seat in a court of thirty inferior judges and the trial began. The plaintiff made a written statement of his case, setting forth his injury and the amount of his damage. The defendant then read what was written, and in writing made his reply. A second written explanation on each side followed, and the documents were then submitted to the judges. When they had deliberated, the arch-judge pointed with the image of Truth towards him whose cause was determined to be just, and the case was over. This method of procedure was adopted because they believed that by the

[1] Clemens Alexandrinus, *Stromateis*, l. vi. In Migne's *Patrologia*, Ser. Græc. vol. ix. col. 253.

harangues of lawyers and the arts of oratory a veil was often cast over the truth, whilst, on the other hand, the passionate pleading of the parties in the suit might excite the pity of the judges, and cause their decision to swerve from the strict line of justice.[1]

Their Advance in Music.

That the Egyptians had made considerable advances in the science and practice of music is proved by the discovery of paintings and portions of harps with from ten to twenty strings, and also of a kind of guitar adapted to produce many tones of different pitch with the limited number of three strings.[2] They were acquainted with the triple harmonies, viz., the harmony of voices, of instruments, and of voices and instruments. The sculptures attest the frequency and popularity of vocal and instrumental performances. Sacred music was studied by the priests. With respect, however, to the place held by music in the education of the youth of the higher classes there is some uncertainty, because an apparent discrepancy exists in the statements made on this point by Diodorus the Sicilian,[3] and by Plato.[4] The historian says that the Egyptian youth were not taught music, as it was considered not only useless, but noxious, and likely to render effeminate the minds of those who listened to it.

[1] Diodorus Siculus, l. i. 75, 76.
[2] See Wilkinson, op. cit. vol. ii. p. 222, et seq.
[3] L. i. 81.
[4] *Leges*, l. ii. p. 656, *d*.

The philosopher, who spent some years studying in Egypt, describes the stringency of the laws relating to the fine arts, which prohibited that any painting, statuary, or music, should be allowed in the assemblies of young people but such as had been legally determined to be of the highest excellence. For this reason, at an early period, fixed types were established in painting, sculpture, and music, from which no departure in the shape of innovations or inventions by later artists was permitted. The inclusion of music in such special enactments shows that it was regarded as a very important art by the State. It seems likely, however, that Egyptian children were not actually taught to sing or to play on any instrument as the part of a liberal education, though they might have learned the rudiments of musical science.[1] Persons of rank did not, like the Greeks, learn music in order to play in society, and at feasts hired musicians were always employed.[2] The practice of music was therefore considered as strictly a profession, but of a lower class,[3] with which amateurs did not meddle. Popular songs there were, of course, such as "Maneros," mentioned by Herodotus.[4] On festival occasions also, general choruses were sung, as, for instance, during the procession to

[1] Wilkinson (op. cit. vol. ii. p. 224) in a quotation evidently transferred from Burney (*History of Music*, vol. i. p. 204) represents Strabo as saying that "Egyptian children were taught letters, the songs appointed by law, and a certain kind of music." Neither author gives an exact reference to the passage (l. x. c. iv. s. 20), from which it may be seen that the geographer is dealing with the institutions of the Cretans and not with those of the Egyptians.

[2] Ibid. p. 241.   [3] Fétis, *Histoire de la Musique*, tom. i. p. 200.
[4] L. ii. c. 79.

Busiris in honour of Isis, when numbers of men and women sailed up the Nile in boats. During the whole voyage one portion of the company kept up a constant singing, whilst the rest played with flutes and castanets.[1]

Notwithstanding the versatility of the Egyptians, and their knowledge of various arts and sciences, nothing at all resembling dramatic representation was ever practised amongst them.[2]

THE GREEKS.

Their Relations with Egypt.—In early Grecian ethnology the most dominant element appears to have been an obscure race, named Pelasgians.[3] Mythically, this people were represented as *autochthonous*, or earth-born, and to have built the city of Argos, considered the most ancient in Greece.[4] Pelasgians, however, are mentioned by Greek authors as dwelling in various other countries besides Greece which had a sea-board on the Mediterranean, such as in Italy,[5] Crete,[6] and Asia Minor.[7] It seems most probable that they were a migratory nation, which travelled in large parties into many countries, and obtained a footing amongst the indigenous inhabitants wherever they went

---

[1] Ibid. c. 59, 60.
[2] Wilkinson, op. cit. vol. ii. p. 259.
[3] See Grote, *History of Greece*, vol. ii. p. 44, et seq.
[4] Pausanias, l. i. 14.
[5] Dionysius of Halicarnassus, l. i. 17, et seq.
[6] Strabo, l. v. c. ii. s. 4.
[7] Homer, *Iliad*, x. 429.

through the possession of superior intelligence and prowess.

Egypt, as the eldest of the countries bordering on the Mediterranean, acted as a fountain of civilization for the nations of the proximate shores, who long regarded her with veneration as an inexhaustible repository of all the arts and sciences in a state of the highest perfection.[1]   Whatever may have been the social condition of the Greeks before the arrival of the Pelasgians, there is little doubt that the advent of the new-comers was attended by a considerable advance in scientific and artistic knowledge.   Herodotus[2] tells us that the Pelasgians introduced Egyptian rites into Greece,[3] and it has been proved beyond dispute, by the archæological labours of Schlieman[4] at Mycenæ and Tiryns, that in the heroic age Egypt was a fruitful source of every kind of knowledge to the Greeks.   Tradition also asserted that the city of Athens was founded in B.C. 1556 by Cecrops, a native of Sais in Egypt, who led a band of his countrymen into Attica.[5]   Even after Greece had emerged from the darkness of mythical times into the broad daylight of a systematic history, her men of letters, amongst them Pythagoras, Plato, and Euripides, made a practice of visiting Egypt to increase their knowledge of science and art.   But the Greeks, the

[1] See Homer, *Odyssey*, l. iv. 229.

[2] L. ii. 51 ; vi. 137.

[3] See Gladstone, *Studies on Homer*, vol. i. p. 148.

[4] *Mycenæ : a Narrative of Researches and Discoveries at Mycenæ and Tiryns*, 1878.   The author shows the identity of the Greek Hera ("Βοῶπις πότνια Ἥρη" of Homer, *Iliad*, i. 568 ; iv. 50, et passim) with the Egyptian cow-headed goddess Isis ; pp. 9, 216.   Numerous specimens of Egyptian glass, porcelain, etc., were found ; pp. 157, 242, 330.

[5] Diodorus Siculus, l. i. 28.

varied and impressive scenery of whose country displayed nature under a more æsthetic aspect than the sandy plains and sun-dried flats of Egypt, soon outstripped their masters in all matters of taste, and their fine arts, with the exception perhaps of music, rapidly attained an excellence which has not since been surpassed.

The Greek Hermes, the " Interpreter," was considered to be identical with the Egyptian Thoth,[1] and was looked on as the god of skilful speech or eloquence and the inventor of music. He it was who first constructed a lyre and sang to it with his voice, but he immediately resigned his invention to Apollo, who afterwards became the chief patron of the fine arts and leader of the muses.[2]

Their Oratory and Voice-Training.

In ancient Greece the city of Athens became the centre of learning and refinement, and at one time or another reckoned amongst her inhabitants all who were most celebrated as statesmen, philosophers, poets, painters, and statuaries. Her political institutions were of such a liberal character that the highest offices in the State were open to any of her citizens who could prove themselves by deed or by word best fitted for the duties of government. He who could command the most eloquent and persuasive language had the favour of the people in their assemblies,

---

[1] Cicero, *De Natura Deorum*, l. iii. 22 ; Herodotus, l. ii. 138.
[2] Homer, *Hymnus in Mercurium*, 420 ; *Iliad*, i. 603.

C

and hence rhetoric flourished and was assiduously studied as an art. The Athenian orators attained to such eminence that it is scarcely hyperbolical to say that the echoes of their voices have not yet died out; for the names of Isocrates, Pericles, Demosthenes, and Æschines, are almost as familiar to modern ears as those of the chief statesmen of the present day.

At Athens there were many schools of rhetoric, and the extant treatise of Aristotle proves how systematic was the cultivation of oratory. Many of the schools were presided over by the class of philosophers called Sophists, such as Gorgias and Protagoras, who afterwards fell into disrepute on account of the superficiality, artifice, and falsity of their teaching.[1] The diction and delivery of the Sophists was characterized by an extreme amount of affectation. They tried to subdue their voices to an almost feminine blandness, and introduced such a variety of intonation into their sentences that their speech most resembled a song.[2] All the abler rhe-

---

[1] See Plato's *Gorgias* and *Protagoras*, and Grote, *History of Greece*, vol. vi. p. 53.

[2] Plutarch, *De Audiendo*, c. 7. Philostratus, *in Vitis Sophistarum*, edited by Kayser. This scholar has diligently collected and formed into a continuous account the various scattered facts relating to the training of the Sophists found in the Lives of Philostratus. In his *præfatio* he describes the minutiæ of the process of education to which youths intended for the profession of Sophist were subjected for several years from boyhood; how their taste was cultivated by study of the best authors; how their judgment was exercised by critical debates and the composition of written dissertations; how their manner in delivery was trained to the exhibition of every kind of emotion, not only by technical practice, but by actual observation

toricians and many of the public disapproved of their
style, which was the frequent aim of satire.[1] In one
instance, however, it is related that a Sophist, named
Pollux,[2] having to deliver an oration before the
dissolute Commodus, so charmed the audience with
his mellifluous tones that the emperor at once
appointed him chief rhetorician at Athens. But
Antoninus immediately silenced Philiscus,[3] an orator
of the same class, and refused to remit his taxes, when
he commenced to address him with an effeminate
modulation of voice.

To the school of the Sophists doubtless belonged
those Greek advocates who treated their vocal organs
with such devotion and delicacy that, as Cicero[4]
observes, they became slaves to their voice. They
passed whole years in sedentary declamation, and
before rising to speak on each occasion commenced
gradually to sound their voice. On sitting down
again after pleading they still continued to emit
tones, leading their voice down from the highest to
the lowest pitch, and, as it were, collecting it into
a state of repose by passing it through a scale.

---

of the habits of mankind; and how their powers of memory were
developed by incessant and laborious exercises. Kayser shows
further that even the mature Sophist still submitted himself to a
severe discipline in order to preserve the readiness of his faculties,
and supplemented his public work by an arduous solitary practice of
his art.

[1] Lucian, *Pseudologista.* Aristophanes, *Nubes.*

[2] Philostratus, op. cit. l. ii. 12, p. 258.

[3] Ibid. 30.

[4] *De Oratore*, l. i. c. 59. Compare Martianus Capella, *De Rhetorica*,
circa finem.

The most celebrated schools of rhetoric were those of Isocrates and Aristotle. Isocrates, finding himself disqualified by a nervous disposition for the duties of a public speaker,[1] confined himself to teaching the elements of his art,[2] and writing orations to be delivered by others. He bestowed an immensity of care on the composition of his written speeches, as is shown by the fact that he spent more than ten years in elaborating and polishing his Panegyric oration.[3] His style was artificial and figurative, and his great aim smoothness of diction[4] and artistic gesture.[5] Hence we may infer that the principal matters he taught his pupils were the construction of mellifluous sentences, and the introduction of pleasing tropes and amplifications as well as a graceful method of gesticulation during delivery. Though a pupil of Gorgias, and deeply imbued with some of the principles of the Sophists, he was opposed to their worst extravagances.[6]

The rhetorical teaching of Aristotle was nearly the opposite of that of Isocrates, and was directed mostly towards inculcating the principles of truth with logical disputation and forcible argument. The

---

[1] Plutarch, in *Vitis Decem Oratorum*, sub *Isocrate*, c. 29, et seq.

[2] His class reached to the number of 100 pupils, each of whom paid him 1,000 drachmæ (about £40) for his course of instruction.

[3] Longinus, *De Sublimitate*, c. 4. It was observed that Alexander conquered all Asia in a less time than it took Isocrates to compose his Panegyric oration on the Persian war.

[4] Ibid. c. **xxi. xxxviii.**

[5] Cicero, *Tusculanæ Disputationes*, l. i. c. iv.

[6] See Dionysius of Halicarnassus, *De Veteribus Rhetoribus Observationes*, sub *Isocrate*.

works of the great philosopher are too well known, however, to require any further comment here.

Distinct from the duties of the rhetoricians were those of a functionary termed the *phonascus*[1] or voice-trainer. The sphere of this professional seems to have extended to the cultivation of the voice both for speech and song,[2] but from a purely physical point of view. It is probable, indeed, that all respectable youths took lessons from such a master, as the Athenians were excessively attentive to accent and tone of voice, and altered the 'ss' to 'tt' in their words, from a dislike to the hissing sound of the former.[3] The *phonascus* taught his pupils the most refined mode of pronunciation, the proper modulations and inflections of the voice,[4] and superintended classes[5] in the daily practice of systematic exercises.[6] Such exercises were undertaken in the morning when fasting, as a belief prevailed that the voice would be injured if exerted

---

[1] Φωνασκὸς (see Stephanus, *Thesaurus Linguæ Grecæ, s. v.*), literally "one who practises the voice." Hence the word was often used as almost equivalent to "vocalist." *Phonasci* are defined by Galen as "singers to the *kithara*, public criers, and actors in tragedy and comedy:" *De Compositione Pharmacorum Secundum Locos*, l. vii. c. i. In this sense it was most commonly employed by later authors, *e.g.*, Quintilian, l. xi. c. iii. 23; Paulus Ægineta, *De Re Medica*, l. iii. c. 28.

[2] Quintilian, l. xi c. iii. 19.

[3] See Lucian, *Judicium Vocalium*. They called persons with a rough voice κυκλοβόροι, from a waterfall near Athens. Aristophanes, *Acharnians*, 381; *Equites*, 137, etc.

[4] Suetonius, *in Vita Augusti*, c. 84.

[5]   "Phonascus—
Instructas docuit sonare classes."
         —Sidonius Apollinaris, l. iv. 11.

[6] Called ἀναφωνήσεις, or *vociferationes*, Galen, *De Sanitato Tuenda*, vol. vi. p. 155. Demosthenes, pp. 449, 14; 328, 11.

after eating.[1]   The object of the voice-practice was to soften the natural asperities of the vocal organs,[2] or to strengthen the chest and throat by reciting or singing verses to a kind of scale.[3]   The pupils were required to have their verses, preferably epic or iambic, off by heart, and manuals containing extracts suitable for the purpose were published.[4]   When about to recite, they commenced gradually by repeating detached sentences of the verses at short intervals, during which they walked about.   Afterwards they proceeded to declamation or vociferation, as it was called, at first on the bass notes, making the voice descend as low as possible.   Then the tones were raised in a measured manner until the highest pitch was reached, whence a gradual descent was made back again to the gravest notes.[5]   For a singing exercise the practice must have been very similar, but the chief efforts appear to have been put forth in order to reach and sustain high notes.[6]

[1] Aristotle, *Problemata*, c. xi. 22.   Compare the following statement of Oribasius (l. i. c. 5): "The voice must not be exercised when great and evident crudities of the stomach are present, lest corrupt vapours be distributed largely through the body."

[2] Alexander Aphrodisiensis, *Problemata*, l. i. 119.

[3] Antyllus apud Oribasium, l. vi. c. 8, 9, et seq.

[4] Diogenes Laertius, l. ii. s. 103, *in Vita Aristippi.*

[5] Antyllus (loc. cit.) states that after long experience he has found exercise of the voice in this manner most healthful and conducive to the well-being of the body.   Cœlius Aurelianus (*De Morbis Chronicis*, l. i. c. 1, 5 ; l. ii. c. 6) also recommends declamation under a master (*adhibito præceptore*) as a valuable sanitary exercise in various diseases.   Several other ancient physicians give similar advice.   For further information on the subject see Hieronymus Mercurialis, *De Arte Gymnastica*, l. iii. c. 7; l. vi. c. 5.

[6] Antyllus (loc. cit. c. v.) warns those who resort to declamation as a sanitary exercise against forcing the voice on the high notes.

As public contests were held at which a prize was awarded to him who could best recite the poems of Homer or other compositions, a great rivalry was established in the matter of declamation.[1] Such trials took place in the open air, during the Pythian games,[2] for instance, and hence one of the principal endeavours was probably to be heard clearly at a considerable distance. In like manner the immense size of the theatres, their general acoustic arrangements, and the device of the masks that were worn, would make it necessary that the actors should deliver their speeches with as great a volume of sound as possible. From such causes the spirit of emulation would incite the performers to practise declamation vigorously and incessantly, and even to carry their efforts to a dangerous excess. Thus we find Plutarch[3] warning his disciples against indulging in violent vociferation, by which the voice is forced and strained to an extraordinary extent, for fear of such calamitous consequences as ruptures and convulsions. That even the orators were not free from the vanity of making an exhibition of a tremendous voice-power appears from the incident related of Carneades.[4] This philosopher used to address his class in the public gymnasium, and often spoke so vehemently, that at length the manager of the hall was obliged to remonstrate with him. Upon which Carneades retorted,

[1] Plato, *Io.* c. 1, et passim.
[2] Plutarch, *Symposium*, l. i. q. iv. 1.
[3] *De Tuenda Sanitate*, c. 16.
[4] Diogenes Laertius, *in Vita.*

an eager contest took place, in order to obtain the best chorus-master.[1]

The greatest pains were taken to ensure a perfect uniformity in voice and action between the different members of the chorus, so that even if one of them was found to sing more powerfully and beautifully than the others he was at once separated from them.[2] The chorus-master accompanied his chorus into the theatre, where he filled the part of *coryphœus*, or leader in the songs and dances.[3]

Their Music.

Singing was a popular and much practised art amongst the Greeks as early as the time of Homer,[4] who describes the virgins that ministered in the temple of Apollo at Delos as having the power to ravish those who listened to them by the sweetness of their voices and versatile faculties of song.[5] But although the Greeks at every period of their history were passionately fond of all kinds of music, there is

---

[1] Demosthenes, *in Midiam*, c. 17.
[2] Aristotle, *Politica*, l. iii. c. 8.
[3] Scholiast in Demosthenis, loc. cit.   Aristotle, *De Mundo*, c. vi.
[4] About 850 B.C.

[5] Κοῦραι Δηλιάδες—
ὕμνον ἀείδουσιν, θέλγουσι δὲ φῦλ' ἀνθρώπων.
Πάντων δ' ἀνθρώπων φωνὰς καὶ κρεμβαλιαστὺν
μιμεῖσθ' ἴσασιν· φαίη δέ κεν αὐτὸς ἕκαστος
φθέγγεσθ'· οὕτω σφιν καλὴ συνάρηρεν ἀοιδή.
    —*Hymnus in Apollinem*, 157—164.

nothing in their extant treatises on the art, or in the fragments of their melodies, which are preserved, to indicate that they had attained such a proficiency in composition as would make their performances agreeable to modern ears.[1] Both Plato[2] and Aristotle,[3] in their philosophical works, devote much time to considering the position that music should hold in the education of youth. Plato especially inculcates the principle that young men should be taught to sing to the lyre in order that their voice and ear may be refined by cultivating the clear and precise perception of sounds that is demanded when learning to render tone for tone. It was absolutely essential that every one who had the entry of good Athenian society should have some practical knowledge of singing or playing on an instrument. As Cicero[4] observes, the Greeks thought that the highest amount of culture was displayed in the graceful performance of vocal or instrumental music. Thus we find that such leaders as Alcibiades[5] and Epaminondas[6] are recorded for the possession of considerable skill in singing to the lyre, whilst Themistocles,[7] in the early part of his career, having declined the lyre when it was handed to him at a banquet, was set down as a person of rude manners.

---

[1] See Burney, *General History of Music*, vol. i.

[2] *Leges*, l. vii. 895.

[3] *Politica*, l. viii.

[4] *Tusculanæ Disputationes*, l. i. c. 1.

[5] Plutarch, *in Vita*.

[6] Cicero, loc. cit.

[7] Ibid. On the high estimation in which the Greeks held music, see Quintilian, l. i. c. x.

The most applauded display of vocal power consisted in singing a class of songs called *orthian*. They were composed only of high notes, and had to be sung with great vigour and intensity. Hence very few could sing them.[1]

Modern musicians are generally agreed that the Greeks had no knowledge of counterpoint, so that in singing or playing in concert they only made use of notes in unison or octaves, and never practised any kind of bass accompaniment. Moreover, the scale employed in the best period of Greek music did not extend beyond eight or ten notes. As they failed to invent a simple and systematic musical notation, their melodies have not been transmitted to us, with the exception of a few fragments which scarcely suffice as a representative sample. These fragments have, however, been reduced to modern notation with considerable precision, and are evidently crude productions, which possess little merit according to our conception of melody.[2] Viewing these imperfections of Greek music, the question may arise whether those who practised it were as liberally endowed with the natural gifts of voice and ear as the moderns. From physiological analogy, no doubt can exist that the Greeks had all the power and executive faculty of voice to sing the most difficult compositions of recent masters, just as they must have had the manual dexterity necessary to perform

---

[1] Aristotle, *Problemata*, s. xix. 37.

[2] See Burney, op. cit. vol. i. p. 89; and Chappell, *History of Music*, ch. viii.

the most rapid and intricate of our instrumental pieces. Similarly, as regards aural appreciation of sound, the quality of their senses in this respect must have been as delicate as it was in other departments of artistic taste, *i.e.,* in poetry, painting, sculpture, etc. There was no deficiency of animal constitution, mental or physical, revealed in the character of Greek music, but an incomplete knowledge of acoustic principles and of the full variety of phases in which sound can gratify the susceptibilities of the organ of hearing. It may seem strange that the Greeks did not attain the same perfection in music as in other fine arts, but our surprise will be lessened if we consider that poetry, painting, and sculpture consist essentially in a faithful imitation of the beautiful in nature, of which the type is everywhere present, whilst the advancement of music more resembles that of experimental physics and is dependent on discoveries which, although they may sometimes be made early by accident, are more often the result of patient investigation and step-by-step progress through a lengthened period of time.

Their Medicine and Hygiene of the Voice.

Not only did the Greeks cultivate the greatest suavity and smoothness of voice by mechanical exercises, but they also had recourse to bathing the mouth and fauces with various emollient potions or medicaments. This practice appears to have been mainly adopted by the Sophists who, whilst speaking, were often accompanied by a servant bearing a flask of demulcent liquid at which they sipped from time to time.[1]   The chief ingredient in these draughts was tragacanth.[2]   Even lawyers resorted to *plasmata*,[3] as they were often termed, in order to soften and sustain their voices whilst pleading.   Some simply took sips of warm water[4] for the purpose, whilst others imbibed a vinous *plasma*.[5]   It was probably a constant custom with singers and actors to drink bland and medicated fluids for the benefit of their voices.   Hence, at a later period, we find St. Jerome[6] accusing certain of the church choirs of bedewing their mouths and throats with sweet medicaments as if they belonged to a theatrical company.   One instance is on record of a member of the dramatic chorus who poisoned himself with a potion taken to improve his vocal powers.[7]   Onions and garlic were considered beneficial to the vocal organs, but

---

[1] Synesius, in Dion, c. 11.   In Migne's *Patrologiæ Cursus Completus*, Ser. Græc. vol. lxvi. col. 1149.

[2] Ibid.

[3] " .   .   . liquido cum plasmate guttur
      Mobile collueris."

—Persius, *Sat.* i. 17.

[4] "At tu multa diu dicis, vitreisque tepentem
      Ampullis potas semisupinus aquam."

—Martial, l. vi. ep. 35.

[5] "Chodanasar capiens plasma vinum;" Hieronymus (Jerome), *Quæstiones in Puralipomenon*, ii. c. xxxvi. 10.   In Migne, op. cit. Ser. Lat. vol. xxiii. col. 1402.

[6] *Commentaria in Epistolam ad Ephesios*, c. v. 19.   In Migne, op. cit. vol. xxvi. col. 528.

[7] Antiphon, *Oratio de Choreuta*.

perhaps the greatest virtues of this kind were attributed to the leek, from which the voice was said to obtain a singular brilliancy.[1] Singers thought they derived great advantage from partaking of leguminous vegetables or pulse, whence they were often familiarly spoken of as "bean-eaters."[2] All kinds of firm-fleshed fish and eels were considered to assist the vocal powers.[3] Yolk of egg was taken for roughness of the fauces.[4] A kind of berry, called *carpesium*, probably cubebs, if held in the mouth was believed to confer clearness of voice and distinctness of pronunciation, wherefore some eminent orators never spoke without it.[5] The property of rendering the voice sonorous was attributed to the waters of a fountain near Zama, and to those of another in the island of Ceos the opposite quality.[6] The Greek physicians had many prescriptions for *arteriacæ*, as they termed combinations and preparations of herbs and drugs, which they conceived would act on the air-passages in such a way as to render the voice clear and tuneful. The ingredients were mostly of a gummy, resinous, saccharine, or oily nature, such as Arabic gum, tragacanth, extract of pine cones,

[1] Aristotle, *Problemata*, s. xi. 39. Plinius Secundus, l. xix. 6 (33) ; l. xx. 6 (21).

[2] Isidorus, *De Ecclesiasticis Officiis*, l. ii. 12. In Migne, op. cit. vol. lxxxiii. col. 792. Rabanus Maurus, *De Institutione Clericorum*, l. ii. 48. Ibid. vol. cvii. col. 362.

[3] Clearchus apud Athenæum, l. xiv. c. 19.

[4] Beroaldus, *Commentarius ad Suetonium*, Lugduni, 1548, *in Nerone*, p. 533.

[5] Hermolaus Barbarus, *Corollaria in Dioscoridem*, l. iv. 759.

[6] Plinius Secundus, l. xxxi. c. 12. Vitruvius, l. viii. c. 4.

honey, liquorice, oil of sweet almonds, thyme oil, linseed, etc.[1]

On the other hand, certain substances were considered injurious to the voice, and were avoided by those who were anxious as to the condition of their throat. Many kinds of fruit were believed to render the voice husky. Figs, especially, were thought to be extremely noxious, particularly if eaten in the middle of the day.[2] The Greeks were excessively fond of figs, and it was popularly supposed that by merely abstaining from them a fine voice might be secured. Thus an instance is related of a man who became an eminent actor through not having touched a fig for eighteen years.[3] Apples,[4] pears, and

[1] Most of these *arteriacæ*, or voice prescriptions, were composed of the class of drugs now called *expectorants*, and were given in coughs and colds, etc. They were generally very complex, often containing twenty or thirty different things. One or two samples of the more simple may be given here, 1. Take: of pure myrrh, 24 parts; tragacanth, 28 parts; liquorice root, 18 parts; resin of turpentine (probably Chian turpentine), 18 parts: the whole to be mixed together and made into pills, *secundum artem*, the size of a bean (about 5 grains each)— Scribonius Largus, *De Compositione Medicamentorum*, c. 75. 2. Take: of pine nuts, almonds, white poppy seeds, each 80 grains; of cinnamon, cloves, liquorice juice, tragacanth, ginger, gum arabic, starch, seeds of gourd, cucumber, pumpkin, and lemon, each 60 grains; bitumen, 20 grains; syrup of violets, 180 grains; add a pint of water, some sugar, and make into a mixture the consistency of honey; a tablespoonful for a dose—Nicolaus Myrepsus, *De Antidotis*, c. 97. Horehound was a favourite voice remedy, and one *nostrum* of which it is the chief article was believed to have been devised by St. Peter— Ibid. c. 90. For a treatise on *arteriacæ*, see the seventh book of Galen's *De Compositione Pharmacorum Secundum Locos*.

[2] Athenæus, l. iii. 18, 19.

[3] Ibid.

[4] Suetonius, *in Nerone*, c. 20.

nuts,[1] were regarded as destructive to the sweetness
of the voice.   Cold drinks were studiously avoided.[2]
Singers and speakers were also very attentive to
their mode of life, avoiding all excesses in eating
and drinking, taking systematic exercise[3] and promoting in every way the purest tone of mental and
bodily health.[4]

THE ROMANS.

Their Relations with Greece.—Before the foundation of the city of Rome, about 750 B.C., central
Italy was inhabited by a number of diverse races
whose former existence is now symbolized by the
survival of such names as Umbrians, Oscans, Sabel-
lians, Etruscans, Latins, or more collectively Tyrrhenians.   The Tyrrhenians were probably Pelasgians,[5]
who played the same part in the early civilization
of Italy as in that of Greece by importing the
germs of her arts and sciences from the more
advanced nations of Egypt and Asia Minor.   In

---

[1] Athenæus, l. ii. 42.

[2] Cicero, *De Oratore*, l. ii. 70.

[3] Martianus Capella, loc. cit.

[4] "Itaque scribit Aristoteles (lib. 7, *De Animal.*), cantores absti-
nere solitos a Veneris obscænitate, ut diutius sine ulla mutatione
vocem retinere possent suavem et canoram, quæ flagitio corrumpe-
retur. Et Caluus orator plumbeos laminas de nocte adhibebat corpori
ad cohibendos libidinum sensus et ludificationes, quæ in somno con-
tingerent, quo vegetior deinde laborem studiorum et dicendi conten-
tionem sustineret." Cresollius, *Vacationes Autumnales*, Lutetiæ
Parisiis, 1620, l. iii. c. 11.

[5] See Lepsius, *Ueber Tyrrhenische-Pelasger in Etrurien.* Leipzig,
1842. Donaldson, *Varronianus*, ch. i. s. 9, 10, etc.

support of this view the historian Dionysius of Halicarnassus,[1] describes the sacred rites of the inhabitants of Falerii, an ancient city of Etruria, as similar to the religious ceremonial of the temple at Argos.

The actual origin of Rome is lost in fable and obscurity.[2] For several centuries the Romans were an uncultured people, who paid no attention to fine arts, but in obedience to strong military instincts thought only of war and conquest.[3] In proportion as they subdued the neighbouring states they adopted their arts and institutions almost as freely as they absorbed their population and territory into their own political system. As soon as the circle of Roman conquest extended to the Greek colonies of Southern Italy and Sicily, called Magna Græcia, the elements of science and learning began to make their way to the capital. In 272 B.C. Tarentum, the home of Archytas, and sixty years later Syracuse, the stage of Archimedes, fell under the dominion of Rome. From this point the history of Roman civilization is no more than an enumeration of what they borrowed from the Greeks. Thus it became a staple observation that "victorious Rome was herself subdued by the arts of Greece."[4] But the Romans had no native genius for the highest mental pursuits; they were mere imitators, who not only never surpassed but never even equalled their masters.

---

[1] *Antiquitates Romanæ*, l. i. 21.
[2] See Plutarch, *Life of Romulus*, ch. i.
[3] See Rousseau, *Dictionnaire de Musique*, art. *Chanson*.
[4] Gibbon, *Decline and Fall of the Roman Empire*, ch. ii.

Their Oratory.

The republican constitution of Rome was well adapted to engender and nurture oratory, and many of her public men, such as Cato the Censor, the Gracchi, Julius Cæsar, and Hortensius, were doubtless fine speakers. Of Tiberius Gracchus it is related that whilst speaking he kept a servant with a pitch-pipe concealed behind him, who sounded a note to stimulate him when languid in his delivery, or to recall him to moderation if he became excited and strained his voice.[1] In Marcus Tullius Cicero we behold the flower of Roman eloquence, and his treatises on rhetoric are a proof of how earnestly he studied and thought about his art. In his philosophical writings the Latin language appears at its perfection, but we look in vain for any originality of conception or addition to the natural knowledge of mankind. Yet few will so far concur in the opinion of Mommsen[2] as to regard him in the light of "a mere advocate and not a good one."

The most celebrated of Roman teachers of rhetoric was M. Fabius Quintilian, who, however, lived somewhat later than the golden era of Latin literature. His *Institutions of Oratory* is the most complete and systematic treatise of the kind that we have inherited from the ancients, and this work is perhaps the only example in Roman art to which the Greeks

[1] Cicero, *De Oratore*, l. iii. c. 60. Plutarch, *in Vita*, etc.

[2] "Cicero hatte keine Ueberzeugung und keine Leidenschaft, er war nichts als Advocat, und kein guter Advocat." *Römische Geschichte*, B. v. c. 12.

Their Music.

The primitive music of Rome was borrowed from the Etruscans, whose form of worship, like the Greek, included a processional chorus of basket-bearing virgins or *canephorœ*, who hymned the gods in the songs of the country.[1] The rude throats of the first Roman soldiery gave utterance to their martial spirit when they improvised a boisterous song to the praise of their general. But in the reign of Numa a more polished choir found voice when the Salii, or priests of Mars, celebrated the virtues of the warrior god to a warlike beating on the sacred shields or *ancilia*.[2] Music, however, obtained no positive footing amongst the hardy Romans of the Commonwealth, and never held a place in the education of their youth. It was only under the undisputed supremacy of the Empire and the establishment of universal peace, when the influx of Greeks and Asiatics rendered the city cosmopolitan, that bands of female singers, instrumentalists, mimes,[3] etc., flocked into the capital from the East and other parts, and were engaged to perform at the banquets of the wealthy.[4] Music was, therefore, always an exotic cultivation at Rome, and its practice in private

---

[1] Dionysius of Halicarnassus, loc. cit. ii. 22.
[2] Ibid. ii. 71.
[3] " Ambubaiarum collegia, pharmacopolæ,
        Mendici, mimæ, balatrones, hoc genus omne."
                                        —Horace, *Satiræ*, i. 2.
[4] Livy, l. xxxix. c. 6.

was at variance with the austerity and simplicity of the typical Roman character.[1] The only notable exception to this rule was furnished by the insensate Emperor Nero, who not only sang in retirement for his own gratification, but also appeared on the stage at Rome and Naples, and even travelled to Greece to enter the lists with his voice at some of the public contests.[2] During the greater part of his career he only spoke or sang under the direction of a *phonascus* whom he kept in constant attendance on his person.[3] He sacrificed his ordinary personal comfort and almost starved himself for the sake of his vocal powers, feeding on leeks [4] and refraining from apples [5] and every kind of food that he fancied might dull the clearness of his voice.[6]

THE MIDDLE AGES.

Transition.—In a measure equivalent to the material success of the Roman arms, the science of Greece obtained the mastery of the world in the domains of thought, and the Augustan age may be regarded as a happy union of the highest bearings of the mind with the physical attributes of political and military supremacy. But the perfection of prosperity and peace, by promoting indolence and extravagance,

---

[1] Cicero, *Tusculanæ Disputationes*, l. i. c. 1.
[2] Suetonius, *in Nerone*, c. 20, 21, 22.
[3] Ibid. 25.
[4] Plinius Secundus, l. xix. c. 33.
[5] Suetonius, loc. cit. c. 20.
[6] "Quamquam exiguæ vocis et fuscæ." Ibid.

gave birth to the corruption of good manners, which achieved the dissolution and hastened the decay of both. Soon, however, the restless faculties of mankind recombined under a new mental phase, which struggled into light through the wreck of all Pagan institutions, and the dominion of the Christian Church was raised over the ruins of Grecian science and Roman conquest.

Preservation of Oratory by the Primitive Church.

By the scriptural authority of the New Testament, and the apostolic example, the fundamental principle of Christianity has always been to preach the Gospel to every creature. The cultivation of eloquence, more or less systematic, was therefore a necessary part of the activity of the Primitive Church, and most of the early fathers, such as Ignatius, Origen, Athanasius, Gregory Nazianzen, Basil, Chrysostom, and many others, had all the qualities of vigorous and polished oratory. At first the delivery of sermons, or homilies, was restricted to the bishops, who alone had the licence to debate and the learning to expound the difficulties of the sacred doctrine. But the great and rapid increase in the number of congregations soon compelled the extension of this office to the presbyters or elders; and after the fifth or sixth century the deacons, or lowest order of ecclesiastical ministers, were authorized to preach to the people.[1] During the Middle, or Dark

---

[1] See Bingham, *Antiquities of the Christian Church*, book xiv. ch. 4.

Ages, as they are often called, from the general deficiency of education, the distinction between the clergy and the laity was at its height, as the advantages of any learning or culture that existed were almost exclusively on the side of the former class. But the irregularity and uncertainty of social and political institutions during the period which intervened between the final collapse of the Roman empire in the West, through the repeated incursions and ravages of barbarians, and the foundation and consolidation of the various states of modern Europe, almost annihilated contemporary civilization. After the twelfth century, however, a revival took place, at first in Italy, and studies of literature and science were energetically pursued, which have culminated in the enlightenment of the present age.[1]

During several centuries in the West the only continuous and consistent students of rhetoric, if any, were the bishops, who had to direct the operations of the inferior clergy. In the seventh and eighth centuries, at least, the writings of Isidorus of Seville[2] and Rabanus Maurus,[3] show some attention to oratory, amongst the other ecclesiastical functions; but in the tenth century the obscurity of ignorance is scarcely penetrated by a single ray of learning. After the restoration of letters the ministers of the Church were probably among the first who felt the influence of an improved education, which they showed in their

[1] For a succinct account of the Renaissance, see Gibbon, op. cit. ch. lxvi.

[2] Op. cit. etc.

[3] Op. cit. etc.

religious discourses.   By studying the Greek and Latin
literature of philosophy and eloquence a spirit of
imitation and emulation was awakened, and from the
elaborate and erudite work of Cresollius,[1] the precursor by nearly a century of Bossuet and Masillon, we
may infer that the prelates of the Church had long
cultivated the arts of oratory with an attentive discri-
mination not unworthy of a rhetorician of ancient
Athens.   Cresollius analyzes with a remarkable learning, grace, and acumen, every motion of the body
and features as minutely and categorically as Rush[2]
studied the inflections of the voice.   He also treats at
length of the tones of the voice and the pronunciation
of the orator, illustrating his remarks at every point
by reference to the highest classical writers.

State of the Drama.

The theatre during the Middle Ages furnishes but
little matter worthy of comment; as in fact it scarcely
had any tangible existence.   Both in the East and the
West the Greek and Latin languages were in a
moribund condition, so that the masterpieces of the
Athenian or Roman stage could only be understood

[1] Cresollius, or Louis Crésol, was born in 1568, and for many years
acted as secretary to the General of the Jesuits.   The work referred
to is entitled, *Vacationes Autumnales, sive de perfecta oratoris actione et
pronunciatione*, Paris, 1620.   He also wrote a *Theatrum Veterum
Rhetorum*, and one or two books of a different class.
[2] *The Philosophy of the Human Voice.*   Philadelphia, 1836; 6th ed.
1864.

by the courtiers of Constantinople or the higher ecclesiastical ministers, whilst at the same time there were no playwrights of genius to create a new national drama in the vernacular tongue. There were, however, certain popular exhibitions of acting, called mysteries, moralities, farces, sotties, etc., most of which were representations of scriptural episodes, or consisted in a display of wit extempore or mere buffoonery. The only interest in these disorderly productions is derived from the circumstance that their licence was probably instrumental in unfettering the modern drama from the strict unities of the classical stage. After the Renaissance an indigenous theatre was soon founded and brought to perfection in the various countries of Europe by numerous authors of more or less merit and celebrity, amongst whom may be mentioned—in Italy, Goldoni, Ariosto, and Alfieri; in Spain, Lopez da Vega, Calderone, and Cervantes; in France, Jodelle, Corneille, and Molière; in England, Massinger, Ben Jonson, and Shakespeare; and in Germany, Schiller and Goethe.[1]

Nurture and Dissemination of Music by the Early Church, etc.

The universality of the use of music in the worship of all nations naturally led the early Christians, and even the apostles, to express their devotion by singing psalms or hymns. As soon, therefore, as the Church became established on a secure footing a regular choral service

---

[1] See Dibdin's *History of the Stage*, vol. i.

was introduced, and vocal music was thus fostered as an ecclesiastical institution during the Middle Ages. It appears that a regular choral service was first instituted at Antioch, about the reign of Constantine, whence St. Ambrose introduced it into the Western churches.[1] For long, however, the science and practice of music only suffered deterioration from its religious adoption, as the Christians merely made use of pagan melodies, which they deprived of their chief force and vigour by transforming them into chants or anthems, and applying them to barbarous hymnal verses.[2] In the seventh century, after the pontifical throne had been consolidated at Rome, somewhat of a revival took place, and Pope Gregory the Great attempted a complete reform of church music. He endeavoured to introduce a system into the choral service, and was the first who separated the singers from the regular clergy. As a consequence of the efforts of Gregory, Rome soon became celebrated as the chief source of musical culture, whence issued learned monks to teach the other European nations a refined method of singing.

1. In 596 A.D. Gregory the Great sent a monk named Augustin[3] to England to convert the Saxons, and he also taught them to chant litanies. The first church in which singing was practised here was in a cathedral built at Canterbury, of which Augustin was the first archbishop.[4] Several other monks from Rome also instructed the Saxons in music, amongst them Theodore, ordained

---

[1] See Hawkins, *History of Music*, vol. i. pp. 283, 287.
[2] Rousseau, op. cit. art. *Plain Chant*.
[3] Bede, *Ecclesiastica Historia*, l. i. c. 25.
[4] Hollingshed's *Chronicles*, ed. Hooker, 1587, vol. ii. p. 120.

Archbishop of Canterbury in 668 A.D. by Pope Vitalian, and John, the Precentor of St. Peter's, who, a few years later, received a mission from Pope Agatho, and established schools to teach singing in many parts of Northumberland.[1] In 677 A.D. Putta, Bishop of Rochester, was driven out of his diocese by Ethelred, King of the Mercians, during some civil commotions, and afterwards supported himself by teaching singing throughout the province of Mercia.[2] The Venerable Bede himself, who was a monk in a monastery of Durham, about 700 A.D. did much to establish the cultivation of music on a permanent basis in England, and wrote some short treatises on the theory of music. After the Renaissance the church choir soon came to be regarded as an important institution, and in the reign of Henry VI. we find that a custom arose, which was maintained for more than a century, of pressing youths to recruit the ranks of the choristers.[3] Under such fostering circumstances a knowledge of music was diffused through all classes, who were therefore encouraged to practise it in private, until singing and playing became as universally studied in family circles as at the present day. Henry VIII. was an amateur musician of some talent. He sang, played the flute, and composed the words and music of several ballads still extant.[4] Queen Elizabeth likewise is recorded for her ability to sing "skilfully and pleasingly" to the accompaniment of a lute.[5]

---

[1] Bede, op. cit. l. iv. c. 18.
[2] Hollingshed, loc. cit.
[3] Rymer's *Fœdera*, tom. xi. p. 375.
[4] Burney, op. cit. vol. ii. p. 573.
[5] Camden, *Annales*, etc., *regnante Elizabetha*, ed. 1717, p. 14.

2. Great difficulty was found in teaching vocal music to the French and Germans. They are described as of gigantic stature, and giving utterance to thunder rather than music when they attempted to sing. From their rude throats, instead of melody, issued such rough sounds as most resembled the "noise of a cart jolting down a staircase."[1] In the eighth century Pope Adrian, at the request of Charlemagne, sent two monks, named Theodore and Benedict,[2] to correct the Gallic chants. They established schools at Metz and Soissons, but found it impossible to get their pupils to sing the Italian music, which contained many florid passages, on account of a great want of natural flexibility in the vocal organs.[3] In course of time, however, the new schools were successful, and the singers of Metz surpassed all those of the neighbouring provinces.

The central figure in the history of mediæval music is Guido of Arezzo, a monk to whom is attributed, amongst other improvements, the invention of solmization, and who was formerly invested with the extraordinary merit of having discovered counterpoint. This celebrated man lived about 1025 A.D., and applied himself vigorously to reform the musical scale, and to root out abuses from the choir-singing of his age. He devised a system of notation of such simplicity, that by its means boys could be taught as much in a few months as they could previously in several years, and he made his pupils practise singing with the aid of the one-stringed instrument called a *monochord*. Before Guido's

[1] John Diaconus, *in Vita S. Gregorii*, l. ii. c. 7.
[2] *Annales et Historia Francorum*. Francofurti, 1594. Sub *Vita Caroli Magni*, p. 260.   [3] Ibid.

time the practice of music was most unmethodical, and the choristers followed only the defective guidance of habit and ear. Guido, therefore, chastised the singers of his day in some bitter invectives, on account of their ignorance of musical science. He denied their title to be called musicians, and stigmatized them as the most senseless class of men of the time.[1]

The rise of popular music in Europe is intimately connected with the practice of minstrelsy, viz., the singing of verses to the harp by travelling musicians devoted solely to such employment. From some such vocations appears to be derived the most primitive form of popular entertainment. The characters of public singer, reciter, or story-teller, in combination or separately, are to be found in the dawning civilization of almost every nationality, as exemplified by the rhapsodists of the Homeric age, the bards of Britain, the scalds of Scandinavia, and the story-tellers of Oriental life. The representatives of this class, who have exerted most influence on modern music, are the Provençal poets or troubadours, who arose in France about the end of the tenth century. The social relations of that period were favourable to these wandering minstrels, who were respected by the populace and welcomed in the houses of the wealthy wherever they went. They sang verses, chiefly of their own composition, to an instrumental accompaniment, but those who had not the gift of voice employed an assistant to take the vocal part of their performance.

[1] See the *Histories of Music* by Burney (vol. ii. ch. 2), Hawkins (vol. i. bk. iv. ch. 6), or Fétis (tom. iv. p. 164).

In this country minstrels flourished for several centuries, and must have done much to engender a taste for vocal music amongst all ranks of the people. By the reign of Elizabeth, however, the state of society to which they owed their existence having become obsolete, they degenerated in manners, and were finally proscribed in an Act of Parliament passed for the "suppression of rogues and vagabonds."[1]

Of all the events in the course of the musical development of the voice, doubtless the crowning achievement is the invention of the lyric drama, where the great power of music to awaken the emotions is applied to the systematic illustration of human passion. The first public performance of a regular opera took place at Florence, in the year 1600, when the *Euridice* of Rinuccini and Peri was represented in honour of the nuptials of Mary of Medicis with Henry IV. of France. Previous to that date plays, with songs interspersed, had frequently been acted in most parts of Europe, but the invention of recitative was still wanting in order to give the musical uniformity which characterizes the modern opera. The merit of this invention belongs to Rinuccini, and from his own statement he was led to it by observing that the actors in the Greek or Roman drama must have employed a kind of vocal intonation on the stage quite distinct from ordinary speaking.[2] After the performance of *Euridice*, the opera soon became a national institution in Italy, from whence

[1] See Percy, in the introduction to *Reliques of Ancient English Poetry;* and Warton, *History of English Poetry*, Dissertation i. et passim.

[2] As exemplified in the case of Roscius, p. 37.

it has gradually spread to almost every country in the world. To reach England it took more than a century, and the first opera represented here was *Arsinoë*, in 1705, a translation from the Italian, with English music and English singers. Having once gained a footing, in less than ten years the great superiority of the Italians in natural vocal powers, euphony of language, and inventiveness of melody, led to the immigration of singers of that nation, and forced the opera to assume the exotic character which it retains in this country to the present day.

Nearly allied to opera is the oratorio, or sacred drama, which is a lineal descendant of the mediæval mysteries or moralities. It was brought to its present state of elaboration about the same time as opera.

Perhaps the most remarkable result of the wide-spread popularity of music, and its advancement as a science in modern times, is the creation of a separate office of musical composer. In ruder ages, and even amongst the Greeks, the poet performed a threefold function, setting his own verses to music and singing them himself. But the separation and specialization of pursuits is one of the main effects of increasing knowledge, which demands that the degree of excellence in performance shall progress at an equal rate with refinement of appreciation. A complex apprehension of phenomena enables us to perceive that individuals have seldom the mental and bodily gifts, or the physical industry, to approach perfection in more than a single mode of action. The crude melody of former ages required no rare faculties for its production, but in our own times the highest

E

vocal endowments would be of little worth without the genius of the composer, the expression of whose conceptions constitutes the only field in which singers can exhibit the musical qualities of their voices. This chapter would therefore be incomplete without recording the names of a few of those who are regarded as having first brought vocal music to maturity.

After the time of Guido we meet with no musician of note for nearly three hundred years, and the first names that fix our attention are those of the Netherland contrapuntists, John Okenheim and his pupil, Josquin des Prez, who lived in the latter part of the fifteenth century. Later on in England by a few decades may be mentioned Taverner, Tallis, and Bird. But those who may be referred to as the chief sources of modern vocal melody are Palestrina of Rome, Scarlatti of Naples, and Henry Purcell of England. Palestrina and Scarlatti flourished about the middle of the sixteenth century, Purcell nearly one hundred years later. The memory and works of the most illustrious composers in whose hands opera attained perfection are still fresh, and here the names of Handel, Porpora, Mozart, Beethoven, and Weber, stand preeminent. The first high efforts in oratorio are due to the genius of Stradella, Handel, and Haydn.[1]

THE TWO FACULTIES OF VOICE—SPEECH AND SONG.

Considering the voice with an analytical regard, we are struck not more by the greatness than by the

---

[1] See Burney or Hawkins, op. cit.

diversity of its powers in two essentially distinct spheres of exertion. The first is the sphere of language, the second that of music. The ruling spirit in the one is reason, in the other emotion.

In the utterances of the speaker we hear the voice as an agent of the brain, as an outward expression of mental activity, making intelligible the workings of the mind. Here sound fulfils a secondary office, acting as a thought-bearer, as it flows onwards like a river crowded in its course with nascent ideas from the brain.

But in the tones of the singer we listen to the voice as an acoustic principle, produced mainly under a material influence. Here sound attracts us in its physical character, and in its infinite qualities of pitch and phase and harmony, arouses in the circling channels of the ear a concourse of responsive vibrations, which flood the emotional sensibilities of the brain.

These two faculties of voice, though clearly definable within theoretical limits, are almost inseparably blended in nature. For even in speech there is music, and the spoken voice to be tolerable must be musical.[1] Nor is the voice ever used as a mere musical instrument. For doubtless the intrinsic charm of song, by which it surpasses all artificial tones, is derived from the coalescence of language with music. Even though the words be not distinctly heard, though the sentences be dissolved in a stream of melody, the underflow of speech, in adding shade and colour and warmth to tone, bestows a timbre of excelling lustre, which renders voice beyond ought else most musical.

---

[1] "For even in speaking there is a kind of obscure song." Cicero, *Orator ad M. Brutum*, c. 18.

CHAPTER I.

SOUND AND VOICE.

TRANSMISSION OF SOUND — VIBRATION — SYMPATHETIC
RESONANCE—QUALITIES OF SOUND AS DISTINGUISHED
BY THE EAR—SOUNDS GENERATED IN TUBES OR
PIPES—REED INSTRUMENTS.

Definition of Sound.—Sound, in our apprehension,
is that which is heard, and therefore our only
means of recognizing its existence is through the
sensation it produces on our ear. Various nerves
have various faculties of appreciating external
influences, as exemplified by sight, touch, etc., but
the auditory nerve alone can perceive sound.

TRANSMISSION OF SOUND.

The physical source of sound is impulse or shock
of some material substance. But unless something
intervenes between our ear and the sounding body
nothing can be heard. Sound therefore cannot travel

in empty space. To illustrate this fact a bell may be placed under the exhausted receiver of an air-pump, viz., in a vacuum. On striking the clapper against the sides no sound is audible. For the same reason, sound produced in rarefied air is greatly diminished in intensity. As we ascend from the surface of the earth, the atmosphere becomes gradually thinner and lighter. On the top of high mountains, such as Mont Blanc, the air is so attenuated, that a pistol-shot sounds like a mere cracker,[1] and the voice also is much weakened. Were it not for the deep silence that usually reigns over such localities, from an absence of all the activities of nature and the bustle of animal life, persons could only hear each other speak at very short distances.[2] But the most striking proof that the voice requires air of a certain density for its normal production may be furnished by inhaling hydrogen. If we empty our chest of air and refil it with this, the lightest of all gases, our voice-power will be found to have almost vanished, and with considerable exertion we can only succeed in producing hollow, faint, and muffled tones.[3]

The rapidity with which sound travels varies according to the density of the medium through which it passes. In air at 32° Fahr. it moves at the rate of about 1,090 feet per second, and at 60° some 30 feet faster, but in water it travels four times, in pine wood ten times, and in iron seventeen times more rapidly.[4]

[1] Tyndall, *Lectures on Sound*, 1869, p. 8.
[2] Herschel, *Encyclopædia Metropolitana*, art. *Sound*, s. 83.
[3] Tyndall, op. cit. p. 9.   [4] Ibid. p. 47.

Sound-Waves.

The mode in which sound propagates itself from
one point to another is one of the most interesting
questions in acoustics. Sir Isaac Newton first suggested that it moves by exciting undulations or waves
in the substance which carries it, and this theory is
still upheld and believed to be correct. In order to
understand this explanation it is necessary to know
exactly what waves are. For this purpose we have
only to watch the surface of a sheet of water when
the wind is blowing. Every one is familiar with the
appearance of the waves as they roll along, of
greater or lesser size according to the force of the
breeze. If a wave comes to a chip of wood, a cork,
or a boat, they rise up one side of the wave to its
crest and glide down the other side, but when the
wave has passed they remain in the same place as
before. This shows us that waves do not consist
of ridges of water that roll over the water beneath
as a ball rolls along the ground, but truly of a
motion transmitted through the water from one
particle to another.[1] To illustrate this point in a
most palpable manner we have only to take one
end of a long piece of string, attached to something
at the other end, and, holding it loosely, shake it
so as to produce a kind of serpentine or wavy
motion. Here we can see waves running along

[1] For diagrams illustrating the actual motion of the water in
waves, see Sedley Taylor, *Sound and Music*, p. 14.

the string, backwards and forwards, whilst the ends always remain at the same distance from each other. The water in waves performs therefore only an upward movement, and has no onward motion whatever.

The surface of water may be agitated not only by ranks of waves all proceeding in the same direction one after the other, but also by many series of waves moving at the same time all in different ways, and crossing each other at angles of every degree in a manner too complex for description. In order to observe this let us select a piece of still water and throw a stone into it. We see a system of small waves, a ripple in fact, produced around the spot, which spreads out in an ever widening circle until it is lost to sight or dies out. Let us now throw in several stones near each other. Immediately numerous circular systems are created which meet each other and cross at many points, dividing the surface of the water into a multiplicity of squares, triangles, and diamond-shapes, to an extent too complicated for the eye to follow.[1]

Precisely similar to what takes place in the water is the state of the air when disturbed by sound-waves, either single or many, propagated from various points. Whenever anything is sounded in air it acts like a stone thrown into water and creates a circular system of waves which spread rapidly in all directions. But as the sound-wave moves on all sides at the same time it must be considered as a spherical layer

[1] For a picture of this condition, see Tyndall, op. cit. p. 255.

produced a second time. This is just the point that
is illustrated by the well-known phenomenon of the
echo. If we stand opposite the face of a tall cliff
and speak with sufficient loudness, the waves from
our voice will rebound from the rock and come back
to us, as if it were repeating the words we said.
The only things to be considered, in order to ensure
the production of the echo, are (1) that if we stand
too near the rock the echo comes back so fast as
to blend into one with our voice, and (2) that if
the face of the cliff does not look straight towards
us the sound may be reflected in some other direction, just as a ball thrown against an uneven wall
does not come back to us, but hops off obliquely
some other way.

VIBRATION.

Sounding bodies are in a state of motion termed
vibration. If we move a finger from side to side it
is vibration, but unless the vibrations are executed
with a certain degree of force the waves of air produced do not reach, or do not strike with sufficient
impulse on our ear, and no sound is audible.

Vibrations may be *simple* or *compound*. A body
performs simple vibrations when it moves regularly
from side to side like a pendulum. Hence
simple vibrations are also called pendulum vibrations. But a vibrating body may execute several
eccentric motions simultaneously, as does the string
of a piano when struck, and in this way com-

pound vibrations arise. Thus, a string, if stretched horizontally, may vibrate not only up and down, but also from side to side, diagonally, and in segments at the same time. Those points or *nodes*, as they are called, at which a vibrating string divides into segments remain at rest, as can be proved by experiment.[1] Vibrational forms can be demonstrated very clearly by observing the motions of heavy and light dust, such as sand and lycopodium, when sprinkled over the surface of a plate of metal or glass fixed by one end horizontally and thrown into vibration by drawing a violin-bow along its edge at different points.[2] Helmholtz[3] has devised a means of observing the motion of a vibrating body by the aid of a combination of lenses, which he terms a " vibration microscope."

Even air itself, in a body partially confined by a cavity or in a stream impelled forcibly onwards, may be thrown into vibration and generate sound-waves in the circumambient atmosphere. Many wind instruments exemplify this fact.

SYMPATHETIC RESONANCE.

The power of exciting sympathetic resonance is a property of sounding bodies, and at first sight might seem identical with the echo. For example, if we lift the dampers from the strings of a piano by means of a pedal and sound rather

---

[1] See Tyndall, op. cit. p. 102. [2] Ibid. p. 124.
[3] Op. cit. p. 128.

strongly a certain note with the voice or an instrument, we shall hear the corresponding string vibrating
audibly in the piano after we cease. Or one
key may be pressed down gently, so as merely to
lift the damper from the string, when by singing
the corresponding note we can provoke its repetition
from the instrument. It is to be observed that no
string can be excited in this way unless we sound
exactly its own note. As a further illustration we
may take a tuning-fork and, having struck it, hold
it to the mouth of a wide-mouthed bottle. If the
cavity of the bottle is of such a size as to give a
note in unison with the tuning-fork, a distinct tone
is heard. If we take a rather large bottle it can
be tuned to the proper pitch by pouring in water
gradually, and testing it at each step with the
tuning-fork. Or a sounding tuning-fork will even
excite a quiescent one of the same pitch.

In order to understand sympathetic resonance we
must suppose that each sound-wave moves slightly
anything against which it impinges in its course. If
a file of waves meet anything, such as a string or a
body of air, which can vibrate so as to produce waves
precisely similar to those that strike it, each successive wave increases the impulse of its predecessor,
till a fresh sound is given forth. Thus the body on
being struck moves at first forwards, then backwards
beyond its original position, then again forwards, but
to a lesser extent than at first, and so on until the
motion is lost. But if a succession of even slight
impulses arrives with such regularity that each one
moves the body forwards as it is starting itself in

that direction from having retained some of the preceding impulse, the result is an accumulation of
force which drives the body to take considerable
excursions. We can see this kind of progressive
motion if we set a pendulum swinging from our hand
by a number of slight jerks properly timed. Helmholtz[1]
illustrates sympathetic resonance by the manner in
which a heavy church bell may be rung by a boy
who pulls periodically at the rope attached to it in
such a way as to increase the effect of each preceding
pull.

The quality of the various tones of the voice
has important connections with the sympathetic
resonance of the cavities of the mouth, nose, etc.,
which will be discussed in another chapter.

QUALITIES OF SOUND AS DISTINGUISHED BY THE EAR.

Our ear readily enables us to divide sounds roughly
into two great classes, viz., into *music* and *noise*. A
musical sound strikes us as being even, smooth, and
melodious, like the tones of all musical instruments,
but a mere noise has the opposite characteristics, viz.,
irregularity, harshness, grating on our senses, such as
the rattle of carriages in the street, the confused din
of a crowd of people talking or shouting, the rushing
of wind, etc.

[1] Op. cit. p. 57.

Furthermore, we can distinguish sounds from each other by three striking qualities, which are especially observable in musical tones. They are :—

    1. Pitch, or relative height;

    2. Force, or intensity;

    3. Timbre.

The first two qualities are sufficiently indicated by their names, but by *timbre*, it may be explained, is meant the peculiar distinctiveness between tones, even if of the same pitch, when produced by different instruments, such as the voice, violin, clarionet, etc.

The difference between these various kinds of sound has been very clearly explained by acoustic researches. Scientifically sounds are separated into *simple* and *compound*.

In a *simple sound* we have a single atmospheric wave or a number of single waves following each other in a given direction. A single sound-wave strikes the ear as a short sound, such as the crack of a whip; a file of waves is heard as a continuous sound, such as a musical tone.

Regularity of wave-formation is the characteristic of musical sounds, irregularity that of noise. Simple sounds will generally strike the ear as musical, because their waves must be regular, but not if they are so low in pitch as to be a mere drone, like the deepest organ-pipes; or so high as to be painfully shrill; or too sudden and powerful, like the report of a gun.

Simple sounds are not very easy to produce, and

are seldom heard in nature.   As nearly approaching
such may be instanced the chirp of the grasshopper,
whistling with the mouth, the sounds of tuning-forks,
flue organ-pipes, flutes, etc.

In *compound sounds* a number of waves, each
formed by the coalescence of two or more sound-waves
having different qualities, are in motion.   Compound
sounds are musical if their waves proceed together
with regularity of relation, whence harmony ;   but
if they disturb each other, giving rise to confused
and unperiodic wave-motions, a discord sometimes
amounting to mere noise is produced, as may be
illustrated by striking together a number of adjacent notes on the piano.   Different sets of sound-
waves may even interfere with each other to such
an extent that the result is silence.   Thus two
simultaneous sounds may so nullify one another that
nothing is heard.[1]

It is a peculiarity of our ear, however, as pointed out
by G. S. Ohm, to resolve compound sounds into their
simple constituents and to hear them all separately
though in the same period of time.   Within the ear
is a peculiar arrangement, called Corti's organ, which
consists of a number of microscopical rods (about
3,000) each of which is tuned, as it were, to vibrate
responsively to a certain note and to none other.   By
their means we are enabled, after a little practice in
directing the attention to the matter, to recognize
the several component notes of any chord that may
be sounded.[2]

[1] See Helmholtz, op. cit. p. 240.
[2] Ibid. pp. 51, 89, 188.

Pitch and Intensity—The Siren.

In order to study sound and understand its physical properties we must have recourse to certain acoustic instruments, one of the most important of which is called the *siren*. The simplest form of siren is that known as Seebeck's, and consists merely of a thin disc of wood or metal with a circular series of equi-distant holes pierced around it near the edge. In order to use it, it must be arranged so that it can be made to revolve rapidly, and at the same time a small bellows must be fixed so as to blow through each of the holes successively according as the disc rotates. When it goes slowly we hear a number of consecutive puffs or pulses of air, which may be considered as separate sound-waves, but as soon as a certain speed is reached they become fused together and a continuous musical note is heard. The great value of the siren consists in its enabling us to ex-plain the most signal of all the qualities of sound, without which music would not exist, at least according to our present acceptance of the term, viz., varying pitch, or the difference between compara-tively low or high notes. In experimenting with the siren we perceive that the puffs do not appear to form a continuous sound until they succeed each other with a certain rapidity, which theoretically should be about sixteen puffs in every second. We also observe the interesting fact that according as we make the disc revolve faster and faster the sound rises gradually from a very low note to a pitch higher and higher, until, if the mechanical arrangements are sufficiently perfect, we can produce notes high up in the musical scale.[1] This teaches us that the pitch of a note depends on the rapidity with which the sound-waves, or vibrations, follow each other, viz., on the number of waves produced by the sounding body per second. Thus, if our siren has sixteen holes in its circumference and we make it revolve at the rate of once in a second, we have sixteen sound-waves produced in each second, viz., one for each hole. The sound which proceeds from this rate of wave-formation corresponds to a very low note, such as would proceed from a 32-foot open organ-pipe, and one octave below the lowest „C^2 on our pianos.[3] In order to .make our siren sound the octave above the note produced by one revolution we must make it perform two revolutions per second; for the next octave higher, four revolutions; for the next, eight, and so on. The octave of any given note contains, therefore, exactly twice the number of sound-waves (vibrations), so that in the present case the series would run as 16, 32, 64, 128, etc. The

[1] The siren can produce about three octaves of good notes, viz.,

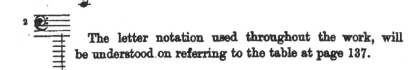

from *A* to *a''*.

[2] The letter notation used throughout the work, will be understood on referring to the table at page 137.

[3] The pitch, however, of the notes on pianos varies a little in different countries, and also according to the maker of the instrument. The London Philharmonic concert-pitch gives 455·2 vibrations (sound-waves) per second for *a'* in the second space of the treble clef.

F

lowest octave or two are, however, hardly distinguishable by the ear as musical sounds, as may be proved by striking the deepest notes of the piano, or listening to those of the organ, which has some deeper still. There is also a boundary to the audibility of sound in the opposite direction, and very high notes cannot be heard, or at least cannot be produced beyond a certain limit. The extent of our sense of hearing seems, however, to be more difficult to define in the upper extreme of the scale than in the lower. Thus Despretz produced and heard the d'''''', three octaves above the highest d'''' on our pianos, having 38,076 vibrations in the second, by exciting small tuning forks with a violin-bow.[1] The range of notes audible as musical sounds comprises about ten or eleven octaves, but varies more or less in different persons, according to the delicacy of their ear.[2]

In order to find out the precise number of vibrations in any note of the scale, sirens of more or less complexity, such as those of Cagniard de la Tour, Dove, Helmholtz,[3] etc., have been constructed, in which, by means of clockwork, the revolutions are registered on a graduated dial with hands.

Whatever means we may adopt for dividing a stream of air, if only it be done effectively, the result will be the same as in the case of the siren. Thus, after the example of Robison,[4] we can arrange a tube through which a blast of air is propelled, so that one

[1] Helmholtz, op. cit. p. 27.
[2] See this point illustrated by Herschel, loc. cit. s. 222.
[3] Op. cit. p. 244.
[4] Tyndall, op. cit. p. 53.

of its extremities shall be opened and shut in rapid alternation, and we shall then have the phenomena of the siren repeated.

The nature of varying *intensity* of sound can also be demonstrated by the aid of the siren, so as to render intelligible the difference between loud and weak sounds. Thus, according as the instrument rotates, we can make the note louder by blowing harder, but no amount of hard blowing will raise the pitch, unless the wheel revolves with greater speed, so as to produce more sound-waves in the same time. Hence we must infer that loudness of sound depends on the height of the sound-waves; not on their length, because that depends on the rapidity with which they follow each other, but on the distance of the crests of the waves from the bottom of the trough between each one. Loud sounds therefore consist of very tall waves with pointed crests and deep furrows between them, but weak sounds are formed only by low air-waves, which have no crests, and pass along like mere undulations or curves on the surface of water.

In order to calculate the *length of wave* proceeding from any given note, we have only to divide the rate at which sound travels in air, 1,090 feet per second, by the vibrational number of the note. Thus, if we take the middle *c* on the piano, with 264 vibrations in each second, we obtain 4 feet $1\frac{1}{2}$ inches as the length of its waves. Because the first wave given off by the note must be at a distance of 1,090 feet at the moment the 264th is generated, and the line of intervening waves will therefore divide the distance into 264 equal parts.

Further on we shall see that the manner in which

the siren when revolving throws the current of air into vibration is similar in principle to what takes place in our own throats every time we speak or sing. Thus, as we drive the air out of our lungs, the mechanism of our vocal organs enables us to divide the stream into a series of puffs, with a variable and almost inconceivable rapidity according to the note produced.

Timbre[1]*—Upper Partial Tones.*

The next point we have to consider is the nature of timbre, and this leads us to a further study of compound tones. Formerly it was thought that the peculiarity of the sounds emitted by various instruments was due entirely to distinctive shapes of their vibrations. But Helmholtz has lately proved that although every form of vibration is rigidly indicative of a particular timbre, yet more than one form may correspond to the same timbre, and that this last quality of sounds is essentially dependent on the measure of certain supplementary tones which are

[1] The Germans call a compound tone a *Klang*, and timbre *Klang-farbe* (tone-colour), which Professor Tyndall has anglicized by *clangtint*. Mr. Ellis, in translating Helmholtz, prefers the expression *quality of tone*. A third writer suggests *acoustic colour* (*Encyclopædia Britannica*, art. *Acoustics*). I have used the French *timbre*, as it is so commonly employed and so well understood in this country. *Timbre* is related to tambour, timbrel, etc. (Littré, *Dictionnaire*, s. v.), to the Latin *tympanum* and the Greek τύμπανον (from τύπτω, to strike), which means anything that is struck or beaten, a signification to which it reverts in French when expressing postage-stamps, post-marks, etc. *Timbre* may, therefore, be applied metaphorically to sound, so as to indicate the peculiar stamp or distinguishing characteristic of the different tones that we hear.

heard in conjunction with the fundamental tone on almost all instruments. The fact, to which allusion has already been made, has long been known, that strings in vibrating do not only swing as a whole, but have also several secondary motions, each of which produces a sound proper to itself. A string when struck, vibrates first in its entire length; secondly, in two segments; thirdly, in three; fourthly, in four, and so on. All of these motions are simultaneous, and the sounds proceeding from them are blended into one note. The lowest note is the loudest, and is called the fundamental or prime tone, and the others are called overtones, upper partial tones, or harmonics. These overtones invariably bear certain definite relations to the lowest note of the string, and constitute an ascending series which contains twice, three times, four times, five times, etc., as many vibrations as the fundamental tone. They are therefore separated by a constantly decreasing interval from the lowest to the highest. The relative succession of the first eight overtones of a string, taking *c* as the prime tone, is exemplified by the following scale :—

The first upper partial is the octave, containing twice as many vibrations as the fundamental tone, the second, the twelfth, containing three times as many, the third, the second octave, with four times the number, and so on; in some cases as high as the fifteenth or twentieth remove, where they do not lie as much as a semitone apart. From this fact, it at once appears that the higher overtones of a string must give rise to a discord, and thus render the timbre disagreeable. They can, however, be got rid of by striking the string in a certain point, which prevents their formation.[1]

As with the notes of strings, so with the tones of almost all instruments. Harmonics are present, but by no means in the same number or position in the series in all cases. Thus one instrument may be particularly rich in the higher overtones, another in the lower ones, whilst a third may select, as it were, a proportion of both, omitting those intervening. In every instance, however, they must bear the direct relation to the fundamental tone of having twice, three, or four times, etc., as many vibrations. On the number of harmonics present and their intensity, according to Helmholtz, depends the proper timbre of any instrument by which we can recognize it from others of a different class. The voice especially is very rich in overtones, and not only possesses a complete series as high as the seventeenth or twentieth, but has probably the power of varying them according to the quality of tone it is desired to produce. To this matter we will return later on.

In order to analyze compound tones and determine the exact number and position of the harmonics proper to any particular timbre, Helmholtz[2] has taken advantage of sympathetic resonance. He has had con-

---

[1] See Helmholtz, op. cit. p. 124.
[2] Ibid. p. 68.

structed a series of glass globes to act as resonators, each with a rather wide mouth on one side, and on the opposite drawn into a short perforated tube which fits the entrance of the ear.[1] Each globe in the series is tuned to a certain simple tone, and resounds sympathetically to that and no other. Whenever the proper tone of any one is sounded, it can, if placed to the ear, be heard to sing into it very distinctly. Thus a delicate means is furnished of ascertaining the presence or absence of simple sounds of any particular pitch in complex combinations of tones. Even amidst the numerous and confused noises of the streets, Helmholtz relates, the proper tones of these resonators may often be heard cropping up.[2]

SOUNDS GENERATED IN TUBES OR PIPES.

As the vibrations which form our voice, before reaching the external air, traverse certain air-chambers, which make up a kind of tube, the acoustic relations of tube-sounds demand notice here. The vibrations in tubes or pipes consist in alternate condensations and expansions[3] of the contained column of air, and, as regards the pitch of the note produced, are subject to

[1] The size of these resonators varies from about 6 in. to 1½ in. of diameter in a range of two and a half octaves, from *g* to *d'''*.

[2] For some objections to Helmholtz's conclusions, see Chappell's *History of Music*, etc. passim.

[3] For a good explanation of this point, see Taylor, op. cit. p. 115.

well-defined laws. The fundamental note of a pipe
open at both ends, such as a flue organ-pipe, a flute,
etc., corresponds to a sound-wave exactly double
the length of the tube. On the other hand, the
wave of the lowest tone produced by a stopped pipe,
such as a reed organ-pipe, or a clarionet, is four
times the length of the tube. Therefore an open
pipe produces the same fundamental note as a
stopped pipe of half its length, and if we stop an
open pipe we lower its tone by an octave, or, *vice
versa*, if we open a stopped pipe we raise its pitch
by an octave.

If we know the length of wave proper to any
note we can tell the length of tube, open or stopped,
required for its production. For example, the middle
c' of the piano, with a wave 4 feet 1½ inches in
length, is the proper note of an open pipe 2 feet
¾ inch long, or of a stopped pipe of half the length.
In order to sound a note corresponding to a deep
tone of the male voice, say *E*,[1] with a vibrational
number of 80, and a wave 13 feet 7½ inches long,
we should want an open pipe of 6 feet 9¾ inches.
Our vocal tube is, at the most, eight or ten inches
long, and it is therefore evident that it cannot produce such deep tones by its own proper vibrations.[2]

[1]

[2] The lowest note that can be produced by our vocal tube or cavity,
i.e., the pharynx and mouth taken together, appears to be *f*
But the walls of our vocal cavity are too yielding to allow of such
condensations of the contained air as are required for the formation

With respect to the overtones of pipes, they are identical in open pipes with those of strings, but stopped pipes have the peculiarity of selecting only the odd harmonics, *i.e.*, the third, fifth, seventh, etc. In such case the resulting timbre has a *nasal* character—that is to say, resembles the tone of our voice in "speaking through the nose." The clarionet is an instance of an instrument with a nasal timbre.

The upper partial tones of pipes are generally weak, rendering the timbre dull, unless reinforced by a reed.

REED INSTRUMENTS.

The production of musical sounds by means of vibrating reeds claims our attention, as instruments of this class bear the nearest analogy to the voice. The reed always covers an aperture which, in vibrating under pressure of air, it alternately closes and leaves partially open for the passage of the current, on a principle identical with that of the siren.

Reeds produce tones, therefore, by dividing the air into a series of puffs, the rapidity of which determines the pitch. Their notes are powerful and highly composite, having distinctly recognizable over-

of strong vibrations. The sounds generated are therefore so weak that they can only modify the timbre of the voice, without being able to govern, in any degree, the vibrations of the vocal bands. Were it otherwise, the formation of vowel-sounds would probably be impossible. See the account of vowel-sounds in Ch. III. p. 142.

tones as high as the nineteenth or twentieth of the series.[1]

Reeds are divided into *striking* and *free* reeds.[2] The former, whilst vibrating, strike the margin of the opening at each excursion, the latter fit the aperture so as exactly· to close it without touching the edges.

Reeds may further be separated into two classes, according as they are used with tubes, as in reed organ-pipes, the clarionet, etc., or as they act only in conjunction with their aperture, that is, like the tongues of harmoniums, concertinas, etc.

Tube reeds, in material, are generally *woody* or *membranous.*

Woody reeds are used either singly or doubly. The clarionet will serve as an example of a tube-instrument with a single woody reed, which belongs to the class of striking reeds, though arranged so as not actually to strike. The tube of a medium-sized clarionet (C) is about twenty inches long, producing for its fundamental tone *e*,[3] with a wave four times

---

[1] Helmholtz, op. cit. p. 150. The fact that the tones of reed instruments are highly compound proves that the sound proceeds from the rapid division of the current of air, and not from the agitated body of the reed itself. Otherwise, as occurs in the case of tuning-forks, simple notes would be produced, because the vibrations of reeds, as examined by the vibration microscope, are of the pendulum kind.

[2] A *reed* is, of course, a kind of tubular grass, and the reed of an organ-pipe is, in fact, a small semi-cylinder against the open side of which the vibrating tongue is fitted. But the latter is the essential part of all reed instruments, and therefore the vibrating lamina, which is the actual agent in producing the sound, has come to be termed a reed.

[3]

its own length, and following, therefore, the law of stopped pipes. The column of air in this tube overpowers the reed and forces it to vibrate sympathetically with it. The reed does not, therefore, emit its proper tone,[1] but merely serves to make the tube speak by its power of rendering the stream of air intermittent. A scale is formed by shortening the tube (by opening side-holes), the amount of shortening required to raise any given note a musical tone being more than an inch. For a compass of an octave, therefore, a shortening of nine or ten inches is necessary. At the same time the reed must also be shortened by pressure with the lips. The timbre of this instrument somewhat resembles that of the soprano voice, probably on account of its nasal character.

The hautboy or oboë is blown by means of double woody reeds, fixed so that the air rushes through a chink alternately opened and closed by their approximated extremities when vibrating. In the production of notes instruments of this class follow the law of open pipes. The fundamental note of the hautboy is, therefore, an octave above that of a clarionet with the same length of pipe.

As *membranous reeds* we have the human lips in sounding brass instruments, such as the horn, trombone, etc. The lips, placed in apposition against the mouthpiece of the tube, generate sound very

---

[1] That is to say, the weak note it would sound if fixed by one end and caused to vibrate apart from any aperture or tube. This sound, though produced in a different way, corresponds, of course, in pitch to the tone that the reed would emit when vibrating at an opening not leading to a tube or cavity.

much like the mechanism by which voice is produced, but their vibrations are commanded by those of the tube. Being thus blown with double reeds, brass instruments follow the acoustic law of open pipes, and produce sound-waves of twice the length of their tube. They have usually very long tubes, for reasons connected with the progression of the harmonic series,[1] and in order to vary the pitch of any note by a musical tone an alteration in the length of the tube of two or three inches or even more is required, according to the size of the instrument.[2]

The brass springs or reeds of harmoniums and similar instruments have no tube, and render therefore the notes proper to their own vibrational number. Each reed is fixed at its aperture, and no alteration in their rate of vibration can be effected. A separate reed is consequently required for each note of the scale. The differences of pitch are obtained by using springs of varying length, breadth, and thickness. In a harmonium of a compass of five octaves the lowest note is produced by a tongue about $3\frac{1}{2}$ inches long, the highest by one of half an inch. In the lowest notes the varying dimensions of the successive reeds are most apparent, but in the highest octave the difference in size of adjacent springs is barely appreciable by the eye. The power and timbre of the tones are well known.

[1] See Helmholtz, op. cit. p. 149.
[2] With membranous reeds, of fixed dimensions and tension, artificially constructed and applied to tubes the result is peculiar. See J. Müller's experiments, *Physiology*, vol. i. Appendix.

In the organ separate reeds are also used for each note, but a tube of fixed· length, which sounds in unison with the reed, is added in order to render the tone more powerful.

In studying the production of musical scales by reeds we observe that when tubes are superadded, the vibrations of the reeds can only be commanded by pipes of considerable length, which require very manifest shortenings to raise their pitch, following, in fact, the natural acoustic laws as determined for vibrations in tubes. On the other hand we see that if reeds are used separately very slight modifications in their size produce remarkable alterations of pitch. Thus, we shorten a tube by an inch or two, and obtain a rise of only one tone or perhaps a semi-tone, but if we diminish the length of a reed by a much less amount the result is a leap of two or three octaves.

The Vocal Reeds.

The economy of nature, taking advantage of the peculiar adaptability of reeds for producing musical tones, and the slight material modifica-tions they require in order to yield a scale of notes, has given us a pair of membranous reeds, the so-called vocal cords, as the essential part of our vocal apparatus. But, compared with artificial reed instruments, the voice appears to exceed them as much in complexity as it does in beauty, combining more or less the mechanism and qualities of them all, and having, in addition, a surplus of powers peculiar to itself.[1]

To brass instruments sounded by the lips compressed together and tightened gradually in ascending the scale, a close likeness is borne by the vocal reeds associated with their tube, which, however, influences not the pitch of their note, but only its timbre.

And again, as the vocal reeds alter their size and shape almost indefinitely, according to the pitch of their vibrations, it may be considered that the vocal scale is formed by a series of separate reeds like those of the harmonium. But, within their own compass, the vocal reeds are infinitely more versatile in giving gradations of pitch than the fixed series of springs of that instrument.

To analyze their peculiarities of constitution, and the delicacies of their action, forms our principal subject for the next two chapters.

[1] See Hullah, *Cultivation of the Speaking Voice*, p. 9.

CHAPTER II.

PHYSICAL CONSTRUCTION OF THE VOCAL ORGANS.

ACOUSTIC CLASSIFICATION OF THE VOCAL ORGANS—THE
CHEST, OR THORAX—THE LARYNX—THE VOCAL
TUBE, OR RESONANCE APPARATUS—THE TONGUE,
LIPS, AND TEETH.

ACOUSTIC CLASSIFICATION OF THE VOCAL ORGANS.

THE anatomical parts concerned, directly and indirectly, in the formation of voice and speech are numerous and complex, whilst most of them present the peculiarity of having often to fulfil several functions in the same moment of time. On this account the ostensible machinery, so to speak, of voice presents an entanglement, in which it is difficult to perceive the essential components, as distinguished from those which merely act in concert with them in relation to other offices.

A mechanical description of the vocal organs, from a purely acoustic point of view, is all that will be here given. With this object they may be separated primarily into two great classes, viz., the organs which produce sound and those which only afterwards modify it. Both these classes, however, require subdivision, because in the former case we have, firstly, the organs which furnish a current of air, and, secondly, those which by reactive vibration divide it into sound-waves; and in the latter case we have the parts which influence purely the musical quality of the tones, and also the organs which stand, psychologically, at the head of the vocal series, *i.e.*, those which form the instrument of articulation.

On these principles the classification of the vocal organs is shown in detail as follows:—

I. ORGANS WHICH COMBINE THEIR ACTION TO GENE-RATE SOUND.

    1. *The air-chamber, commanding the motor element.* The chest-walls, with their proper muscles; the lungs; the bronchial tubes; and the trachea or windpipe.

    2. *The larynx, containing the vibrating element.* The laryngeal cartilages sustaining the vocal reeds, and the intrinsic and extrinsic muscles acting on them.

II. ORGANS WHICH MERELY MODIFY SOUND.

    1. *The resonance apparatus, or vocal tube.* The ventricles and vestibule of the larynx, the pharynx, mouth, and nose with its accessory cavities. Also certain moveable parts of the boundaries of the vocal tube, viz., the epiglottis, soft-palate, and lower jaw.

    2. *The articulating instrument.* The tongue, lips, soft-palate, teeth, and lower jaw.[1]

[1] It may be objected to this classification that the lungs and larynx also modify sound, the former in force or intensity, the latter in

The consonant action of all these parts is required for the perfect formation of voice and speech, but the first class, in their proper functions, are essentially independent of the second, whilst the second class can only perform their office with the co-operation of the first. Secondary relations of a similar character exist between the first and second groups of organs in each pair of subdivisions.

THE CHEST, OR THORAX.

The chest-walls consist of a bony and cartilaginous framework, of which the various apertures are covered in by numerous muscles and membranes. The osseous portion is formed by the twenty-four ribs, twelve on each side, which are seamed together, behind by the spinal column, and in front by the breast-bone and costal cartilages. Above and in front the collar-bone, or clavicle, and behind the shoulder-blades also contribute to the bony consolidation of the chest-walls. In front the ends of the ribs are joined to the breast-bone by several slips of cartilage, except the two last or lowest on each side, which are therefore called floating ribs.

pitch. The main acoustic action of both is, however, to produce sound, and as regards the larynx every note must, I think, be considered as a separate production, and not as a modification of sound, primarily existing in another form. A further difficulty in separating the various organs into classes is seen in the necessity of including some of them in more than one group. Thus the soft-palate, whilst having a special function as regards the timbre of the voice, also plays an important part in articulation. (See pp. 134, 188.)

G

The space thus partly enclosed has a somewhat conical shape, being broad and open below at the abdomen, and narrow and almost shut above at the neck. The reason of this is that the opposite pairs of ribs increase gradually in length, and embrace successively a larger circle from the first, or highest, to the last two or three.

The joints of the ribs with the spine admit of a considerable degree of motion; the articulations of the cartilages with the breast-bone are also moveable, but to a lesser extent, and not at all in old age.

The ribs are well clothed with muscles, which perform the double duty of completing the closure of the chest, and altering the dimensions of its cavity by their contractions. They consist of two classes, viz., muscles of *inspiration* and of *expiration*. Both classes are also subdivided into two groups, namely, *abdominal* and *costal*.

Muscles of Inspiration.—There is only one *abdominal* muscle of inspiration. It is called the diaphragm,[1] because it acts as a partition between the chest and the abdomen, forming the floor of the upper cavity, and the roof, as it were, of the lower one. It is a large, flat, and thin muscle, shaped like a fan, and attached all round to the inside of the lower ribs. When relaxed its under surface is concave, and its upper surface is arched upwards into the thorax.

The *costal* muscles of inspiration may be divided into *ordinary* and *extraordinary*.

The *ordinary* consist of a set of muscles, called *intercostals*, which fill up the long parallel spaces between the ribs, and also of another set, twelve in number on each side, which run from the back part of each rib in an upward direction to the spine. These latter are named *Levatores costarum*, or elevators of the ribs. Lastly, three small muscles (*Scaleni*) belonging to this group extend up the neck on each side from the first two ribs.

---

[1] From διάφραγμα, a partition.

Of the *extraordinary* we have the *Serratus magnus*, or Great serrated, a large muscle which is attached on each side to the first nine ribs and to the base of the blade-bone. Behind, another large muscle, the *Latissimus dorsi*, stretches, one for each side, from the spine and back of the lowest three or four ribs to the shoulder. In front, the strong *Pectoral* muscles cover the upper part of the chest from the collar-bone as low as the sixth or seventh rib, and are fixed on each side to the shoulders. A rather strong muscle (*Sterno-cleido-mastoid*) stretches on each side, from the junction of the breast-bone and clavicle, along the neck to the base of the skull, just behind the ear. Finally, a muscle of no great size (*Serratus posticus superior*) is attached to the backs of the upper five ribs on each side, and passes up the back of the neck to the skull.

The *muscles of expiration* do not require special enumeration here. They are few and weak in comparison with those of inspiration, because the chest once filled can empty itself by force of gravitation and contractile elasticity alone.

The chest contains the *lungs, bronchial tubes, heart,* etc. At the top of the chest the windpipe, or trachea, divides into two bronchial tubes, one for each side, which pass outwards from each other for a few inches, and then divide gradually into numerous small branches, like those of a tree. The ultimate branches are no thicker than a pin, and terminate each in a group of little cells, called air-cells. All these little tubes and cells collected and connected together into a mass on each side of the chest form the lungs, which are thus of a spongy nature. They are also very elastic, and if distended with air, will re-contract to their previous size.

THE LARYNX.

The windpipe is about 4½ inches long, and at the upper part of the throat undergoes expansion and modification so as to form the essential organ of voice, the larynx. Under the chin the larynx can be seen and felt as the prominence called "Adam's apple." It consists of five principal cartilages, namely, the *epiglottis*, the *thyroid*, or shield-cartilage, the *cricoid*, or ring-cartilage, and two *arytænoid* cartilages.[1]

Fig. 1.

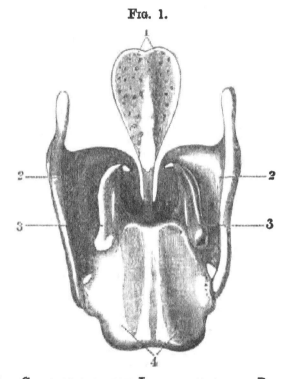

THE CARTILAGES OF THE LARYNX SEEN FROM BEHIND.

1. The epiglottis. 2. The thyroid cartilage, its wings and horns. 3. The arytænoid cartilages tipped with the cartilages of Santorini. 4. The cricoid cartilage, its body.

---

[1] These names are of Greek origin, *i.e.*, from ἐπιγλωττίς, *upon the glottis*, or space between the vocal reeds; θυρεὸς, *a shield*; κρίκος, *a ring*; ἀρύταινα, a vessel of a doubtful kind, probably *a spouted ladle* (see Stephanus, *Thesaurus Linguæ Græcæ*, s.v.). In the latter instance the resemblance is most likely that of the whole upper outlet of the larynx, the epiglottis forming the spout.

The *epiglottis* is the highest cartilage, and stands erect against the back of the tongue, above and in front of the other parts of the larynx. In shape it much resembles a leaf, being broad and expanded above, and dwindled below into a stalk-like extremity.

The *thyroid* cartilage is the largest, and forms the front and sides of the larynx. It is quite open behind, where its wings, as they are termed, terminate in rounded margins, which are prolonged upwards and downwards into horns, four in number, two on each side, two above and two below. In front it is cloven down the centre for half its length, and the rest of the central part has a peculiarly elastic structure[1] and gives attachment inside to the vocal bands.

The *cricoid* cartilage is very like a signet-ring, with a broad, thick part behind, and forming a slender half hoop in front, just under the lower edge of the thyroid cartilage. At this place an elliptical chink exists between the two, which are thus separated for about a third of an inch from above downwards at the widest part. Behind, the lower horns of the thyroid cartilage embrace the thick part or body of the cricoid like two short fingers, and a hinge-like joint is thus formed. The back part of the cricoid, therefore, projects upwards, not quite half way, into the open space of the thyroid.

The *arytænoid* cartilages are a pair, and form two small, irregular, three-sided pyramids, about half an inch in height. Their apices are above, and their

---

[2] Luschka, *Der Kehlkopf des Menschen.* Tübingen, 1871, p. 67.

bases rest, about a third of an inch apart, on the upper thick edge of the body of the cricoid, where two smooth surfaces or *facets* are prepared for them. They stand between and close to the posterior margins of the thyroid cartilage, and thus tend to fill up still more its open space. In front and below they run into rather long points, called the vocal processes, because the vocal bands spring from them. They turn and glide freely on the smooth part of the cricoid, to which they are fastened by ligamentous fibres.

In addition to these great cartilages there are also several small ones, called *sesamoid*, some not larger than a pin's head. Two such (*Capitula Santorini*) form the apparent apices of the arytænoid cartilages. Another pair (*Cartilagines Wrisbergii*) lie in the folds of membrane (*ary-epiglottic*) which form laterally the upper margin of the larynx. The others will be noticed wherever they appear to bear on the mechanism of voice.

The soft parts of the larynx consist of the vocal bands, muscles, blood-vessels, nerves, etc., the whole being clothed with mucous membrane,[1] which induces a smoothness and uniformity of surface.

The *vocal bands,*[2] *or reeds,* to which all the other structures are subservient, consist at their edges, which move from side to side, to and from each other, of strong, whitish, and highly elastic tissue. Behind,

[1] The red, moist membrane which covers the internal surfaces of the body is called *mucous membrane.*

[2] Generally called vocal *cords* in this country, but, as this term conveys a false idea of their acoustic nature (see p. 108), it seems to me preferable to call them vocal *bands* (like the German *Stimmbanden*) or *reeds.*

they are attached to the vocal processes of the arytænoid cartilages, and in front to the thyróid cartilage, quite close together, running into each other in fact. The space between them, the glottis, is therefore triangular in shape, because the vocal bands

Fig. 2.

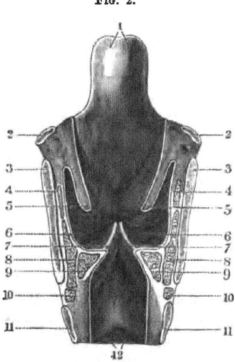

Transverse Vertical Section of the Larynx seen from Behind.

1. Epiglottis. 2. Tongue-bone. 3. Thyroid cartilage. 4. Thyro-ary-epiglottic muscles. 5. Ventricular bands. 6. Ventricles. 7. Vocal bands. 8. Ext. and sup. thyro-arytænoid muscles. 9. Int. ditto. 10. Lateral crico-arytænoid muscles. 11. Cricoid cartilage. 12. Trachea.

can be drawn widely apart posteriorly, but are fixed to the one spot anteriorly. A space exists between each vocal band and the inside of the wings of the thyroid cartilage, which is filled up with muscle.

Taken with this muscle, which is intimately connected with them, the vocal bands resemble a pair of prisms, fixed by their base, horizontally and parallel to each other, to the cartilaginous side-walls of the larynx, and projecting towards one another with their free sharp edges. Three of the little cartilages mentioned are generally found imbedded in the substance of the vocal bands where they are attached to the thyroid cartilage, one at the point where they run into each other, and one at the extremity of each just before they join.[1]

Near the position where the stalk-like process of the epiglottis is attached to the thyroid cartilage there is an eminence, called the cushion of the epiglottis, which projects over the anterior extremities of the vocal bands.

The upper surfaces of the vocal bands are flat, and in order to give them breadth a deep hollow is scooped out of the fleshy part of the larynx, just above them on each side. These cavities are called the *ventricles*, or pockets of the larynx. The upper edges of the ventricles are somewhat thickened and cord-like, wherefore they were formerly thought to be a second pair of vocal cords. On this account they are now

[1] Luschka, op. cit. p. 80. Henle found them to be condensed elastic tissue, not actually cartilage—*Handbuch der Eingeweidelehre*, Braunschweig, 1866, p. 239. Seiler (*The Voice in Singing*, Philadelphia, 1868, p. 60 and Appendix) describes a pair of small cartilages which project into the posterior ends of the vocal cords, and states that they are also mentioned by Wilson. They are not, however, noticed by Wilson or any other anatomist, and I have never found anything of the kind in the situation indicated. They must, therefore, have arisen from some error in the writer's dissections.

generally called *false vocal cords.* But a better name for them is "ventricular bands."[1]

The larynx has several muscles attached to it, which may be considered in two sets, *i.e.,* an *intrinsic* and an *extrinsic,* or the muscles which move the vocal bands and those which draw the whole larynx up and down in the throat. The names of these muscles usually imply the cartilages to which they are attached.[2]

The *intrinsic* muscles are mostly attached to the little arytænoid cartilages, because in moving them about the vocal bands are moved. We have seen that the body of the vocal bands is formed by a muscle (*Thyro-arytænoid*). This muscle consists of a complicated entanglement of fibres, the most apparent division of which is into an internal, an external, and a superior set. A few fibres of the superior portion curve upwards anteriorly towards the epiglottis, and appear to act as a depressor of that cartilage. A muscle (*Arytænoideus*) extends between the backs of the arytænoid cartilages, thus closing up the space between them. A pair of muscles (*Lateral Crico-arytænoids*) run from the posterior external angles of the arytænoid cartilages to the upper edges of the sides of the cricoid cartilage. And from the same angles another pair of long, slender muscles (*Constrictores vestibuli,* or *Thyro-ary-epiglottic*) pass upwards and inwards in a slanting direction, right across each other to opposite sides, and round the outside of the points of the arytænoid cartilages to the edges of the epiglottis. On each side a muscle (*Crico-thyroid*) stretches obliquely forwards and downwards from the lower margin of the wings of the thyroid cartilage to the thin part of the cricoid, limiting the lateral extent of the chink between the two cartilages. A pair of slender muscular fascicles is occasionally found extending downwards and slightly inwards from the extremities of the lower

---

[1] Like the German *Taschenbanden* (pocket bands): first proposed by Mackenzie (*The Laryngoscope,* etc. p. 74).

[2] It may be mentioned here that generally muscle must be fastened to something by each end. Its action is to bring the two points of its attachment closer together by its power of contracting or shortening its length, at the same time increasing in thickness, rigidity, and also in temperature.

horns of the thyroid cartilage to the sides of the body of the cricoid. Merkel[1] has given them the name of *Kerato-cricoids*. The last pair of intrinsic muscles (*Posterior Crico-arytænoids*) to be noticed are totally different in action to all the others, as they draw the vocal bands away from each other, in order to widen the glottis for the passage of air. They extend from the posterior external angles of the arytænoid cartilages (the third pair from the same point) to the back of the body of the cricoid cartilage.

Fig. 3.   Fig. 4.

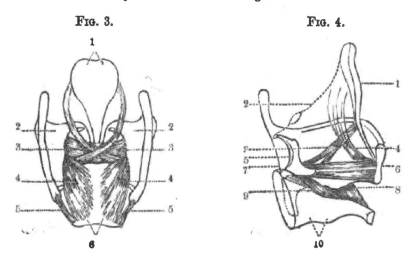

DIAGRAMS OF THE INTRINSIC LARYNGEAL MUSCLES.

Fig. 3.—View from Behind. 1. Epiglottis. 2. Thyroid cartilage. 3. Arytænoideus, crossed by the Constrictores vestibuli. 4. Posterior crico-arytænoids. 5. Kerato-cricoids (most frequently absent). 6. Cricoid cartilage.

Fig. 4.—Section showing the Lateral Muscles from the Inside. 1. Epiglottis. 2. Line of the upper margin of the larynx. 3. Superior thyro-arytænoid. 4. Depressor epiglottidis, or Dilator vestibuli. 5. Arytænoid cartilage. 6. Prismatic mass of the internal and external Thyro-arytænoids tipped by the vocal band. 7. Thyroid cartilage. 8. Crico-thyroid. 9. Lateral Crico-arytænoid. 10. Cricoid cartilage.

The *extrinsic* muscles are those which draw the whole larynx up or down. Above, the larynx is attached by a pair of strong muscles (*Thyro-hyoids*) to the tongue-bone, and hence, practically, to the base

---

[1] In 1857 Merkel claimed to have discovered these muscles, but, as Luschka has pointed out (op. cit. p. 129), they were really first noticed by Naumann in 1857, under the name of *Posterior Crico-thyroids*.

of the tongue. Behind, from the posterior margin of the wings of the thyroid cartilage two pairs of muscles (*Inferior constrictor of pharynx* and *Palato-pharyngeus*) pass up to the base of the skull and palate. Below, the corresponding pairs are separated by the whole width of the larynx, but approach each other as they ascend, and unite together.[1] A third pair (*Stylopharyngei*), having similar attachments, do not approach or unite. The principal muscles (*Sterno-thyroids*), which draw down the larynx, pass from the outsides of the wings of the thyroid cartilage to the upper part of the breast-bone. The extrinsic muscles are assisted in their action by several other muscles which are not attached directly to the larynx.

In addition to the muscles mentioned, which are generally sufficiently obvious in their direction and attachments, an examination of various larynges will frequently discover bundles of muscular fibres which are neither constant in their presence nor easily determinate as to their course.[2]

Variations of the Larynx in Age and Sex.—The larynx undergoes a great and rapid increase of size in the male sex, in about the fifteenth year of life. The voice then "breaks," and descends in pitch by nearly an octave. The same phenomena occur in females, but not to a marked extent, and the depression of vocal pitch is only about a tone or two. In adult age the male larynx is always much larger than that of the female; its cartilages are much firmer, and are pronouncedly angular in shape. The female larynx is more delicate in the structure of its cartilages, which are also curved in their outlines. The average length of the ligamentous portion of the vocal reeds

[1] The *inferior constrictor* is considered usually as one muscle, because the fibres immediately unite at the back part of the pharynx by means of a central sinewy seam. This muscle is also attached to the sides of the body of the cricoid cartilage, where its fibres run horizontally, but they increase in upward obliquity in the upper part of the muscle.

[2] The greatest amount of detail respecting these will be found in Luschka, op. cit.

is in the male nine, and in the female six lines.[1] After middle life the laryngeal cartilages gradually undergo ossification, whence in old age they become so rigid that much of the power of varying the tension of the vocal bands and inflecting the voice is lost.

The Vocal Tube, or Resonance Apparatus.

This consists mainly of the pharynx, mouth, and the double set of passages in the nose. The soft palate, pillars of the fauces, and lower-jaw may also be mentioned in this connection. There are also some auxiliary cavities, such as the portion of the larynx, about three-quarters of an inch deep, above the vocal cords, into which the ventricles open, and also some chambers in the thick bones of the head and face. Further, even the trachea and lungs may be ranged under this heading.

The *pharynx* extends from the upper part of the larynx to the base of the skull, forming the open space at the back of the mouth, and also at the back of the nose. Its dimensions vary in different persons. On an average it may be said to be 4½ inches from top

---

[1] The preparations in the Museum of the Royal College of Surgeons illustrate very well the variation of size in different larynges. See, for example, No. 939 P, a female larynx with ventricles that appear as mere chinks, and No. 939 P,a, a male larynx, the ventricles of which are almost large enough to contain the first joint of the little finger. For tables showing numerous comparative measurements of various parts of the larynx, see Béclard, *Dictionnaire Encyclopédique des Sciences Médicales*, Paris, 1868, art. *Larynx*, p. 555, etc.

to bottom, $2\frac{1}{2}$ from side to side, and $1\frac{1}{2}$ from behind forwards at its widest part opposite the base of the tongue. Its size and shape can be altered by movements of the various parts by which it is bounded.

The *mouth* requires no special description. Its capacity can be greatly varied by the action of the tongue and lower jaw.

The cavity of the *nose* is peculiar, and may be regarded as a collection of six small tubes. Each nostril is separated into three channels, running horizontally from before backwards to the upper part of the pharynx, by projections on its external wall formed by ridges of spongy[1] bone. The floor of the nose is formed by the upper surface of the hard-palate, or roof of the mouth.

The *soft-palate* is attached to the back of the hard-palate, and hangs down towards the back of the tongue, separating the mouth and pharynx. From its centre depends the uvula, a small body like a grape, as its name implies. The pillars of the fauces are two ridges of muscle on each side of the pharynx. They terminate above in the soft-palate, of which they form the greater part in arching across to unite with each other from opposite sides. Between them on each side lie the large glands called tonsils. The pair of posterior pillars consist of the muscles before-mentioned (*Palato-pharyngei*), which spring from the hind edges of the thyroid cartilage, and converge towards each other in

---

[1] "Spongy" in appearance only, being of a cellular structure, but not capable of being squeezed like a sponge.

passing upwards to unite at the palate over the uvula. The lower-jaw assists to open and shut the mouth, thereby altering its capacity and resonance properties.

The Tongue, Lips, and Teeth.

The tongue, lips, and teeth, superadded to the oral portion of the vocal tube, render possible articulate speech. The tongue and lips are almost wholly composed of muscular substance, which, being capable of infinite combinations of contractions, bestows on them a great versatility of motion. They, with the soft-palate and lower-jaw, may be considered as the active organs of articulation. The teeth take a passive part, acting as a kind of fulcrum for the tongue and lips.

Fig. 5.

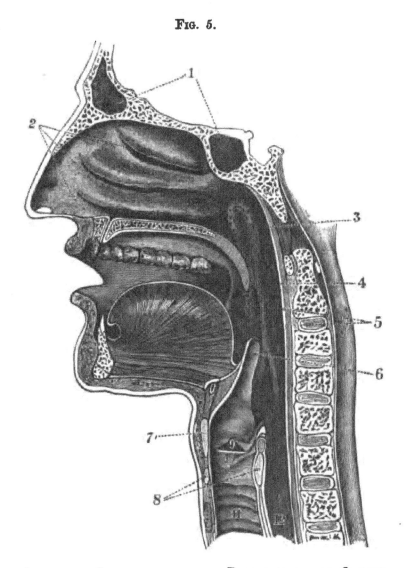

ANATOMICAL SECTION SHOWING THE RELATIONS OF THE ORGANS
OF VOICE.

1. Cavities in the bones of the head (frontal and sphenoidal cells). 2. The channels of the nose (sup., mid., and inf. meatus). 3. Entrance of Eustachian tube (leading to ear). 4. Uvula. 5. Pillars of the fauces with the tonsil between them. 6. Epiglottis. 7. Thyroid cartilage. 8. Cricoid cartilage. 9. Ventricle of larynx. 10. Vocal band. 11. Trachea (windpipe). 12. Œsophagus (gullet).

CHAPTER III.

PHYSICAL ACTION OF THE VOCAL ORGANS.

ACTION OF THE AIR-CHAMBER (RESPIRATION) — ACTION
OF THE VIBRATING ELEMENT (VOCAL REEDS)—THE
RESONANCE APPARATUS (VOCAL TUBE) — COMPASS
OF THE VOICE: INDIVIDUAL AND SEXUAL DIF-
FERENCES: REGISTERS—ARTICULATING APPARATUS.

In this chapter we have to consider the share taken
by the various parts of the body just described in
the production of voice and speech. In accordance
with the classification adopted, the action of the
thorax—the air-chamber or wind-chest—which initi-
ates the giving forth of sound, first claims notice.

THE AIR-CHAMBER (RESPIRATION).

The muscles attached to the chest-walls have the
power of enlarging the cavity of the thorax, so as
to draw air through the windpipe into the lungs,
which thus become inflated. The lungs have not in
themselves any ability to increase their capacity, and
are merely blown out by force of the air which rushes

into them, according as the chest expands, in order
to prevent the formation of a vacuum. As there are
two principal ways in which the thorax can be enlarged, inspiration is divided into (1) *abdominal* and
(2) *costal.*

In *abdominal breathing* inspiration is performed by
means of the diaphragm, which, when relaxed, projects upwards into the chest. By contracting it
greatly diminishes the amount of its upward projec-
tion, thus rendering the chest more capacious below,
at the same time that it presses downwards the
stomach and other abdominal viscera. When it
again relaxes the tendency of the abdominal organs
to return to their former position is sufficient to thrust
it up and expel the air introduced. In men ordinary
quiet breathing is chiefly diaphragmatic ; but in
women this muscle is used to a much less extent.[1]

Costal, or *rib breathing,* is accomplished by raising
the ribs, each of which can move, as on a pivot,
at its joint with the spine. During this action the
ribs are drawn up closer together in front and at the
sides, so as to lessen the vertical measurement of the
spaces between them, and the breast-bone is made to
advance. Behind, of course, the ribs merely rotate
on their heads, and cannot approach nearer to each
other, owing to the nature of their vertebral articula-

---

[1] Merkel thinks the activity of the diaphragm and its share in
respiration much overrated—*Anatomie und Physiologie des menschlichen
Stimm- und Sprach-organs,* Leipzig, 1857, p. 33. Hermann, on the
contrary, states that this is the principal respiratory muscle—*Human
Physiology,* trans. Gamgee, 1878, p. 196. The latter opinion seems
to me to be nearest the truth.

H

tion. The lower ribs also move much more than the upper ones, the first rib being, in fact, almost fixed. In costal inspiration the thorax is enlarged laterally and in front, because the larger ribs in being raised are made to occupy the place of the smaller ones. The ordinary costal muscles are generally sufficient for respiratory purposes, and only in taking a long breath —in forced inspiration—is the action of the extra-ordinary set required. The extraordinary muscles of inspiration are nearly all attached to the shoulder, and their real object is to regulate the motions of that part. If, however, the shoulders be elevated, they can raise the ribs, but only to a comparatively small extent, because their power is mostly exerted over the upper ribs, which have little freedom of motion. In some diseased conditions the movements of the dia-phragm and lower ribs are very much restricted, and in compensation the upper ribs are called on to work to their utmost. This is sometimes called *clavicular breathing*, because the motions of the chest are principally in the region of the collar-bone or clavicle.

With respect to *expiration*, when all the muscles of inspiration relax, the ribs fall by their own weight, the abdominal viscera returning to their position thrust back the diaphragm, and the lungs by con-tracting assist to drive out the superfluous air that is in them. Much of the act is therefore automatic, but if more force is wanted the muscles which pass from the lower ribs down the abdomen and flank can pull the ribs down strongly, and at the same time can press the abdominal organs up against the bottom of the chest. In this manner a forcible expiration can be performed.

The air of respiration may be divided into four different complements. In the first place we have the air which passes continually in and out of the lungs during quiet breathing. This is called *tidal air*. Next we have that which can be forced into the lungs when expanded to their full extent by drawing a deep breath. This gives the *vital capacity* of the chest. Thirdly, there is the complement of air that can be pressed out of the lungs when emptied by a strong effort of expiration, called *residual air ;* and lastly, there remains some air which cannot be squeezed out by any exertion during life, nor even after death without the direct application of such mechanical force to the lungs as would rupture their air-cells. Hence it may be called *fixed air*, or air which cannot be removed.

THE VIBRATING ELEMENT (VOCAL REEDS).

The column of air as it rushes out of the lungs through the trachea is rendered sonorous by the vibrations of the vocal reeds. Without these membranous bands man would be voiceless, or at least could only speak in a whisper, as is frequently seen in cases where they are paralysed or destroyed through disease. Before, however, examining minutely into the powers of the larynx to generate sound by the light of modern science, it may be instructive to glance at the opinions entertained by some of the earliest philosophers regarding the nature of voice, and to trace briefly the evolution of our knowledge of the subject from ancient times to the present day. A volume, indeed, might easily be filled with these matters alone, as the interest of such questions has always led many to attempt their solution, whilst the former deficiencies of anatomical and acoustic science and the difficulties of empirical observation rendered the numerous conjectures conflicting and many of them baseless.

Survey of Principal Pre-laryngoscopic Theories of Voice.

Hippocrates, 460 B.C.[1]   Though always paying great attention to the condition of the voice in disease,[2] as an index to the state of the patient, he had yet no definite idea of the existence of any special physiological arrangement that could be termed a vocal organ.   In the age of the "father of physic" the position of the lungs and the windpipe was known, but their functions were so little understood that it was generally supposed that liquids passed down the trachea. Hippocrates, however, was in advance of such an erroneous idea, and argues against it with considerable clearness, showing that he had made experiments in order to ascertain the truth.[3]   He frequently uses the word "larynx," and knows its site, but does not connect it

---

[1] The dates appended to the names of the various writers are actually or approximately those of birth.   The authors are arranged according to the order of their contributions.

[2] *E.g., Prædicti,* l. i. c. 2, et seq. *De Victu Acutorum,* c. 37, etc. etc.

[3] *De Corde,* c. 2.   *De Morbis,* l. iv. c. 30.

with the vocal powers. His ideas of the production
of voice he sums up in the following passage : "We
speak by means of the air which is drawn into the
whole body, but which mostly accumulates in the
cavities.   In rushing outwards through the vacant-
space[1] it makes a noise, for the head resounds. The
tongue articulates by moving into the fauces and by
pressing against the palate and teeth, thus producing
distinctness of voice.   If the tongue did not always
act in such a manner, man would be without language,
and would be confined to a monotonous sound."[2]

Aristotle, 384 B.C.   Nearly a century later than
Hippocrates, he shows a great empirical knowledge
of the varieties and peculiarities of voice in his
treatises on natural history and his problems relating
to voice and sound.   His general idea of acoustics
is expressed by the statement that "a loud voice
arises from a great motion of the air, an acute one
from a rapid, and a grave one from a slow motion
of the air."[3]   He also knows the position of the
larynx, its cartilaginous structure, and even recognizes
it as the part whence voice proceeds.[4] He makes no
mention, however, of the vocal bands, though he
evidently regards the sound as arising from the stream
of air being opposed in some manner in its passage
from the lungs.[5] He also states that the larynx emits
vowels, but the tongue and lips form consonants.[6]

---

[1] τὸ κενόν.
[2] *De Carnibus*, c. 19.
[3] *Problemata*, c. xi. 3.
[4] *Historia Animalium*, l. i. c. 12, 16.
[5] Ibid. l. iv. c. 9.
[6] Ibid.

Galen, 130 A.D. After an interval of more than five centuries, which are not represented by any extant work to mark the progress of physiological research, we come to Galen, the most voluminous writer and the most industrious and scientific observer of all the ancient physicians. So important a faculty as voice could of course not escape him, and he devoted a treatise to its elucidation. Unfortunately this work in its entirety is lost, but fragments remain sufficient to show what were his ideas on the subject.[1] He knew that the larynx was composed of separate cartilages, but thought that the arytænoids formed one piece. Further, he had some notion respecting the action of the vocal bands, as he states that " in the interior of the larynx is a body which resembles no other part of the animal structure, but is very similar to the tongue of a flute,[2] especially if regarded from above." " This," he continues, " is the first and most important organ of voice, for, in order that the animal may emit sound, a narrowing of the laryngeal channel is necessary, and such is exactly the office of this part, which I therefore call the *glottis*, or tongue of the larynx." Proceeding with his description, Galen describes also the ventricles of the larynx, and alludes to the secondary use of the vocal bands in closing the windpipe in order to hold the breath, an action in which he thinks the ventricles assist.[3] He mentions,

[1] Apud Oribasium, l. xxiv. c. 9.

[2] A kind of ancient flute, which probably resembled the oboë in being sounded by means of a double reed.

[3] See Appendix i.

in addition, that the uvula has a great effect on the power and beauty of the voice.[1] Galen knew the position and action of the muscles of the larynx well enough to enumerate them almost completely, and to divide them into an intrinsic and extrinsic set.[2]

Fabricius of Aquapendente,[3] 1537. After Galen no writer of original research added anything to the literature of the voice for fourteen centuries, a period which carries us through the Middle Ages and beyond the Renaissance into the beginning of our own times. Fabricius,[4] having mastered all previous knowledge of the subject, made a careful anatomical examination of the larynx and thought carefully over the nature of sound. He discovered that the arytænoid cartilages formed a pair instead of a single piece, and analysed the possible action of the various muscles of the vocal apparatus. He noticed especially the power of the inferior constrictor of the pharynx to press together the wings of the thyroid cartilage, and observed that the thyro-arytænoid muscle (the intrinsic muscle of the vocal bands) contained several distinct sets of fibres which must give it many essentially different modes of action. But the science of acoustics was scarcely born in his day, and he relied mainly on the vague notions of Aristotle. His ideas respecting

---

[1] Apud Oribasium, l. xxiv. c. 10.

[2] *De Usu Partium,* l. vii. c. 12 ; l. xvi. c. 4.

[3] Vesalius may be passed over, as, although he describes the larynx in his great anatomical work (*De Humani Corporis Fabrica,* Basileæ, 1543, l. i. c. 38), he goes no further than Galen, and his researches on this side did not enable him even to recognize the duality of the arytænoid cartilages.

[4] *De Larynge Vocis Instrumento,* partes iii. Venetiis, 1600.

the formation of voice were therefore necessarily in-
conclusive and erroneous. He believed that the vocal
bands acted like the lips in whistling, and that pitch
was determined by the size of the aperture between
them, and also by alterations in the length and width
of the vocal tube, *i.e.*, the pharynx, etc., consequent on
the motions of the larynx and trachea. In comparing the voice to artificial instruments he regarded it
as partly similar to an ordinary flute, but possessing,
moreover, some analogy to the trumpet, the player on
which varied the compression of his lips to produce
different notes.[1] Though Fabricius advanced on his
predecessors in practical acquaintance with the vocal
organs, yet his theory of voice was retrograde to the
shrewd guess of Galen, who compared the larynx to
a reed-flute.

Fabricius also studied the phenomena of articulate
speech,[2] and illustrated his observations on this subject
by an analysis of the vocal power of animals.[3] He
described the movements of the vocal organs in the
production of vowels and the different classes of
consonants with an accuracy which has scarcely been
surpassed by any modern physiologist.

Mersenne, 1588. This French philosopher and
Jesuitical priest was a diligent student of almost
every science, and also a voluminous writer. Being
well acquainted with music and musical instruments,[4]

---

[1] Op. cit. pt. iii. c. 11.
[2] *De Locutione et ejus Instrumentis.* Patavii, 1603.
[3] *De Brutorum Loquela.* Patavii, 1604. See Appendix iii.
[4] See his treatises—*Harmonicorum,* Libri viii. and *De Instrumentis
Harmonicis,* Libri iv. Lutetiæ Parisiorum, 1635.

he possessed some of the prime qualifications necessary for the analysis of the laws of voice production, though not being a physician or anatomist he could not carry his speculations to a definite issue. In his *Treatise on Universal Harmony*[1] he discusses the nature of voice, and his practical acoustic knowledge enables him at once to reject the supposition of Fabricius that the alterations of pitch are due to changes in the dimensions of the vocal tube, and leads him to attach more importance to the immediate action of the vocal bands. He almost concludes that voice is produced by the vibrations (*tremblements*) of the vocal bands, but is uncertain whether they can be considered as reeds or strings. He even hesitates to decide whether they move themselves or merely cause the air to vibrate by forming a passive interruption as it rushes by. He is clear, however, as to the action of reeds, and remarks: "Had we not the example of reeds, which make us understand the movements of the tongue (*languette*) of the larynx which anatomists call *glottis*, it would be difficult to know how the voice of man can have a compass of three or four octaves."[2]

Dodart,[3] 1634. Dodart was one of the court physicians in the reign of Louis XIV., and was a man of considerable scientific acquirements, though not of much original research. In 1700, nearly at the end of his life, he turned his attention to the elucidation of

---

[1] *De l' Harmonie universelle.* Paris, 1637, l. i. prop. 13, etc.

[2] Ibid. prop. 16.

[3] Some years previous to Dodart, Perrault, his preceptor, wrote an essay on sound in which he emitted a theory of voice, but he introduced no new idea—*Essais de physique*, tom. iii. p. 146. Paris, 1680.

voice,[1] and after making some anatomical observations came to the conclusion that the glottis alone produced sound. At the same time he allowed that the resonance of the mouth and nose might affect the quality of the tones. His conception of the function of the muscles of the larynx was, however, very imperfect, and he absurdly supposed that their action was too coarse to allow them to participate in the production of voice, and that the elastic fibres of the vocal bands possessed a peculiar power of contraction unexampled in any other tissue of the body. " Voice," he remarks, " arises from the vibrations of the lips of the glottis, the number of which vibrations depends, not on their dimensions, but on their tension and the swiftness of the air as it rushes out." According as higher notes are given forth he thinks that the glottis becomes gradually narrower, and the falsetto voice is formed by a glottis constricted " beyond measure." Dodart supposed, in short, that for low notes the lips of the glottis stood apart about a line and approached each other by degrees with elevation of pitch, the rise of the notes being aided by the force with which the wind was expelled from the lungs.[2] He also considered that the glottis acted similarly to the lips in whistling, which he therefore calls a " labial glottis." He can find no artificial instrument to which the voice

---

[1] *Histoire et mémoires de l'Académie Royale des sciences*, 1700, p. 17 and p. 238; 1706, p. 15 and p. 388; 1707, p. 18 and p. 66.

[2] Dodart calculated that the width of the slit between the vocal cords during phonation varied from one line to complete approximation, and that the action of the glottis was so delicate that by its adjustment it could divide this small space into 9,632 parts, rendering at each point a separate tone—op. cit. 1700, pp. 23, 264.

may be likened, though he inclines to the reed theory, and instances the fact that "Filidor *père* can render all the tones and semi-tones of an octave from the mouthpiece alone of a bassoon merely by varying the pressure of his lips." He can only compare the action of the vocal bands to that of the edge of a piece of paper pasted over the crevice of a badly-fitting window-sash when thrown into vibration by the draught of air (*châssis bruyant*). Such an arrangement, in effect, would constitute a kind of membranous reed, but Dodart's acoustic science was too insufficient to enable him to mature his comparison.

Ferrein, 1693. Also a physician, and the first who made actual acoustic experiments on the natural larynx.[1] He showed that voice was produced by the vibrations of the glottis, as by touching the vocal cords so as to stop their movement the sound was extinguished. He also demonstrated that the intensity of the tones depended on the force of the blast of air. He believed, however, that the vocal bands acted like a pair of strings set in motion by the stream of air, which he compared to a violin-bow, and that the elevation of pitch was caused solely by a progressive increase of tension. He was led to these conclusions by observing in his experiments that the notes of the vocal bands were raised by shortening or by stretching in a manner analogous to stringed instruments. But failing to perceive any natural provision for shortening the vocal bands, he could only think

---

[1] *Histoire et mémoires de l'Académie Royale des sciences*, 1741, p. 51 and p. 409.

that the compass of the voice was obtained entirely by altering their tension. When Ferrein had definitely formed these ideas he bestowed the name of "vocal cords" on the lips of the glottis, which, though conveying a false notion, is still universally employed in this country.

Cuvier (*G.*), 1779. The illustrious naturalist, not being a practical acoustician, could only surmise generally as to the formation of voice when it was necessary to adopt some view of the subject in his comprehensive work on *Comparative Anatomy*.[1] He supposes that the glottis acts in conjunction with the vocal tube like an ordinary reed instrument, such as the clarionet, in which the pitch of the note is determined by the length of the pipe.[2] At the same time he allows that the amount of shortening that the vocal tube can undergo is inconsiderable.

Dutrochet, 1776. A physician, he made a careful study of sound, and compared the action of the glottis to that of the lips in playing the horn (class of brass wind-instruments), but he maintained that pitch was dependent only on changes in the vibrating element. He introduced a new question into the debate by asserting that the muscular portion of the vocal bands alone generated the sonorous vibrations,

---

[1] *Leçons de l'anatomie comparée*, tom. iv. pp. 496, 522. Paris, 1880, etc.

[2] He says: "Leur effet (les rubans vocaux) est de faire varier l'anche de l'instrument vocal, de manière à produire les tons harmoniques de chaque ton fundamental déterminé par la longueur du tube de cet instrument." *Ibid.*

whilst the fibrous (ligamentous) tissue only served to shield their edges.[1]

Liscovius, 1785. A German physician who, like Dodart, deviated into the false track of supposing that complete approximation of the vocal bands was not a necessary factor for the emission of tone. He advocated that for low notes a considerable aperture remained between the lips of the glottis, which became narrowed as the pitch was elevated.[2]

Geoffroy St. Hilaire, 1772. This celebrated French philosopher and naturalist devised a rather fantastic theory of sound,[3] and agreed with Ferrein that in the chest-voice the larynx acts as a stringed instrument. Falsetto notes were produced like those of a flute. He explains in detail the movements of the vocal organs in forming different tones, but his notions are purely imaginative.[4]

Savart, 1791. This eminent acoustician magnified the errors of Dodart and Liscovius, and promulgated a theory of voice entirely at variance with the truth.[5] He believed, in fact, that if the vocal bands were brought close together during phonation, speaking would be attended with too great an effort. He concluded, therefore, that the glottis always remained open, and that sound was produced by the action of the true and false vocal cords, so called, with the ventricles between them, on the current of air. In

---

[1] *Essai sur une nouvelle theorie de la voix*, Thèse de Paris, 1806.
[2] *Theorie der Stimme.* Leipzig, 1814.
[3] *Philosophie anatomique*, p. 284. Paris, 1818.
[4] Ibid. pp. 304, 358, et seq.
[5] *Annales de chimie et de physique*, 1825, t. xxx. p. 64.

this manner the glottis, according to his idea, sounded analogously to a kind of hunter's whistle, or bird-call, which consisted of two small perforated plates with a short tubular cavity between them of much larger diameter than their apertures.[1]   In general he thought the principle of voice was that of a flute, but, having discovered that a tube with thin elastic walls could be made to yield a variety of tones through alteration in its rigidity alone, he attributed to varied tension of the trachea a remark-able influence on pitch.   The supposed resemblance, however, between such a tube and the trachea, constructed for the most part of firm cartilaginous rings and built up nearly all round with solid tissues, is but slight, and amounts practically to nothing.[2] Savart, however, adhered to his theories with great tenacity, and even when it was demonstrated to him that reed tones could be artificially produced from the detached larynx on bringing the vocal bands together, he rejected the proof with the expression, " *Ce sont bien des sons d'anche, mais ils sont criards.*"

Magendie, 1783.   A professional physiologist, he established by a vivisection that the vocal bands actually vibrated like reeds during phonation.[3]

Malgaigne, 1806.   The eminent surgeon, who sup-ported the reed-theory and endeavoured to construct an artificial larynx, imitating the vocal bands with

---

[1] In children's toys which sound by pressing a kind of bellows, and in hollow india-rubber toys, the whistling noise is generally produced by such a contrivance.   The pitch rises merely by increasing the force of the blast of air.

[2] See Müller, *Physiology,* vol. ii. p. 10.

[3] *Précis de physiologie,* t. i. p. 301.   Paris, 1838.

strips of parchment. He thought the falsetto voice was produced by the contraction of the soft-palate cutting off the nasal portion of the vocal tube.[1]

Lehfeldt, 1811. A German physician who was the first to state, what is still believed to be correct, that in the falsetto voice the vibrations of the vocal bands are confined to their edges.[2]

Johannes Müller, 1801. A great German physiologist who made the most exhaustive and ingenious experiments with the natural detached larynx and artificial imitations of it.[3] He showed conclusively

[1] *Archives générales de médicine*, t. xxv. 1831, pp. 201, 327.

[2] "Et vocularum falsarum sonos in larynge ipso formari, inde videtur effici. . . . . . In larynge quoque vibrationes non per totam latitudinem expansæ, in marginibus tantum se continentes multo tenuiorem tenerioremque efficiunt sonum."—*Nonnulla de Vocis Formatione*. Berolini, 1835, pp. 64, 65.

[3] *Elements of Physiology*, trans. by Baly, London, 1837, vol. i. Appendix, and vol. ii. sec. 3. Müller's experiments have often been repeated and confirmed: in this country most carefully by Wyllie (*Edinburgh Medical Journal*, vol. xii. 1866, p. 214). It may be stated, however, that the action of the laryngeal muscles cannot be imitated with any exactitude on a detached larynx, but the artificial production of a scale from the vocal reeds alone by progressive tension is sufficient to nullify the theory that changes of pitch are obtained by shortening or lengthening the vocal tubes in a manner analogous to opening or closing side-holes on a flute or clarionet, or to drawing in and out the sliding tube of a trombone, as was advocated by Despinay de Bourg in his first essay (*Thèse de Paris*, 1821, No. 46, p. 12). All that acoustic experiments can perform with the detached larynx can doubtless be done much more perfectly and effectively by the living muscles. We may except, however, the tension of the vocal reeds, which can be increased artificially until they are ruptured, whereas in the natural state there is a safeguard against such an accident. Thus Müller tightened the reeds of a male larynx until he produced the note

; an octave higher, probably, than the subject in life could have sounded by such means.

that a compass of a couple of octaves could be obtained from the vocal bands merely by varying their tension when approximated. He attached small weights to them, and by increasing gradually the amount of weight found that pitch rose in proportion. He also experimented with membranous reeds, some of animal tissue,[1] some of caoutchouc, and made it clear that a greater length of tube was required to affect their pitch and produce a series of notes than could be furnished by the vocal passages. In addition, he showed how unlikely was Savart's idea that alteration of tension in the walls of the trachea would influence pitch of voice.[2]

The Laryngoscope and its Revelations.

After the researches of Müller but little was left in the way of direct experiment to be done by his successors, although conflicting theories of voice were still held, owing to the difficulty of obtaining the absolute demonstration or ocular proof of any one set of deductions. The increase of acoustic science gradually threw a light over many obscure points, but it was only on the discovery of the laryn-

---

[1] Such as the middle coat of arteries.

[2] These sketches of the opinions of pre-laryngoscopic authors on voice are only a few selections of the principal names which might easily be multiplied fourfold. For a complete bibliography of the subject, with short allusions to the theories of the various writers, see the work of the younger Liscovius, *Physiologie der menschlichen Stimme*, Leipzig, 1846, p. 71, et seq.

goscope that most of the doubts and absurdities were finally resolved and laid to rest.[1] Many unsuccessful, or perhaps disregarded, attempts to see the action of the living larynx had been made prior to 1854, when Manuel Garcia, a teacher of singing, actually caught sight of his own vocal bands in a small dentist's mirror pushed into the back of his mouth. Continuing his observations on his own throat, he was at the end of a year enabled to read a paper at the Royal Society [2] on the formation of voice as elucidated by means of his invention. Garcia's device did not, however, attract much immediate notice, and it was only at the end of two years that Czermak, a German medical professor, commenced a systematic practice with the instrument, on himself and on patients, and showed finally the feasibility and facility of viewing the living larynx. As soon as Czermak had satisfied himself as to the actual value of the invention, he travelled into the chief cities of Europe, and, by

---

[1] It would be impossible and even unprofitable to recount within the limits of this work the numerous baseless and absurd opinions relating to voice that have been put forward from time to time by theorists unacquainted, on the one hand, with acoustics, or on the other, with anatomical and physiological observations ; some, indeed, ignorant on both sides of the question. Such suppositions, for instance, as that the falsetto voice is produced by a new glottis formed above the larynx (Colombat de l'Isère, *Traité medico-chirurgical des maladies des organes de la voix*, Paris, 1834, p. 85), or that the musical tones of the voice are formed at the bifurcation of the trachea, as in birds (Romer, *The Physiology of the Human Voice*, London, 1845), or that the falsetto notes are produced by blowing into the ventricles of the larynx, as a schoolboy whistles with an excavated nut (Illingworth, *Students' Journal*, London, 1876 ; a series of papers otherwise well digested), etc. etc.

[2] *Proceedings of the Royal Society of London*, vol. vii. No. 13, 1855.

I

giving laryngoscopic demonstrations before the principal physicians and surgeons of each town, achieved the introduction of the laryngoscope into medicine as an indispensable adjunct to the local study of disease.[1]

The laryngoscope, as now used, consists simply of a small mirror, from half an inch to an inch in diameter, fixed at the end of a stem of sufficient length to allow it to be passed to the back of the mouth (middle part of pharynx). It is held there at such an inclination as to reflect the parts of the throat below. Some practice is required in order to be able to place it quickly at the proper angle, which in fact differs somewhat in almost every individual, and also in order to manipulate it so delicately as not to irritate by pressure the tongue, palate, and other parts adjacent. The tongue should be protruded during the examination, as the larynx is thus drawn up higher in the throat. It may be held out gently with a small cloth. Of course a strong light must be thrown on the surface of the mirror, and for this purpose various kinds of accessory apparatus are employed.

The Vocal Reeds.—On inspecting the larynx with the laryngoscope, the rim of its upper outlet, surmounted in front by the epiglottis, which generally stands erect against the back of the tongue, is plainly visible. But the most striking objects are the vocal bands which are seen at a short distance below, projecting opposite each other from the sides of the inner

---

[1] For a full account of the labours of Garcia and Czermak in relation to the laryngoscope, see P. Richard, *Notice sur l'invention du laryngoscope*, Paris, 1861.

wall of the larynx, and of a pearly whiteness which
contrasts strangely with the redness of the surrounding
parts. Between them is the oblong aperture through
which the air continually passes to and fro, the glottis,
of dimensions varying at every moment, for the vocal
reeds are never absolutely at rest during breathing, but
with deep inspiration separate widely until they almost
disappear from sight behind the ventricular bands,
and with expiration gradually approach each other, so
as sometimes almost to touch. If the person under
observation speaks in an ordinary tone of voice they
draw together so closely as to reduce the glottis to a
mere thread-like fissure, and as the sound issues forth
the eye can perceive that they are in a state of
vibration. At one point they touch, viz., posteriorly,
where they join the tips of the vocal processes of the
arytænoid cartilages. Behind this the chink of the
glottis is continued backwards for a short distance, about
three lines, between the inner edges of the base of the
arytænoid cartilages (*cartilaginous glottis*), but this portion is probably incapable of vibration, and cannot properly be considered as forming part of the vocal reeds.

The theory of the generation of sound by our vocal bands is as
follows :—By the contraction of the expiratory muscles of our chest
we propel a stream of air from our lungs through our windpipe.
Impinging against the closed glottis from below, the current drives
the vocal bands apart sufficiently for a puff to escape. This relieves,
momentarily, the pressure of the air below, and the vocal bands at
once spring back towards each other by their own resiliency. The
glottis is thus again shut, the pressure re-accumulates below, and a
second puff escapes. By a continuance of this action the current
of our breath is divided into a series of puffs, variable in rapidity at
will, according to the height of the note, and a tone is produced in like
manner as is observed to occur when experimenting with the siren.

The Larynx as Viewed with the Laryngoscope.

Fig. 6.

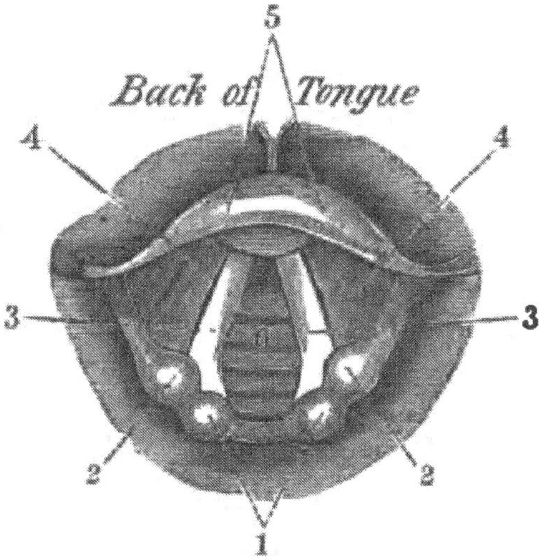

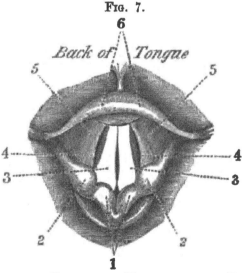

The Larynx during Quiet Breathing.

1. Arytænoid cartilages. 2. Cartilages of Wrisberg. 3. Vocal bands. 4. Ventricular bands. 5. Epiglottis with its cushion below. 6. Trachea.

Fig. 7.

The Larynx when Sounding a Note about the Level of the Ordinary Speaking Voice.

1. Arytænoid cartilages. 2. Cartilages of Wrisberg. 3. Vocal bands. 4. Entrance of ventricles. 5. Ventricular bands. 6. Epiglottis.

Considerable alterations take place in the appearance of the vocal reeds and the upper outlet of the larynx, during the production of a scale of notes from the lowest to the highest pitch. Whilst sounding the deepest notes of the *chest-register* the glottis is open in its whole length, and forms an elliptical slit, which, in a bass voice, may measure as much as a line at its widest part, when the vibrations strike outwards. After ascending two or three tones the tips of the vocal processes become visible, projecting towards each other across the chink, and on a rise of two or three tones more they come by degrees into contact. At this moment the glottis is seen to consist of two parts ; the main portion in front, forming a linear fissure between the vocal reeds of from a third to half-an-inch in length, and a small triangular space behind separating the arytænoid cartilages. This condition of the glottis occurs about the level of the ordinary speaking voice. In mounting a few notes higher, the posterior triangular space diminishes, until at last it is quite closed, and in this state it remains during the emission of the upper three or four chest-notes. At the same time the progressive narrowing of the anterior fissure, the actual vibratory glottis, continues until it is reduced to a mere dark line between the borders of the vocal reeds.[1] Concomitant with

[1] Mandl thinks the vocal cords vibrate in their whole length for every note of the chest-voice, and that the cartilaginous glottis never becomes quite closed till falsetto tones are produced (*Traité pratique des maladies du larynx*, Paris, 1872, p. 270). If it remains open in the upper notes, it is only for a hair's breadth, and as to this it would be impossible to pronounce dogmatically. Merkel divides the chest-register into two parts, in the lower of which the triangular space

these changes the vocal bands seem to be lengthened; they are so, in fact, by being stretched, but greater than their real is their apparent lengthening, which depends on their coming more into sight in the laryngeal mirror, according as the gamut is ascended. Their actual lengthening may be about a line,[1] their apparent increase of length twice or three times that amount. In the lowest notes the epiglottis generally conceals from view the front of the glottis; in the middle notes the cushion of the epiglottis still covers the anterior ends of the vocal bands, but at the top of the chest-register their tension is very evident, and appears to draw them away from their attachment to the thyroid cartilage, so as to bring their full length into sight. In mounting the scale of chest-notes, therefore, the outlet of the larynx undergoes enlargement, and its margins expand so as to afford a complete view of the interior. When a note is swelled to its maximum of loudness, the vocal reeds perform more ample vibrations in the same

is open and in the upper closed (*Die Functionen des menschlichen Schlund- und Kehlkopfs*, Leipzig, 1862, p. 96). My own general view accords closely with that of Krishaber (*Dictionnaire des sciences médicales*, Paris, 1868, art. *Laryngoscope*, p. 506). I have, however, observed various different appearances, dependent probably on the kind of voice, such as bass, tenor, etc., which could only be definitely explained by the examination of a large number of practised singers by an expert laryngoscopist. Two facts I believe to have ascertained in this connection, *i.e.*, (1) that in the tenor voice the cartilaginous glottis is closed in almost the whole compass, and (2) that in the alto (male) voice there is a hyper-development of the anterior sesamoid cartilages (see p. 86), which gives a special facility for shutting the ligamentous glottis in front for nearly a third of its length; an equivalent, in fact, to an anterior cartilaginous glottis.

[1] Probably less; their tension could not, of course, be effectively increased if they stretched too readily. See Illingworth, loc. cit.

period of time, their edges cannot be seen in such sharp definition, and the glottic aperture assumes a hazy appearance.

In the *falsetto-register*, the laryngoscopic appearances are in many respects the reverse of those just described. The rim of the larynx, instead of becoming dilated, suffers a progressive and marked constriction in proportion as the pitch rises, until at last only the edges of the vocal bands can be seen through the narrow

Fig. 8.

THE LARYNX DURING THE EMISSION OF FALSETTO NOTES
(MIDDLE OF RANGE).

orifice that remains. The object of the movements seems to be to shorten the glottis and limit the vibrating portion of the vocal reeds as much as possible. As soon as their tension can be increased no further by the means resorted to for the formation of chest-notes, a change occurs in the physiological mechanism for the purpose of obtaining a higher scale of tones by gradually reducing the size of the reeds. The aperture during the emission of the lower falsetto notes occupies the centre of the ligamentous glottis, and appears to be

from a quarter to a third of an inch in length, but
somewhat wider and more elliptical than at the highest
level of the chest-register.   It diminishes in length as
the sound mounts up, but at the same time its width,
if anything, rather increases.   At a certain elevation
of pitch, which, of course, varies considerably in
different individuals, the power of ascending any
higher is lost.

Action of the Laryngeal Muscles.

The *intrinsic muscular movements*,[1] by which the various positions and
conditions of the vocal reeds are determined, are, of course, only generally distinguishable by the laryngoscope, and can only be definitely
understood by the aid of anatomical dissections.   It is difficult, however, to gain an exact idea of the combination of actions requisite for
the production of the different pitches and qualities of voice.   Indeed,
to complete our knowledge of the physiology of the larynx it would be
necessary to have the means of observing the under surface of the
vocal reeds.   There are, therefore, gaps in our apprehension of the
subject which can only be filled by surmise.   The main action to allow
of phonation is to approximate the reeds, and this is done very well by
the contraction of the lateral crico-arytænoids which cause the arytænoid cartilages to rotate towards each other on their bases, so as to
bring the tips of their vocal processes close together or into actual
contact.   The same object can be effected by the thyro-arytænoid
muscles which form the bulk of the vocal reeds, whilst the arytænoid
cartilages can be drawn together so as to close the hinder part of the
cartilaginous glottis by the arytænoid muscle which passes between
them at their back.   The deepest notes are probably produced by the

---

[1] All Schech's careful experiments failed, except in the instance
of the posterior crico-arytænoids, to establish anything conclusive
respecting the action of the laryngeal muscles.   Many of them,
however, furnish a thread of probability to such of the above statements as depend on surmise.   See his work, *Experimentelle Unter-
suchungen über die Functionen der Nerven und Muskeln des Kehlkopfs.*
Würzburg, 1873. (Republished in the *Zeitschrift für Biologie*, Bd. ix.
1873.)

contraction of the external fibres of the thyro-arytænoid which approximate and at the same time relax the vocal reeds by drawing the arytænoid cartilages forward towards the thyroid cartilage, whilst the internal fibres of the same muscle, by remaining loose, favour slow and ample vibrations. In addition, a gentle contraction of the arytænoid muscle may narrow the cartilaginous glottis and assist in giving the necessary fixity to the arytænoid cartilages. The ascent of the next two or three tones is obtained merely by the gradual relaxation of the external thyro-arytænoids, which permit the reeds to regain their ordinary state of tension. A point is thus reached at which the vocal reeds are simply held together by the arytænoid muscle, assisted perhaps by the lateral crico-arytænoids. A fresh process now commences for the purpose of progressively tightening and stiffening the reeds and at the same time bringing them into close contact. The increase of tension is obtained by the action of the crico-thyroid muscle,[1] which draws the cricoid cartilage up towards the thyroid,[2] thus making the distance greater between the anterior and posterior attachments of the vocal reeds. In this way the chink between the two cartilages, which was stationary[3] during the emission of the deepest notes, becomes closed by degrees, as can be felt by placing a finger on it at the front of the neck. The contraction of the internal thyro-arytænoid commences, and gives firmness to the body of the reeds[4] and also holds them approximated, whilst the lateral crico-arytænoids cause the vocal processes to approach and finally to touch. Lastly, the arytænoid muscle contracts firmly, and completely shuts the cartilaginous glottis. The three latter muscles also steady the arytænoid

---

[1] Paralysis of the crico-thyroid or of the thyro-arytænoid destroys the power of forming a musical scale, and a gruff, monotonous voice results. See Magendie, op. cit. p. 302; Luschka, op. cit. p. 120; Ziemssen, *Cyclopædia of Medicine*, vol. vii. p. 940, 973; etc.

[2] Schech's view, which, as it appears to me, he has proved to be the correct one.—*Zeitschrift für Biologie*, Bd ix. 1873, p. 277. It is usually stated that the crico-thyroid muscle draws the thyroid cartilage down to the cricoid.

[3] Or perhaps somewhat dilated, through the thyro-arytænoid muscle causing the thyroid cartilage to rotate upwards and backwards on the cricoid, an action in which the kerato-cricoids, when existent, would assist.

[4] Some of the fibres of this muscle run obliquely, and are inserted into the edge of the vocal band. See Battaille, *Nouvelles recherches sur phonation*, Paris, 1861, p. 9.

cartilages so as to enable them to resist the traction made on them by the crico-thyroid. Finally the crico-thyroid space is quite closed, and the opposing margins of the cartilages are pressed forcibly together, whilst the vocal reeds are rendered tense and stiff to the utmost extent. Here results then a kind of dead-lock, and any further elevation of pitch by these means is impracticable. Such is the position at the top of the chest-register.

Fig. 9.

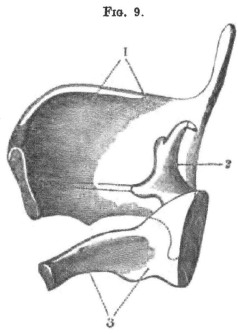

SECTION OF THE LARYNGEAL CARTILAGES SHOWING HOW LONGITUDINAL TENSION OF THE VOCAL BANDS IS EFFECTED.

1. Thyroid cartilage. 2. Arytænoid cartilage. 3. Cricoid cartilage. The dotted lines from the vocal process of the arytænoid cartilage to the thyroid indicate the position of the edge of the vocal band, which is tightened by progressive closure of the chink below, between the thyroid and cricoid cartilages.

The muscular actions called into play for the production of the falsetto tones are even less certain than those of the chest-voice. When it is required to ascend beyond the highest note of the chest-register, a change in the mechanism for forming the tones is necessary, and many, or all, of the previously contracted muscles suddenly relax, as is evidenced by the re-opening of the crico-thyroid space. A different and more complex method of putting on the voice is then adopted which yields a higher scale. For the lowest falsetto tone the vocal reeds are drawn tight and the space again closes, though not to the same extent as for the top chest-note.   The cartilaginous glottis is tightly shut, and the combined contraction of the external and superior thyro-arytænoids and the thyro-ary-epiglottic presses the vocal reeds firmly together, especially in front, where their rigidity is greatest owing to the presence of the sesamoid cartilages.   The constrictive action of the same muscles causes the external walls of the ventricles to encroach on the upper surface of the reeds, so as to reduce their breadth and limit the vibrations to their edges, producing at the same time the approach of the ventricular bands and circumferential narrowing of the laryngeal orifice so apparent in falsetto tones.   When these movements become extreme the highest limit of vocal pitch is reached.

A special question to be decided is the condition of the internal thyro-arytænoid muscle throughout the compass of the voice.   I have supposed it to be relaxed in the deepest notes and contracted during about the upper two-thirds of the chest-register.   It is probably relaxed again in the falsetto scale, as whilst in a loose state it could not vibrate if the ligamentous edge were simultaneously tightened. Such an arrangement would be an important factor in confining the vibration to the margins of the vocal reeds.   Merkel's[1] view of the matter is that this muscle, being contracted in the chest-register, renders the edges of the reeds thick, a favourable condition for the production of low and full tones, whilst its relaxation in the falsetto voice allows the formation of a thin, sharp margin which is specially adapted for rapid vibration.

On the whole, I think it most in accordance with observed facts to suppose that the falsetto range is produced by a truly sphincter-like

---

[1] *Physiologie der menschlichen Sprache*, Leipzig, 1866, p. 20.   The Tonic Sol-faists have made use of this idea to substitute the terms "thick" and "thin" for chest and falsetto-registers.   See Curwen, *Teacher's Manual of the Tonic Sol-fa Method*, 1875, p. 170, et seq.   Helmholtz suggests that "the head (falsetto) voice is probably produced by drawing aside the mucous coat below the vocal cords, thus rendering their edge sharper"—op. cit. p. 150.   It is only necessary to mention the hypothesis of Fournié, viz. :—" Nous sommes pleinement autorisé à conclure, que les vibrations sonores sont exclusivement produites par la petite portion de la muqueuse, qui récouvre le bord interne des rubans vocaux."—*Physiologie de la voix et de la parole*, Paris, 1866, p. 389.   Such an assumption is plainly opposed by physiology and acoustics.

action of all the constrictive glottic muscles. [1]   In such case the effect
would be a progressive concentric narrowing of the glottis, during
which it would tend to pass from an elliptic to a circular shape. [2]
Thus the aperture, until it had attained the circle, would be seen to
diminish in length and increase in breadth during the ascent of the
scale, and elevation of pitch could proceed, *cæteris paribus*, until the
reduction of the opening to a mere pin-hole. The remarkable delicacy
and elasticity of the cartilages of the female larynx is precisely the
condition most favourable to such an operation, and an explanation
would thus be afforded of the extraordinary range in the highest
register so often met with in female voices. [3]

Since writing the above I have become acquainted with some
researches of Professor Oertel on the vibrations of the vocal bands
when viewed laryngoscopically by a powerful intermittent light. [4]
He sums up his results as follows:—" According to the foregoing
observations the notes in the chest-register are produced by vibration
of the vocal bands as a whole, whilst the tones of the falsetto-register
originate by longitudinal division of the plane of the vocal bands
into aliquot parts through the formation of nodal lines." It does
not, however, appear to me that such aliquot division of the vocal
bands would account for the falsetto scale, which can be graduated
with the utmost delicacy from the *lowest* to the *highest* tone, but
only for a harmonic series, the practicable part of which would not
form a gamut. The phenomena, therefore, seen by the Professor
can scarcely be considered as conclusive without further elucidation.

---

[1] Such, in fact, as pointed out by Henle, is the fundamental action
of the set of muscles which close the glottis. *Handbuch der Eingeweidelehre*, Braunschweig, 1866, p. 249.

[2] I have not had an opportunity of observing laryngoscopically the
highest notes of the female voice, but the figure in Seiler (op. cit.
p. 58) depicted from autoscopic examination is in exact accordance
with the view propounded.

[3] See page 179.

[4] *Centralblatt für die medizinischen Wissenschaften*, Berlin, 1878, pp.
81, 99. Oertel recommends the electric light or the lime-light, which
may be caused to intermit by means of a circulating plate, perforated so as to let in and shut off the light in rapid alternation as it
rotates. The number of intermissions must coincide with the vibrations of the note sounded by the voice or with the octave of it. Oertel
calls this method of observing the larynx the " laryngostroboskopische
Untersuchungsmethode."

His description also of the ascent of the falsetto scale appears to indicate that the appearances were by no means certain, being invisible except " under favourable illumination with exact intermission ; " whilst the figure given is only put forward as " something like " (*entspricht etwa*). Some of Oertel's remarks are conformable to my own view, as when he says that in ascending the falsetto scale " the length of the vocal bands is seen to become shorter through both vocal processes being firmly pressed together, whilst the zone formed by the edges of the vocal bands, indicating the progressive elevation of pitch, becomes continually narrower." Altogether I surmise that the appearance of aliquot division may be due to secondary vibrations propagated over the entire surface of the vocal bands, whilst the main vibrations are confined to a comparatively small portion of their length and breadth. I do not, therefore, think it necessary to modify my previous opinions without additional researches on the points raised by Professor Oertel.

The *extrinsic muscles* of the larynx are in full activity during phonation. They move the larynx up and down in the throat, whilst they modify the vocal tubes for purposes of resonance and articulation. They also slightly alter the position of the larynx with respect to verticity. Their functions, therefore, are manifold. One of their chief offices is to steady the larynx in order to prevent its wavering in its place with the force of the blast of air. In sounding the deepest notes this is done by the sterno-thyroid, which at the same time probably draws asunder the wings of the thyroid cartilage so as to increase the breadth of the vocal reeds. This muscle also causes the larynx to descend towards the sternum about one-eighth of an inch. According as the tones become elevated the progressive retraction of the soft-palate calls into play the palato-pharyngeus muscle, and the larynx is gradually raised. When the falsetto scale is reached the inferior constrictor of the pharynx begins to contract and contributes to the elevation of the larynx, but its main action seems to be the compression of the wings of the thyroid cartilage,[1] in order to facilitate the peculiar closure of the glottis demanded in

---

[1] Advocated by Wyllie (loc. cit. pp. 228, 236) and Fournié (op. cit. p. 404), but denied by Mandl (op. cit. p. 372). This action of the inferior constrictor seems to me a very obvious one. Indeed, as Wyllie remarks, it is possible to gain a note or two of falsetto by pressing the wings of the thyroid cartilage together with the fingers. The cleft anteriorly evidently exists in order to allow mobility to the wings.

this register. Throughout the whole compass of the voice the thyro-hyoid muscle is in a state of contraction, and is most instrumental in giving the necessary fixity to the larynx. Its activity is greatest at opposite extremes of the scale. On account of the intimate attachment of the larynx to the tongue-bone, it follows very closely the movements of the tongue during articulation,[1] and these motions, as Mandl[2] has pointed out, have often been erroneously set down as exacted by the alterations of pitch. The sum of the excursions of the larynx from the deepest chest-note to the top of the falsetto-register amounts to less than an inch, but if the tongue be kept at rest a great part of the scale can be sounded without any material change in the position of the organ.

The *ventricular bands* (called also superior or false vocal cords) appear to come down on the upper surface of the vocal reeds during the emission of falsetto notes, as first observed by Mandl.[3] In this way they may limit the vibrations of the reeds. It is impossible, however, to speak decisively on this point, as they cannot be viewed obliquely enough with the laryngoscope to see whether they actually touch. In the upper chest-notes they are stretched, and are curved slightly upwards by the force of the passing sound-waves. Their main use seems to be to close the larynx during holding the breath, swallowing, and coughing. Under these circumstances they are tightly approximated.

RESONANCE APPARATUS [4] (VOCAL TUBE, ETC.).

The Ventricles.—The existence of these small cavities

---

[1] Thus in whispering (which does not require any vibration of the reeds) a succession of vowels from the lowest to the highest (see p. 144) a progressive rise of the larynx may be felt.

[2] Op. cit. pp. 255, 265.

[3] Ibid. p. 271.

[4] I have excluded the thorax from a place amongst the resonance apparatus, because it is scarcely possible to estimate how far it reinforces the vocal tones. The voice can be heard to resound on applying the ear to the chest of a person who is speaking or singing, but it is doubtful whether this resonance is audible with the sound issuing from the mouth. Deep notes create an impression of distance, high tones of proximity, and therefore we speak of "chest" and "head"

appears necessary in order to allow a proper breadth to
the vocal reeds. In man, their acoustic influence on
the voice must be unappreciable on account of their
limited area; but in the *mycetes*, or howling monkey,
they communicate with several large pouches on each
side of the throat, and with excavations in the body of
the tongue-bone, so as to impart to the cries of these
animals a degree of resonance which renders them
louder than the roaring of lions.[1] On the other hand,
that they are absolutely unessential in conferring an
extraordinary voice-power, is proved by the fact that
the lion, tiger, ox, and many other animals that do not
lack in this respect, have neither ventricles nor
ventricular bands.[2]

The Epiglottis.

Viewed with the laryngoscope, the epiglottis presents
considerable variability of size, shape, and position in
different persons. Sometimes it forms a mere projec-
tion of the anterior margin of the larynx of less than
three-quarters of an inch, and stands erect against the
back of the tongue; or it may extend backwards over
the larynx, like a roof, for nearly an inch, so that its
surfaces are almost horizontal. It may appear round,

notes. Acoustically, however, these terms appear arbitrary and
meaningless. See Woiliez, quoted in *The Medical Record*, 1879,
p. 193.

[1] See Owen, *Anatomy of the Vertebrates*, vol. iii. p. 597.

[2] Béclard, loc. cit. p. 572. See also, however, Bishop, *Cyclopædia
of Anatomy and Physiology*, 1854, vol. iv. p. 1490.

square, or folded so that its upper edge resembles a horse-shoe. In singing the scale it seems to have little or no proper motion, but the movements of the larynx make it apparently shift its place. Approximation of the vocal bands draws the posterior margin of the larynx slightly towards it. In the lowest notes the larynx moves downwards and forwards, so as to cause it to intercept the view,[1] whilst in the upper range of the chest-register the larynx is seen to pass away from it in a direction upwards and backwards as the glottis comes into full sight. During the contraction of the vestibule of the larynx, of which it forms the anterior part in the falsetto scale, it becomes gradually doubled up, and its lateral edges approach nearly in the highest notes. At the same time it is drawn more over the glottis than at the top of the chest-register, but if naturally erect its upper edge remains everted towards the back of the tongue. Being closely connected with this organ, it follows its movements during articulation. Thus it is depressed when the vowel-sound *aw* (as in *law*) is pronounced, and drawn away from the glottis by the enunciation of *ee* (as in *feel*).

This valve is capable of closing the upper outlet of the larynx, to which it acts as a kind of operculum or

[1] Five causes may combine to produce a depression, apparent and real, of the epiglottis in low notes. (1) The arytænoid cartilages being drawn nearer to the thyroid. (2) The thyroid cartilage being rotated upward and backward. (3) Descent and (4) forward movement of the whole larynx. (5) Action of those fibres of the thyro-arytænoid muscle called *Dilator vestibuli* (Luschka, Fig 4, 4), which may also depress the epiglottis. In this last instance the slight depression of the epiglottis might assist the slackening of the reeds, whilst the full patency of the outlet would be preserved.

lid, if pressed down upon it, as occurs during the act
of swallowing, when the larynx is drawn upwards and
forwards, so that the base of the tongue rolls over it.
Food and drink are thus prevented from passing into
the windpipe. Such is certainly the physiological purpose of the epiglottis; but in those animals who have
well-developed ventricular bands it appears to be superfluous, unless we can regard it as a vocal appendage.
The presence, however, of an ample epiglottis in
animals for the most part voiceless,[1] such as marsupials (kangaroo, etc.), and cetaceans (whale, dugong,
etc.), argues against this supposition, which is further
controverted by its small size and comparative immo-
bility during phonation in man.[2] It has been suggested[3]
that it acts as a "tuner," a resonator, and that it

[1] Owen, op. cit. p. 582, et seq. Amongst reptiles that have no
vestige of vocal ligaments the epiglottis is frequently found, *e.g.*, in
several snakes, such as *Boa constrictor*, *Crotalus durissus* (striped rattle-
snake), etc. See Henle, *Beschreibung des Kehlkopfs mit besonderer
Berücksichtungen des Kehlkopfs der Reptilien*, Leipzig, 1839, p. 50, Taf.
iii. 1, 45, etc.

[2] In the *mycetes*, above mentioned, the epiglottis is four inches
long and two inches wide, *i.e.*, about twelve times larger than the
human epiglottis. In these animals it may, therefore, have some
acoustic effect, but this is apparently the only instance of the
kind.

[3] See Walton, *Journal of Physiology*, Sept. 25, 1878. The writer
appears to me to have concluded too hastily from a few experiments
on dogs that the epiglottis is of no value in swallowing throughout
the animal series. Some of the experiments prove indeed that were
the ventricular bands deficient or absent, as is frequent, the valve
would be indispensable during deglutition. Just as hastily does he
leap to the inference that it must be an important factor in phonation. But his observations, in many other respects assailable, have no
element of conclusiveness, on account of being confined to a single
individual. No allowance is made for circumstances of sex, voice,

K

modifies the timbre of the voice. But the vocal reeds, with almost infinitesimal powers of altering their tension and dimensions, do not seem to stand in need of such a tuner, whilst their great resonator is the concavity of the hard-palate, the roof of the mouth.[1] It may modify timbre, and give something of the peculiarity of voice by which we recognize different persons, as when it is large and depressed, or small and erect; but, apart from lingual articulation, it has no motion to enable it to vary the quality of any particular note. It certainly, however, has the office of directing the sound-waves against the back of the pharynx, to be thence reflected, under the variable arch of the soft-palate, on to the hard-palate, especially when the most resonant vowel-sounds, such as *aw* (as in *law*), are pronounced.[2]

or idiosyncrasy, and in the next case Mr. Walton examines he may find a contradiction of most of his first views. On the whole, I am inclined to believe that, if he could submit phonation to the same tests as he has done deglutition, he would find that the singer would experience little inconvenience from the loss of the projecting part of his epiglottis. On this point see Liscovius (the elder), loc. cit. p. 34; Müller (J.), op. cit. p. 1022; and Wyllie, loc. cit. p. 229; etc.

[1] Magendie (op. cit. t. i. p. 308) conceives that the epiglottis may act like the loose tongue or flap introduced by Grenié into some of the pipes of his *orgue expressive* (see Fétis, *Biographie universelle des musiciens*, sub *Grenié*). The fact, however, that this tongue was used only for flute-pipes, in order to compensate their characteristic tendency to vary in pitch under altered pressure of air, entirely destroys the supposed parallel. Reeds when properly fixed do not change their pitch in proportion to the strength of the blast, but merely the amplitude of their vibrations, *i.e.*, the intensity of their sound. Grenié's invention does not appear to possess any general value. See Hopkins, *The Organ*, etc. pp. 108, 112, 115.

[2] The production of the *tremolo* has been referred to the epiglottis, but I think erroneously. See Béclard, *Traité élémentaire de physiologie*, Paris, 1862, p. 736.

The Pharynx.

The share taken by this cavity in voice-production is scarcely capable of separate definition. The vibrations of the vocal reeds do not appear to derive any special modification from it, except in the utterance of certain guttural speech-sounds. It allows of the extrinsic movements of the larynx necessary for the elaboration of a musical scale. The tongue encroaches on or recedes from it during articulation of vowels. Under ordinary circumstances it extends, with the laryngeal vestibule, directly from the vocal reeds to the back entrance of the nasal channels, but by the action of the soft-palate it may be caused to pass most directly into the mouth, with which it usually forms a single resonance chamber. The alterations of its capacity, so evident to any one who observes it during singing, induced some former physiologists and physicists to believe that it bore the same relation to the voice as the tube of a flute or clarionet to the sounds generated at the embouchure.[1] A knowledge of the acoustic laws of

---

[1] Cruveilhier says: " La longueur du pharynx est de quatre pouces à quatre pouces et demi ; mais cette longueur peut être portée jusqu' à cinq pouces et demi et même six pouces et demi, par l'effet de la distension, et réduite à deux pouces et demi par l'effet du plus grand raccourcissement possible, et ce raccourcissement est mesuré par le contact de la base de la langue et du voile du palai devenu horizontal ; d'où il résulte que le pharynx peut présenter dans sa longueur une différence de quatre pouces environ ; résultat aussi prodigieux qu'in attendu."— *Traité d'anatomie descriptive*, Paris, 1852, t. iii. p. 268. Were our vocal tube sufficiently long (a couple of feet perhaps) and rigid to command the vibrations of the vocal reeds as the tube of a brass wind

sonorous vibrations in tubes and cavities has, however, reduced this hypothesis to a nullity.[1]

The Mouth.

The most harmonious tones of the voice are obtained by the action of the mouth, as resonance chamber. In this cavity the power and volume of the voice are greatly augmented by secondary vibrations, to the formation of which the solid arch of the hard-palate mainly contributes. The highly composite clang proceeding from the vocal reeds is reinforced in those upper partial tones which are nearest and most consonant to the prime, namely, its octave, the fifth above that, and the second octave, etc. Such is probably the succession of overtones which are brought out distinctly when the most resonant of vowel-sounds are pronounced or sung. But the reinforcement of the upper partial tones is altered by every motion of the tongue, lips, etc., during articulation, and hence results a pleasing diversity of timbre which prevents the ear being fatigued by monotonous repetition.

instrument governs those of the lips, even this rather exaggerated view of the changes of size of the pharynx would scarcely account for a variation in pitch to the amount of half a dozen tones.

[1] Helmholtz remarks: "The air-chambers connected with the larynx are not adapted for materially altering the tone of the voice-bands. Their walls are so yielding that they cannot allow the formation of vibrations of the air within them sufficiently powerful to force the voice-bands to oscillate with a period which is different from that required by their own elasticity. The cavity of the mouth is also far too short and generally too widely open to serve as a resonance chamber which could have material influence on pitch"—op. cit. p. 149.

The Nose.

The office of the nasal cavity in phonation is also to give increased intensity to upper partial tones. Consisting, however, of a number of small channels which have little intercommunication, its own proper sounds must be high and shrill.[1] The overtones, therefore, that it can reinforce lie generally at a great distance above the prime tone of the vocal reeds; not nearer probably in any part of the chest-register, than the eighth or tenth in the harmonic series, *i.e.*, more than three octaves from the fundamental note of the voice. Beyond this height the rapidly-diminishing intervals between the successive overtones soon render them dissonant, both with each other and with the prime tone. When, therefore, the voice resounds fully in the nose, the fundamental note is impoverished and nearly drowned by the predominance of high partial tones. Hence the well-known discordance, the jarring "twang," of an exalted nasal intonation which, disagreeable in speaking, is utterly ruinous to melodious singing. A due proportion, however, of the nasal harmonics must generally be present[2] (invariably with *m* or *n*), and when the gap is bridged over by a proper pre-

[1] The lengths of the nasal meatus average—inf. 3-ins., mid. 2¼-ins., sup. 1½-ins. The proper notes of such tubes (open) would be respectively about *c♯‴*, *d⁗*, and *e⁗*. The selection of alternate overtones peculiar to closed pipes gives a nasal timbre, probably because the upper harmonics, being numerous and close together, suffer less than the lower, which are few and distant from each other.

[2] On this point see Malgaigne, loc. cit. p. 225.

ponderance of oral resonance they are of real value in adding to the brilliancy and variety of vocal timbre.[1]

The Soft-Palate.

The use of this pendulous and mobile portion of the palate is to cut off the communication between the upper part of the pharynx and the nasal cavity during the act of swallowing or in phonation. To effect this purpose its muscles draw it backwards and slightly upwards till it meets the back wall of the pharynx. Whilst singing a scale, this movement goes on progressively, from the deepest chest-note to the highest limit of the falsetto, when the retraction is nearly complete. A sufficient opening, however, remains almost to the last to allow of some nasal resonance. For every note of different pitch, therefore, the soft-palate occupies a separate position, which is determined by the direction of the sound issuing from the glottis. In ascending the scale, the successive changes of place of the larynx tend to project the column of aërial vibrations, so that they rebound from the back of the pharynx more and more vertically upwards towards the posterior nares. Step by step the motions of the soft-palate counteract this tendency and divert the course of the sound-waves to the arch of the hard-

---

[1] The cavities in the bones about the nose, viz., the antrum, and the frontal and sphenoidal sinuses, have a certain, though undetermined effect on voice. When they are undeveloped, as in many of the Australian aborigines, a noticeable want of vocal resonance has been observed. See Owen, op. cit. vol. ii. p. 563.

palate. It is quite possible to sing all the chest-notes without moving the soft-palate, but, as a consequence, there is a great loss of resonance, and an insupportable predominance of nasal timbre.[1] The effect is somewhat similar to blowing a trumpet from which the bell has been removed; a "tin-kettle," or "cracked-pot" tone is the result. But when the falsetto scale is reached it is no longer practicable to restrain the retraction of the soft-palate, although these notes would probably suffer least from a surplus of nasal harmonics. The action of the palato-pharyngeus muscle seems indispensable, in order to approximate the wings of the thyroid cartilage, and consequently the falsetto register cannot be produced without the palatal motions. In cases, however, where the soft-palate has been destroyed by disease, the power of producing the falsetto-notes is not abolished, as the lateral parts of the palato-pharyngeus and the inferior constrictor are still able to fulfil their office.[2] It is thus demonstrated that the gradual occlusion of the posterior nares in this register is merely an accidental phenomenon without any acoustic necessity for its occurrence.

[1] The larynx scarcely rises in ascending the scale in this manner, as the principal action which draws it up is in abeyance. The experiment also appears to indicate that the pharynx and epiglottis have little separate power of rendering the vocal tones sonorous. Phonation in this manner seems to be what Fournié (op. cit. p. 421) calls *voix de tête*.

[2] For reports of cases illustrating this point, see Rush, *The Philosophy of Human Voice*, Philadelphia, 1845, p. 108; and Ségond, *Hygiène du chanteur*, Paris, 1846, p. 56.

COMPASS OF THE VOICE—INDIVIDUAL AND SEXUAL DIFFERENCES—REGISTERS.

The compass of the voice from the lowest note of the male to the highest of the female includes about four octaves, viz., from E^1 to c'''^2. Many gifted singers can, however, exceed both these extremes by several tones, and males may even descend to F^3 whilst females can sometimes attain f''',[4] a range of five octaves. The voices of individuals, of infinite variety as regards timbre, present also numerous diversities in compass, but they can always be relegated to some one of six different classes, the precise extent of which is not strained. Men's voices are termed *bass, baritone,* and *tenor ;* and women's *contralto, mezzo-soprano,* and *soprano,* in regular succession, from the bottom to the top of the vocal scale.[5] The bass and soprano are more than an octave apart, whilst the tenor and contralto lie for the most part over the same notes. The range of each kind of voice is shown in the adjoining table, according to the conventional acceptance. The compass

[5] In determining to what class a voice belongs, attention is often directed more to its timbre than to its actual compass. A first-rate baritone, for instance, may be able to deliver g' from the chest, whilst a good tenor may be unable to rise beyond that note. But an unmistakable difference of timbre at once decides the question.

COMPARATIVE SCALE OF DIFFERENT CLASSES OF VOICES.

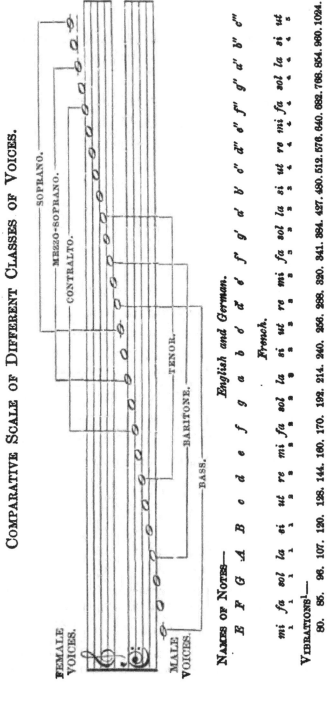

FEMALE VOICES.

SOPRANO.

MEZZO-SOPRANO.

CONTRALTO.

MALE VOICES.

TENOR.

BARITONE.

BASS.

NAMES OF NOTES—

English and German.

E F G A B c d e f g a b c' d' e' f' g' a' b' c" d" e" f" g" a" b" c"'

French.

mi fa sol la si ut re mi fa sol la si ut re mi fa sol la si ut

VIBRATIONS[1]—

80. 85. 96. 107. 120. 128. 144. 160. 170. 192. 214. 240. 256. 288. 320. 341. 384. 427. 480. 512. 576. 640. 682. 768. 854. 960. 1024.

[1] The vibrational numbers here given are those of the so-called natural scale, which assumes the lowest sound audible as a musical note, to have sixteen vibrations per second—fractions are omitted. In the French notation the above numbers would be doubled, as in France the to-and-fro motions of a vibrating body are reckoned separately.

here apportioned to the various voices is, however, only such as the composer would regard when writing music for different classes of singers, and is far from representing the physiological limits of each kind. From merely acoustic considerations, for instance, we might suppose that the bass voice would be capable of producing not only the deepest notes, but also those of the highest pitch, on the same principle that an imitation of the violin can be performed on the violoncello, though the notes are not of the same musical value as the proper tones of the instrument. In either case, the only faculty required is an unlimited power of shortening and tensing the strings or vocal reeds. The truth of this hypothesis is exemplified, as regards voice, in the fact that a bass or baritone singer may have such an extent of falsetto notes as to be able to counterfeit the vocal performances of a soprano.[1]   Similarly the male alto voices employed in cathedrals for choral service are generally, if not always, of bass or baritone range fundamentally, but with an unusual facility for falsetto singing.[2]   In these instances the upper voice may embrace ten or twelve notes.[3]

[1] "Dans une scène *de la Prova d'un opéra seria*, Lablache, imitant un soprano, chante une cavatine entière en voix de fausset." Ségond, op. cit. p. 86.

[2] In the alto voices I have examined there has been a remarkable power of closing the anterior third or more of the ligamentous glottis, due to a hyper-development of the sesamoid cartilages at that point. Owing to the latter cause, probably, there was also an impoverishment of the chest-notes, through a hindrance to full-length vibration of the vocal reeds.

[3] From *a* 𝄞 to *d″* 𝄞.

Male and female voices differ not merely in degree, *i.e.*, in lower or higher pitch, but also in kind. They are characterized by a peculiarity of timbre, so that the dullest ear is in no danger of mistaking a man's voice for that of a woman, even on notes of the same pitch. The falsetto tones of a male voice have little resemblance to their equivalents in the musical scale when sung by a female, and the woman's voice is remarkably more brilliant and full in its sound. The causes here are obscure, but one of the greatest is undoubtedly superior resonance. The air-chambers connected with the female larynx are better adapted to reinforce high tones. The circumstance that the retraction of the soft-palate cuts off the nasal part of the vocal tube in woman to a lesser extent for notes of similar pitch than in man may have some influence. But principally we must regard the fact that the female larynx is formed for a treble instrument, and produces tones naturally and with ease which the male organ can only emit, if at all, with more or less of a strain. A man singing in falsetto is, therefore, in a position somewhat similar to a violinist who should endeavour to draw the highest notes from the fourth or lowest string of his instrument.

Having dealt with the question as to the mechanical formation of the chest and falsetto notes, it remains to consider at what level of the voice the break[1] between the two usually occurs. We should naturally

[1] The falsetto register can generally be carried down two or three notes below the highest level of the chest scale. Some tones can, therefore, be produced with either quality of voice. In this position the so-called "mixed voice" is said to occur.

expect that this point would bear a similar relation to the bottom of the chest-register in every individual, not occurring at any determinate point in the musical scale, but moveable according to the notes embraced within the compass of each particular class of voice. Anatomical and physiological observations point clearly to such a conclusion. Amongst singing-masters, however, it is usually considered that the falsetto scale commences at or near *g'*,[1] whatever the kind of voice and whether the singer be male or female. I do not know whence this hypothesis originated,[2] but it appears to rest on the basis that in women's voices there is often a break more or less pronounced in that position, and a marked difference of timbre between the ascending and descending series of notes. In many cases, on the other hand, the break and change of timbre are scarcely perceptible. It is difficult to believe that the finest notes of the soprano voice are produced in a manner strictly analogous to the falsetto tones of the male,[3] and the fact that the female voice presents a second break near its upper limit, where the so-called "head" voice begins, renders the proposition extremely doubtful. Such a view would also allow no falsetto notes to a bass singer who could not rise beyond *d'*[4] from the chest, whilst

[1]

[2] Its elaboration and dissemination are due in great part to Seiler, op. cit.

[3] "Madame Grisi, par exemple, qui n'emploi pas un seul ton du régistre du poitrine." Ségond, op. cit. p. 85.

[4]

151 n.364
BOD Old Class

Missing	☐	Bound together	☐
Poor condition	☐	Uncut	☐
Publication date	☐	Oversized	☐

Thursday, 17 August 2006

OC95216

ARTICULATING INSTRUMENT.

Speech is produced by modifying the capacity of the vocal tube and by altering the size and position of, or entirely closing, its outlets, through the instrumentality of the mobile parts contained within it or forming its boundaries. The various sounds, or phases of sounds, which are joined together in almost endless combinations to build up words, are represented in written language by letters, and classified according to the peculiarities of their formation. Almost at first consideration letters fall naturally into two great divisions. The first comprises those that consist of continuous sounds of characteristic timbre, called *vowels;* and the second embraces the series of interruptions or complete stoppages, enunciative or terminal, of the current of breath or sound, named *consonants.*

Nature of Vowel-Sounds and Mechanism of their Production.

In 1780 the Imperial Academy of St. Petersburg awarded a prize to Kratzenstein[1] for an essay on

mainly on aural observation, must be accepted with some reserve. During laryngoscopic inspection, I have never seen the female larynx assume the form for falsetto tones on the subject being told to pronounce a vowel, not even when the attempt to sound *ee*, which usually prompts the emission of a high note, was made. My practical and literary researches are against the admission of three registers, strictly so-called, in female voices.

[1] *Journal (Observations) de physique*, vol. xxi. 1782, p. 358.

the nature of vowels, illustrated by a reed instrument of purely empirical design which sounded a
recognizable imitation of them. About the same
time Kempelen[1] pursued an inquiry of a similar
kind, and published a treatise containing his results.
In 1828 Willis,[2] treating the question more scientifically, made a series of experiments by attaching
cylindrical chambers to a reed-pipe, and showed that
the prime tone could be thus modified, so as to produce a number of sounds closely resembling the
vowels of speech. Some few years later a consideration of these phenomena led Wheatstone[3] to suggest
that in such instances the vowels are formed by the
feeble vibrations arising in the short tube, which,
especially should its resonance correspond to one of
the multiples (*i.e.*, overtones) of the prime tone given
by the reed, thus confers the effect of a superadded
musical note. A further step was gained in 1857
by Donders,[4] who discovered that for the various
vowels the cavity of the mouth is tuned to different

---

[1] *Le mécanisme de la parole suivi de la description d'une machine
parlante*, Vienne, 1791. These were not, however, the first or only
attempts to construct a talking machine. Albertus Magnus, Friar
Bacon, the Abbé Mical, and others made, or are accredited with
having made, heads that could utter sentences. See Kircher, op. cit.
t. ii. p. 305 ; *Biographia Britannica*, t. i. p. 359 ; Rivarol, in the notes
to his essay *De l'universalité de la langue française*, Paris, 1797,
p. 60 ; and Borgnis, *Traité complet de mécanique*, t. viii. Paris, 1820,
p. 160 (an interesting account of acoustic imitative machines, etc.).
See Appendix ii.

[2] *Transactions of the Cambridge Philosophical Society*, vol. iii. 1830,
p. 231.

[3] *London and Westminster Review*, vol. xxviii. 1837, p. 36.

[4] *Archiv für die holländischen Beiträge zur Natur- und Heilkunde*,
vol. i. 1857, pp. 157, 354.

pitches by observing the whistling noise produced in whispering.

Subsequently many investigators directed their attention to the subject, but for the most complete experimental elucidation hitherto we are indebted to Helmholtz.[1] According to this physicist the essential origin of vowel timbre is the reinforcement of a fundamental tone by the superadded note of a resonance chamber, which for the same vowel always yields the same note, although the fundamental tone may undergo a considerable, but not unlimited, change of pitch. When the note of the resonance chamber corresponds to one of the partials of the fundamental tone the vowel is best heard; but in proportion as it recedes from this measure the vowel loses character, until it becomes imperceptible.

Thus, in the case of spoken vowels, the pharynx and mouth constitute a short tube, which resounds during phonation, not so as to yield a distinctly separate musical note, but only so that a weak secondary sound of determinate pitch is heard blended with the laryngeal tones. Within certain limits the capacity of this vocal tube can be altered to any required extent by the action of the tongue and lower jaw with the effect of lowering or heightening its proper note, the pitch of which is still further governed by the size of the orifice circumscribed by the lips. The smaller the aperture of the mouth the lower the resonance pitch of its cavity.

For the vowel U (*oo* in *pool*) the vocal tube is

[1] Op. cit. p. 153.

arranged to give its lowest pitch of resonance; the tongue is collected into the smallest space at the bottom of the mouth, and the lips are protruded so as to lengthen the cavity, at the same time that they leave a narrower opening than for any other vowel. Under these circumstances the shape of the vocal tube corresponds to that of a bottle with a small orifice and without a neck. For O (*o* in *note*) the lips retract and enlarge the opening, so that the pitch of the cavity is considerably raised. For A (*a* in *father*) the oral aperture is still further increased in size, and for A (*a* in *bath*) the mouth is wide open. The elevation of the resonance pitch of the vocal tube, taken as a whole, has now been brought to its maximum, and beyond this point we pass into another register, so to speak, of vowel-sounds. To produce A (*a* in *fate*) a part of the tube is cut off by the tongue, which was quiescent hitherto, rising near to the hard-palate, whilst the lips remain so far separated that the front of the mouth loses all power of resonance. The shape of the vocal tube now resembles a bottle with a narrow and rather long neck, as the tongue forms with the roof of the mouth an elongated channel which leads back to the more capacious pharynx. As a consequence of this adjustment of the articulating apparatus, a double vowel resonance arises, because a comparatively low tone is generated in the pharyngeal cavity and a higher one in the narrow pipe which leads out of it in front. For I (*ee* in *feet*) the tongue is applied to the hard-palate, so as to reduce the anterior channel to the smallest possible

L

dimensions, and the highest limit of vowel resonance is reached. Diphthongs are sounded by the rapid consecutive formation of two different capacities, and other vowels (such as are used in Continental languages) are obtained by various gradations of the positions described. In the speech of every nation, and even in that of provincials and individuals, distinctions of vowel timbre are found, which, of course, depend on the production of diversities in the size and resonance of the vocal tube. The vowel-sounds distinguishable as separate by the ear may, therefore, be considered as more numerous than consonants, although in each language they are always relatively few.

Various efforts have been made to determine the precise note to which the vocal cavity resounds for each vowel as pronounced by the natives of different countries. The results for vowel-sounds, the same or almost similar, coincide very nearly according to some authors, but diverge considerably according to others. The best and most trustworthy experiments have been performed by Helmholtz by means of his resonators, which he has employed to ascertain what upper partials are reinforced most strongly whilst different vowels are sung. He also uses tuning-forks, which, on being struck, are held close to the opening of the lips when the mouth is shaped for the emission of each vowel. The vocal tube thus acts as a resonance chamber, which will reinforce sympathetically the vibrations of a tuning-fork that sounds the same note, speaking for itself, as it were, in this way as to its own pitch. After repeated observations by the combined aid of both these methods, which, however, in the case of the highest and lowest vowels had to be supplemented by aural observation, Helmholtz is inclined to fix the pitch of the mouth for the various vowels used by the North Germans according to the following notation :—

U   O   A   Ä   E   I   Ö   Ü [1]

Helmholtz has found the pitch of the mouth for the same vowels invariable in all ages and sexes. In women and children, the want of capacity of the vocal tube is compensated by diminishing the opening at the lips.

An interesting point in the consideration of the subject is the existence of an antagonism between certain combinations of vowel and laryngeal sounds. Helmholtz, whilst confessing the incompleteness of his observations on this side, advances the proposition, implied above in the enunciation of his theory, that particular vowels cannot be sounded properly on certain notes of the voice because of an acoustic difficulty in producing a vowel resonance concomitantly with laryngeal tone, which does not afford it a sufficient base in the natural series of partials. The evidence is too incomplete to follow this question further here,

[1] The first six of these vowels are most near'y represented in English by the six described in the preceding paragraph, in the same order. The last two are unpronounceable in English, and correspond nearly, *ö* to the French *eu* in *peuple* and *ü* to *u* in *pu.*

and it will suffice to allude to the well-known fact, to singers at least, that all voices find a difficulty in forming vowels and syllables at the extremes of their compass. From my own observation, I am led to conclude that the obstacle in this case is in great part, if not altogether, of a mechanical nature. Pronunciation is most distinct at the level of the speaking voice, and becomes imperfect according as the laryngeal notes move away from this pitch in an upper or lower direction. In the lowest notes the contraction of one group [1] of the extrinsic muscles of the larynx fixes the base of the tongue and greatly impedes the motions required for articulation. In the highest notes the tongue is also tied down by muscular activity, whilst the constriction of the pharynx and isthmus of the fauces hinders still more the various and rapid modifications of the vocal tube necessary for fluent speech.[2]

Consonants—Their Formation and Classification.

Consonants, as their name signifies, can only be sounded in conjunction with a vowel. They comprise in fact a number of methods, each characteristic,

[1] Sterno-thyroid, sterno-hyoid, and thyro-hyoid.

[2] For objections that may be urged against Helmholtz's vowel theory see Von Quanten, Poggendorf's *Annalen*, Bd. cliv. 1875, pp. 272, 522. No doubt our knowledge of the subject is by no means complete, but Helmholtz's explanations may be regarded as in the main correct, so far as they go. See further Ellis' observations on vowels, with his answer to Von Quanten, in the appendix to his translation of Helmholtz, p. 724, et seq.

of putting on or cutting off more or less completely the current of vocal sound, modified to the timbre of some one of the various vowels. The most obvious means of classifying consonants is derived from acoustic considerations, and from this point of view they admit of division into *explosives, aspirates, resonants,* and *vibratives.* They may be further subdivided by regarding the anatomical disposition of the articulating apparatus required for their enunciation. Hence they are also arranged as *labials, dentals,* and *gutturals.* Finally, consonants possess a third characteristic, which admits of their being distinguished as *breathed* and *voiced.*

I. 1. In *Explosives* the vocal tube is, for a moment, completely closed at some part of its course during phonation. Their enunciation is therefore accompanied by a kind of burst or explosion, occasioned by the sudden release of the confined air which is forced against the point of constriction by the chest. The explosive consonants form a class specially distinct from the rest, which, in opposition, may be grouped together under the term *continuous.*

2. In *Aspirates* the vocal tube is only partially stopped and the breath pours out, accompanied by a faint wind-rush, through the point of constriction.

3. In *Resonants* the vocal tube is completely closed at some position of its main, *i.e.,* oral, channel in the same way as occurs during the formation of explosives, but a free secondary passage is still left by the inaction of the soft-palate, and the voice passes out with a peculiar resonance through the nose. These consonants might also, therefore, be called *nasals.*

4. In *Vibratives* the action of the articulating apparatus is a combination of that required in pronouncing explosives and aspirates, *i.e.*, at one moment the breath is stopped and at the next allowed to force its way through, in continued alternation. They consist, therefore, of a series of explosions, and the opposing surfaces at the point of constriction act as membranous reeds (like the vocal reeds themselves), which, however, vibrate too slowly and momentarily to give the sensation of a musical note. A kind of " purr " is all that is heard.

II. 1. In *labials* the vocal tube is closed by the approximation of the lips, or by the lower lip being pressed against the upper row of teeth.

2. In *dentals* the tip of the tongue is pressed against the back of the upper front teeth, or against the part of the hard-palate which borders on them.

3. In *gutturals* the back of the tongue is approximated to the soft-palate.

III. The difference between *breathed* and *voiced* consonants is, that the former are accompanied at the moment of their pronunciation merely by a wind-rush, whilst the latter have a base of audible laryngeal vibration. These qualities are not so easily determined as the distinguishing characteristics between the various consonants of the explosive class on account of their momentary duration, but continuous consonants can easily be recognized as breathed or voiced by attentively observing their sound when prolonged indefinitely. Testing in this way, for example, S and Z, the former, when prolonged, is found to consist of a mere " hiss," whilst the latter has a strong foundation of tone proceeding from the larynx. Otherwise their formation is precisely similar.

After this description of the various qualities of consonants, the following table, showing them ranged according to their respective groups, will be intelligible :—

EXPLOSIVES.

	Breathed.	Voiced.
Labials	P ...	B
Dentals	T ...	D
Gutturals	K ...	G

ASPIRATES.

	Breathed.	Voiced.
Labials... ...	F ...	V
Dentals...	{ S, L, Sh, Th hard, Greek θ) }	Z, L, J, Th (soft)
Gutturals	{ Ch (German, Greek χ) }	Y (beginning a word)

RESONANTS.

					All Voiced.
Labial ...	...	...	...	...	M
Dental ...	...	...	...	...	N
Guttural	...	...	...	...	N G

VIBRATIVES.

Labial[1] (not used as a definite letter).

Dental ...	...	...	...	...	R
Guttural	...	...	...	...	R

[1] The sound which may be reckoned as the labial R, is the trill of the lips, which appears to be so important a factor in equine language, as everyone knows who has observed a man grooming a horse.

A few words of explanation are required respecting some letters which are omitted in this table, and also as to some others which have special characteristics.

H is a breathed aspirate, but differs from all other letters in being formed in the larynx itself by the glottis, narrowed so as to produce a wind-rush, but not sufficiently so as to allow the vocal reeds to be thrown into vibration. It is therefore called the *spiritus asper*, or "rough breathing"—denoted in Greek by a comma turned the reverse way (')—whilst words beginning with a vowel that are pronounced without this preparatory wind-rush are said to have the *spiritus lenis* or "smooth breathing."

C is redundant, having at one time the power of K, at another that of S; also Q which is equivalent to K, but is only used before the vowel U; and X which is the same as Ks at the end of a syllable, and as Z when beginning a word.

L is formed by the passage of the mouth being left permeable at both sides of the tongue whilst the centre is stopped by the tip of the organ being pressed against the hard-palate. The English L is always voiced; the breathed L is used by the Welsh and is represented by the Ll, so well known in their local names of places.

Sh is the breathed equivalent of the voiced J, as it occurs in the French word *jamais*.

Th is formed by placing the front edge of the tongue between the two rows of teeth; the voiced Th would be more decidedly represented by Dh. They can be sounded less distinctly by pressing the tip of the tongue against the back of the upper front teeth, when they tend towards S and Z.

The English Ch is not a guttural aspirate, but a consonantal diphthong, sounding when breathed as TSh, when voiced as DZh or rather DJ. The latter is the sound of the English G soft, and also of J.

The dental R is produced by trilling the tip of the tongue against the hard-palate, at the rate of about thirty vibrations in the second; the guttural R is formed by the uvula vibrating about nineteen times in the second against the back of the tongue.[1]

In *whispering* the vocal reeds are approximated so as to produce a wind-rush, like the *spiritus asper* continued indefinitely. This suffices to render recognizable the pitch of the note to which the mouth is tuned for the various vowels, and articulation is carried on in the same manner as in sonorous phonation. The distinction, however, between breathed and voiced consonants is for the most part lost; and B becomes P; D, T; etc., if entirely deprived of laryngeal tone.

[1] See Donders, *De Physiologie der Spraaklanken.* Utrecht, 1870, p. 18.

CHAPTER IV.

THE PHYSIOLOGICAL PRINCIPLES OF VOCAL CULTURE.

GENERAL CONSIDERATIONS — MANAGEMENT OF THE MOTOR ELEMENT (RESPIRATION)—MANAGEMENT OF THE VIBRATING ELEMENT—MANAGEMENT OF THE RESONANCE APPARATUS — MANAGEMENT OF THE ARTICULATING APPARATUS.

The Subject Defined.—The cultivation of the voice amongst civilized nations has for its object the complementary development of the powers of organs which have already attained a high degree of perfection in the performance of their functions. Through the exertion of influences acting from without, and not directly controlled by the will, man proceeds instinctively and intuitively as a mere agent to the evolution of speech and language. But here, as in many other of his relations, beyond a certain point the unerring guide of nature leaves or only follows him with a perpetually widening interval, and his further advance is made voluntarily and with self-consciousness of his aim under the direction of his own clear mental perceptions. The growth of complex senses, indefinitely progressive, generates exalted faculties of appreciation which lead him beyond the sphere of mere utility into a world of æstheticism, and his life becomes one of artificiality, where the useful can no longer exist apart from the beautiful.

Hence we may recognize two grades in the employment of the voice; the first necessitated by the conditions of social life as a means of intercommunion; and the second undertaken with a view to the æsthetic observation of the listeners. In speaking, the voice is used in both degrees to a variable amount according to the circumstances, the effort to please being strongest in addressing an audience or when declaiming in the theatre; but in singing the vocal powers are almost invariably put forth under a purely æsthetic impulse.

GENERAL CONSIDERATIONS.

The technical training of the voice lies immediately in the hands of teachers of elocution and singing. On their taste and genius, as well as on the aptitude and natural vocal gifts of their pupils, depends in the greatest measure the success obtained and the perfection of the result. But, whatever methods be adopted, the base of operations is vital organization and action, of which the true apprehension and normal guidance must lead most directly and certainly to the desired end. Hence questions become involved which are a proper subject for the physiologist.

In listening to the voice as an acoustic instrument,

apart from its expression of thought, we notice certain qualities, namely, its *force, timbre, compass,* and *duration,* which, according to their musical or forensic value in different voices, affect the ear in various degrees, pleasurably or otherwise. Each of these qualities originates physiologically in special muscular mechanisms and in peculiar anatomical conformations of the vocal organs.

Force, or loudness of voice, which includes volume, arises from (1) power of muscular contraction of the chest, which drives the air in a current of variable strength through the glottis; (2) breadth, elasticity, and perfection of form of the vocal reeds, which allow them to vibrate at a maximum of amplitude and regularity at any required rate of rapidity; and (3) the capacity for resonance of the vocal tube and other parts capable of reinforcing the laryngeal tones.[1]

Timbre takes its character from (1) the physical qualities of the vocal reeds whence they derive their amount of aptitude for isochronous vibration; (2) anatomical configuration of the vocal tube, which bestows special powers of reinforcing certain overtones and extinguishing others; (3) voluntary arrangement of the articulating apparatus for the production of particular vowel-sounds; and (4) inherent individual

---

[1] Loudness of sound may be considered as a compound quality, constituted by two factors, viz., intensity and volume. In voice, intensity is primarily governed by breadth of the vocal bands, and volume by capacity of the resonance chambers. In persons, therefore, with a powerful voice the laryngoscope will show a remarkable width of the upper surfaces of the vocal reeds, and a striking amplitude of the pharynx, mouth, and nasal cavities will also be observed. In the opposite case the appearances will be the reverse.

or national peculiarities in the management of the vocal organs, as when deficient employment of the soft-palate permits a preponderance of nasal resonance, etc.

Compass indicates the extent of the contractile powers of the laryngeal muscles, which enables them to make the utmost amount of variation in the vibrative capacities of the vocal reeds. But persons whose voices possess an unusual range of notes, have probably supernumerary fascicles of muscular fibres in the larynx.[1] The fundamental pitch is, of course, determined by the length of the vocal bands natural to different individuals.

Duration, which marks the power of prolonging the laryngeal vibrations, without taking breath, depends on the capacity of the chest, which must form an ample reservoir for air.

Furthermore, we notice, *in speaking*, the precision of action of the muscles of articulation, as evidenced by distinctness and fluency of pronunciation; and *in singing*, the precision of action of the laryngeal muscles, as shown by the rapidity and perfection with which they accomplish manifold changes of pitch in florid passages of music, *i.e.*, the execution of the singer.

From this summary and the preceding remarks, we may perceive that the various factors whence the qualities of voice are derived can readily be resolved into three groups. Thus we have influences in their nature, (1) *mental*, (2) *muscular*, and (3) *morphological.*[2]

---

[1] Great vertical measurement of the crico-thyroid space might possibly confer a higher range of chest notes, by allowing hyper-extension of the vocal bands.

[2] A fourth, a material factor, is practically included in the muscular.

1. The *mental* factor, which includes aural perceptiveness, is the genius of the speaker or singer who, according to the subtlety of his appreciation of various vocal effects when listening to them, has a measure of success in reproducing and improving on them with his own voice.

2. The *muscular* influence is the strength and activity of the muscles concerned in phonation.

3. The *morphological* factor depends on the form and size of the different parts of the vocal organs.

After this analysis we are in a position to understand approximately the physiological nature of the process which is being carried on in training the voice, and to estimate in what direction success may be obtained, together with its amount. We know, for example, (1) that the powers of the mind are highly improvable when impelled to habits of observation and study; (2) that muscles can gain greatly in strength and in rapidity and certainty of action by being subjected to definite courses of exercise; but (3) that the morphological configuration of any organs of the body can seldom be modified to a marked degree by methods of training.

Applying these facts more intimately to the cultivation of the voice we may come to the following conclusions :—

a. Force may be increased so far as it depends (1) on vigorous and consonant action of the thoracic muscles, (2) on the laryngeal muscles maintaining the larynx and vocal reeds firmly in the most favourable position for producing sonorous vibration, and (3) on the judgment and muscular power of the individual to adapt the vocal tube so as to give the strongest resonance. But as each person possesses a natural power of voice, which is governed strictly by the development of the several portions of the vocal organs, training can seldom bridge a wide gulf between the vocal powers of different subjects as regards force.

b. The *timbre* of the human voice is almost entirely under the control of the will, on account of the great and varied alterations that the muscular boundaries of the resonance chambers can induce in their capacity, and must therefore owe much of its character to the taste of the speaker or singer. Cultivation of the ear and general intelligence must consequently be attended with great refinement in this respect, but of course individual or national peculiarities of timbre can be modified or eradicated only with great difficulty, as they arise to some extent from a special morphological conformation of the vocal organs.

c. Compass may be extended by practising the laryngeal muscles, as they can gain in power of contractility.

d. Duration.—The ability of sustaining the laryngeal tones without taking breath may be augmented, because the capacity of the chest can be enlarged by exercising its muscles, which, as they gain in contractile power, will cause the ribs to execute wider motions, and thus the lungs will be compelled to expand beyond their primary limits.

e. The *executive faculty* of the articulative or laryngeal muscles can be largely developed by definite courses of practice.

From a careful consideration of such principles any system for the training of the voice must be elaborated. It is necessary, however, to bear in mind that the advance in any given direction, even where nature seems most pliable, must be checked at limits not very far distant from the starting-point, the barrier being closest in relation to morphological conformation, and probably furthest removed in the case of muscular increment. A number of voices cannot, therefore, be regarded as capable of being all trained up to a certain maximum of excellence; as if by adding to one voice a small complement of cultivation and to another a large amount they could all in the end be equalized in the perfection of the various qualities that constitute first-class merit. The natural vocal gifts of each pupil must then be considered as a separate zero, from which the voice may be improved upwards so many degrees of which the totals in different instances can seldom be very dissimilar. The most marked success may perhaps be expected where the mental powers are greatly in excess of the physical endowments; the least result under the reverse circumstances.

It is only requisite to mention that the age of the pupil is a matter of the extremest moment, youth being an indispensable ally in order to succeed in mental or physical training; for when the organs of the body are in course of formation they are more impressionable by external influences, and portions of the bones are soft, so that their growth may be encouraged in one direction or restrained in another. At the same time it must be remembered that the youthful organs are exceptionally delicate and susceptible to too severe a strain. Their task must be adapted to their capabilities, and they must be carefully guarded from over-exertion. The object of systematic training is to stimulate the vital forces in the required direction, so that nature may attain to a more luxuriant maturity than she herself designed; but excessive labour will, instead, crush vitality and reduce the flourishing scion to a dwarfed and sapless stem.

And, again, it is important to observe that training should always proceed slowly and methodically. The success of rapid measures can only be superficial and partial, especially when dealing with youth, for the animal fabric will only yield to prolonged influences which affect it without intermission at every step of its growth. The vital tendencies cannot be forced aside by a short-lived attack, however vigorous; they must be guided gently and measuredly along the path it is desired they should follow.[1]

An opinion as to the probable amount of success to be attained in particular instances from a course of vocal training cannot at present be formed with any precision from general physiological data, but must be arrived at by empirical observations, by noting down many separate results and afterwards comparing them together.

Having dealt so far in generalities, I will now

[1] For some important physiological remarks on training, see Aitken, *On the Growth of the Recruit and Young Soldier*, pp. 25, 41, etc.

M

endeavour to specialize this part of the subject by considering, with as much detail as the present state of our knowledge will allow and as appears of practical importance, the action of the vocal organs in the æsthetic production of voice. Under this aspect the movements of the vocal organs appear as governed by artificial impulses instead of being ruled merely by the exigencies of their physiological purpose. As a matter of consequence an antagonism may result which will counter-balance and render void the efforts of unsystematic training. The end, then, of this inquiry is to discover a path which, if pursued, will enable us to steer clear of obstacles and to harmonize, without disturbing, nature and art.

MANAGEMENT OF THE MOTOR ELEMENT

(RESPIRATION).

Measure of Breathing.

During quiet respiration the chest expands and contracts, *i.e.*, we breathe, about seventeen times in every minute, as the tidal air flows in and out of the lungs. Under these circumstances inspiration and expiration occupy each less than two seconds, whilst the chest is seldom filled to its vital capacity or emptied of its residual air. But phonation completely alters this process, because voice is only produced during expiration. In speaking or in singing it is necessary for the continuity of sentences or phrases of music that expiration should be prolonged as much as possible. And lest utterances of words or notes intended to be delivered in close succession should be separated by an intolerable gap, which would give a disjointed character to a whole speech or song, it is also required that inspiration should be performed as quickly as possible. And further, as breath cannot be drawn in at any moment, but advantage must be taken of places where a pause occurs in the flow of words or stream of melody, the acts of respiration during phonation are of unequal length in contrast to the regularity of ordinary breathing.

Hence we see that in speaking or singing the function of respiration, instead of being carried on by a number of short breaths in which inspiration and expiration are duly proportioned, consists of a few long breaths, five or six in the minute or even less, where the relations of inspiration and expiration are very disproportionate. In such cases the balance as regards the quantity of air required by the lungs for their vital operations is maintained by supplying them more copiously each time, and the chest is expanded more by inspiration, and generally parts with some of its residual air during expiration. And, moreover, voice production occasions a greater activity of the respiratory muscles during expiration than mere breathing, for if a soft tone is desired, the tendency of the chest-walls and lungs to contract has to be counter-balanced by the action of the muscles of inspiration,[1] whilst the expiratory

[1] Termed by Mandl the "*lutte vocale.*"—*Hygiène de la voix*, Paris, 1876, p. 12.

muscles are called on to labour vigorously whenever loudness of voice is required.

Under these circumstances the taking of breath demands the direct attention of the speaker or singer at every moment, and on his judgment and train-ing depends the accomplishment of the function with ease and absence of embarrassment. On the one hand, he must be quick to notice the occurrence of all the pauses, and must even look out for them beforehand, and, on the other, he ought to be well acquainted with the capacity of his own chest in order to decide when the opportunities may be taken and when he can afford to let them pass by. It is in music especially that the artistic management of the breath is of the greatest importance, because in speaking the attention of the audience is not so much concentrated on sound as on sense. If the singer neglects a proper occasion he may have to squeeze all the residual air out of his chest before he can find another, or else mar the effect of a phrase of melody by a cacophonous gasp. And the evil may not terminate in a momentary difficulty if the chest is exhausted, for it must after-wards be replenished by a very long breath in order to prevent a repetition of the same trouble. A pause, however, which will allow of an extra-ordinary inspiration may not occur, and the vocalist may be kept for the rest of his song breathing at the lowest limit of his respiratory capacity. Now the expulsion of the residual air from the chest demands a considerable muscular effort, which increases up to the point where the lungs are emptied of all but their fixed air. In such case the stream of air cannot be propelled with sufficient steadiness through the larynx, a wavering sound will be produced, and it will be evident to the audience that the singer is straining himself. Such muscular straining, of course, soon creates fatigue, and as the consequence of a single mistake the singer may not regain his freedom of breath through a whole song, or perhaps during the length of an evening. And such awkward management of the breath may be habitual with vocalists who have not had the advantage of technical training, and they may exhaust their lungs unnecessarily, through inexperience, on each occasion that they sing.

The converse of the preceding proposition may now be considered, viz., the practice of filling the lungs too full at each inspiration, and singing always with a chest expanded almost to its vital capacity. The result here is nearly similar to that just described. Powerful muscular contractions are required in order to inflate the chest to the utmost, and of course the chest-walls when released tend to return with great force to their state of normal equilibrium. Consequently the command over the current of air, to be thrown into sonorous vibration as it passes the glottis, is lessened, and the singer quickly becomes tired through over-exertion.

The foregoing remarks apply also to the speaker, but not always with equal force. For the orator or actor, during passionate declamation, may exhaust his breath, whilst the evident severity of his labour will only serve to constrain the attention and rouse the feelings of the auditors, so as to impress them most strongly with the importance or reality of the theme. Yet the actor will perhaps do better by imitating vividly the appearance of natural excitement, than if, by yielding entirely to the force of his representation and identifying himself with the presented character, he agitates and tires his system as violently as if torn by the convulsions of a veritable passion. For in the one case, indeed, he seems to practise that art which can conceal art, but in the other to abandon himself to an irrational phrensy. And though the orator may sometimes allow himself to be carried away by the depth and sincerity of his impulses or the loftiness of his subject, on ordinary occasions, such as lecturing, for example, on a scientific topic, he must manage his breath with as much delicacy as a singer. Because when the understanding alone of the audience is addressed they will be more attentive to a smooth and consecutive flow of sentences, whilst their taste may be offended by an abrupt and gasping delivery.

Mode of Breathing.

We have seen that there are three sets of muscles which are capable of enlarging the thoracic cavity in different directions for inspiration. Now, in practising respiration with the mind turned towards the mechanism of the act, it is possible to use one or two of these sets almost to the exclusion of the remaining respiratory muscles, and it therefore happens that, on false theoretical grounds or by accidental proclivity, a vicious habit of breathing, the so-called "clavicular," may be adopted. Thus a departure occurs from what ought to be the standard rule, *i.e.*, to breathe always naturally and to fill the chest in the manner which comes easiest. If this simple rule were invariably adhered to there would be no occasion to compare the various kinds of breathing, and to decide from physiological data which is the most proper to be chosen. This question, however, must be briefly discussed here, in order to show why clavicular breathing should be generally prohibited.

During *abdominal respiration* the expansion of the thorax is obtained with the least expenditure of muscular energy. The only muscle concerned is the diaphragm, which descends by contraction, and thus shifts the lower chest-wall further down into the abdomen. The opposition to this act is but slight, as the only parts moved are the abdominal viscera, which gravitation assists to carry downwards. Therefore this mode of breathing can be employed for a long time without fatigue, and by man, in fact, for an indefinite period, because the diaphragm, through constant action, gains an amount of endurance practically inexhaustible. But in woman the diaphragm is not brought so continually into play, for physiological (obstetric) reasons, of which, however, the potency, under ordinary circumstances, is probably considerably over-estimated. We may, indeed, conclude that the custom of confining the waist with a rigid corset, which compels the upper part of the abdomen in its whole circumference, and probably the last two ribs, to inaction, has generally the greatest share in restricting the abdominal breathing of females.

Costal or *lateral respiration*, where most of the ribs have to be raised *en masse* proportionately to the increase required in the capacity of the chest, is accompanied by no small degree of muscular effort. But, as the ribs to be elevated are sufficiently mobile and not hampered by superincumbent parts, this kind of breathing can be accomplished to its full extent without any excess of strain being put on the muscles engaged. Consequently, it forms a salutary exercise for the chest and for the body generally, so that it may be practised habitually, though not exclusively, with advantage to health. The respiratory capacity included in the range of combined abdominal and costal breathing gives air enough for all the requirements of the artistic exercise of the voice, and a well-trained speaker or singer can rarely be obliged to exceed such limits.

Clavicular respiration, as already stated, is performed by a number of muscles which are not primarily intended to move the chest-walls. Their position and attachments constitute a kind of respiratory reserve which nature presses into service, if at any time an extraordinary effort of breathing be demanded, or when disease obstructs the motions of the diaphragm or lower ribs. And as these muscles act chiefly on the upper ribs, which not only possess little mobility on account of their size and stiff joints, but are, moreover, restrained by the bones and soft parts of the shoulders and neck being superimposed on them, clavicular breathing can only be effected by a kind of a struggle. For the muscles which are capable of lifting the shoulders off the upper part of the chest must first contract before room can be obtained for the elevation of the superior ribs. The consequence of such labour is rapidly supervening fatigue, which is greatly disproportionate on the side of excess to the trivial amount of respiratory movements executed. Hence we can perceive the error and injury of attempting to substitute clavicular breathing for the more natural and facile methods. And it may also be affirmed with confidence that no speaker or singer can practise it to any extent without showing a marked deficiency of endurance which must lead to a complete defeat of his strength if called on to use his voice for a lengthened period, such as when engaging energetically in a protracted debate, sustaining a leading part in a five-act play, or singing through an opera.

Clavicular breathing is always betrayed by the motion it necessarily gives to the shoulders, which are alternately drawn up towards the ears and depressed. Should the habit be formed, it must then be got rid of by paying attention to keeping the shoulders immovable during respiration. Any difficulty in attaining this object may be surmounted by practising breathing with the back to a wall having projecting ledges, which can fix the shoulders and prevent their moving upwards, or the same purpose may even be effected by crossing the arms behind a chair and holding on to the rail behind.[1]

Respiratory Gymnastics.

Every action of the body accelerates the circulation, and is also, therefore, an exercise for the chest, because the more rapid flow of blood through the lungs causes them to demand a larger supply of air. This demand may, however, be met simply by quickened respiration, so that instead of seventeen breaths in the minute, thirty, forty, or even more may be taken. In such case there is no influence at work which can increase the lung capacity, and it therefore becomes necessary to organize a system of gymnastics with the direct object of developing the chest.

The first point to which attention must be directed, is to obtain a proper position of holding the chest, whereby the ribs may be allowed, as much as practicable, a free and extensive mobility. For when the muscles of the trunk are not vigorous, the various parts which it is their office to support

[1] Mandl was the first to demonstrate the evil of clavicular breathing—*Gazette médicale de Paris*, 1855, pp. 244, 275, 294. Previously many teachers of note actually encouraged this mode of respiration, and the Paris *Conservatoire* promulgated the absurdity that in singing the breath should not be taken in the same manner as in speaking. " Quand on respire pour parler ou pour renouveler simplement l'air des poumons, le premier mouvement est celui de l'aspiration, alors le ventre gonfle et sa partie postérieure s'avance un peu. . . . . Au contraire, dans l'action de respirer pour chanter, en aspirant il faut aplatir le ventre et le faire remonter avec promptitude en gonflant et avançant la poitrine."—*Méthode de chant du Conservatoire de musique*, p. 2.

are abandoned to gravitation, and a stooping posture is maintained. Thus the shoulders, with the arms dependent from them, droop forward and lie passively on the top and upper parts of the sides of the chest, whilst the spine, instead of preserving its forward curve at the hinder part of the abdomen (small of the back), relaxes to verticity, so as to lower the thorax, laterally and in front, until the last ribs rest on the pelvis (hips). In this way, as the pelvis rests on a seat or through the legs on the ground, the muscles are relieved in great part from their task of sustaining the body erect. But, as a consequence, the chest is built up in such a manner by its contiguous structures that its osseous case is rendered nearly immobile.

Hence it appears that the preliminary action in respiratory gymnastics should be *to draw the shoulders backwards, and to advance the chest forwards and upwards, by giving the spine a strong forward curve at the hinder part of the abdomen.* At the same time the arms should not be allowed to hang against the sides of the chest.

The next proceeding should be to practise the different modes of breathing. The activity of the diaphragm, as evidenced by the power of protruding and retracting the abdomen during inspiration and expiration, whilst the ribs are retained nearly motionless, should be encouraged. And when the pupil has drawn a full abdominal breath, costal inspiration may follow, and occasionally, at the last, the chest may be expanded to the utmost by a clavicular effort. But the natural sequence of the different kinds of respiration should never be disturbed. It should be seen that the abdomen is first expanded, then the lower ribs, and only at the extremity of inspiration should any motion of the shoulders be permitted, so that the lungs may be inflated to the maximum extent. As a rule the exercise should be restricted to the abdominal and costal breathing, but an occasional clavicular inspiration in its proper place may be allowed, in order that the pupil, by being accustomed to the highest limit of chest expansion, may be enabled to practise the intermediate movements with more facility.[1]

Furthermore, it is important to observe that this factitious breath-taking should not, especially at the commencement of a course of training, be pushed too far at each lesson. After every two or three efforts it ought to be alternated with movements of the arms, and with pacing up and down for a few steps with an erect carriage. By thus engaging the pupil in a positive muscular exercise, a natural incentive is obtained to increased respiration, and the breath-training will proceed more effectually. Otherwise, to draw a number of long breaths for reasons that are purposeless as regards the immediate requirements

---

[1] *Holding the breath* may also be occasionally included in the respiratory training. Not the *spiritus cohibitio* practised by the ancients until the gorged veins of the body stood out in thick ridges (*Hieronymus Mercurialis*, op. cit. l. iii. 6, l. vi. 4), and in some cases even recommended by Galen (*De Sanitate Tuenda*, l. iii. c. 1), Cælius Aurelianus (*De Morbis Chronicis*, l. iii. 1, l. iv. 7), and by other classic physicians, as a sanitary and curative exercise; but a retention of the breath by fixing the chest-walls after a moderate inspiration by the power of the inspiratory muscles, whilst the glottis remains wide open. See Root, *Normal Musical Handbook*, p. 101.

of the animal economy, cannot fail to upset the pulmonary and vascular equilibrium and to produce a transient exhaustion.[1]

MANAGEMENT OF THE VIBRATING ELEMENT (VOCAL REEDS).

Whilst our knowledge of the physiology of the larynx is incomplete, a considerable part of this division of our subject must be given up to empirical treatment, and the ear must be guided by results to act as chief·arbiter of the utility of many practices relating to voice training. In all cases the ultimate appeal must be to the ear, but a basis for the successive steps of any process of voice development must nevertheless be sought for in physiology. Where such a basis is wanting, the result often fails to justify the means adopted, and the object which from the first was aimed at is not attained.

The cultivation of the laryngeal powers has for its purpose, (1) *to augment the force of the sounds that can be produced,* (2) *to modify their timbre,* (3) *to extend their compass, and* (4) *to increase the executive faculty of the laryngeal muscles.*

In training the speaking voice, power and timbre only, so far as the larynx is concerned, claim close

---

[1] The most accurately systematized series of breathing exercises, very much in accordance with the principles enunciated in the text, will be found in Monroe's *Vocal and Physical Training*, Philadelphia, 1869, p. 19, et seq. See besides, Frobisher, *Voice and Action*, New York, 1867, p. 59, et seq. Much useful advice on breathing will also be found in Guttmann, *Gymnastik der Stimme gestüzt auf physiologische Gesetze*, Leipzig, 1861, p. 98, et seq.

attention, because the sounds employed are concrete and the range of pitch is limited. Thus the voice glides up and down without marking the intervals that form notes, whilst its excursions seldom comprise the compass of an octave.

In singing, on the contrary, discrete sounds are emitted, so that changes of pitch are effected by leaps of not less than a semitone,[1] whilst the entire range of notes of which the voice is capable is often traversed. Hence every activity that the larynx possesses is called into play, and the physical training of the organ is, therefore, of a much more complicated description.

Force and Timbre.

Force and timbre, as far as the vocal reeds are concerned, may be treated of together, because in the larynx they are practically inseparable and only modifiable by identical and simultaneous efforts. Force of voice depends very much on the firmness and elasticity of the vocal reeds, and on the accuracy with which their opposing edges fit together, as they are thus most apt for the isochronous vibration which is the characteristic of musical tone. They must be homogeneous in density, and the muscular contractions which hold them together and regulate their tension must be exactly balanced, so that all their parts may respond alike to the current of air

---

[1] A glide, called *portamento*, is, however, occasionally admissible in singing. Quarter tones are used in Oriental music.

issuing from the lungs. Should their edges be uneven, their substance hard in one spot and soft in another, or their tension dissimilar on opposite sides, the pressure of the air has a different effect according to the part at which it strikes, irregular sets of vibrations are generated, and, instead of a tone of fulness and volume, a harsh, jarring sound, a mere noise in fact, is produced. As far as physical inequalities of the vibrating element are concerned these phenomena may be dismissed without further notice here, because in the normal state the vocal reeds are always homogeneous in structure and symmetrical in form.[1] One of the chief causes of a rough, unmusical voice is disparity of action between the various pairs of laryngeal muscles. The tone of the voice is, therefore, governed almost wholly by the will of the speaker, and according to the delicacy of his ear will be tuneful or the reverse. That the ear is mainly instrumental in producing refinement of vocal tone is proved by the example of persons who, being born incurably deaf, have been taught to speak, as in such cases the voice remains harsh to the highest degree. On this account the voice becomes an index of mental and social status by which we can distinguish the uneducated from persons of culture, as the aural perceptions are generally in a state of development proportionate to that of the other senses.

Persons in trying to speak with a sonorous voice

---

[1] An elevation of the edge of one of the vocal bands, causing an unsteadiness of pitch when singing, sometimes exists without any evidence of past or present disease.

too frequently strain the muscles of the chest and pharynx by violent efforts to expel the air with excessive force, whilst the action of the vocal reeds is entirely disregarded. But the best way to fill a large hall is to contrive to press as many regular and ample vibrations as possible into each syllable uttered,[1] on which account the words should be somewhat more prolonged than in ordinary conversation. In singing, though the same fault may occur, it is guarded against to a great extent, because so much more watchfulness is demanded over the musical quality of the notes.

In voice practice, therefore, with the view of obtaining a full and pure tone, attention should at first be mainly fixed on the laryngeal vibrations. For this purpose the exercise of vocalization, *i.e.*, the exclusive emission of vowel-sounds, as adopted by the old Italian school of singing, and still kept up by some modern teachers, seems most plausible. By this means the observation can be concentrated on the character of the laryngeal tones without being turned aside at every moment by other actions, because the vocal tube and articulating organs either remain completely at rest or execute very slight movements according as a single vowel or a succession of vowels are employed.

An action of the vocal and ventricular bands, encouraged by many teachers of singing, and termed the "stroke of the glottis" (*coup de glotte*), appears

---

[1] Allowing, of course, for pitch. Apart from the choice of resonant vowels, such is the only mode I can conceive physiologically of producing the so-called "orotund" voice. See Rush, op. cit. passim.

well adapted to steady the working of their muscles either for speech or song. Usually at the beginning of phonation the vocal bands approach during expiration and commence to vibrate as soon as they come near enough to interrupt without absolutely breaking the continuity of the issuing stream of air.[1] But in practising the stroke of the glottis the ventricular bands,[2] simultaneously with the vocal reeds, are first tightly approximated, so that a condensation of the air in the thoracic cavity precedes the emission of tone, which consequently commences by a slight explosion, arising thus in a manner mechanically similar to the explosive consonants. The notes begun in this way strike the ear with an initial sharpness of definition and firmness of tone which add to their musical effect. This stroke of the glottis should, of course, be produced without any more marked effort than occurs in the pronunciation of *p* or *b* by the lips. To attain the perfect execution of it the pupil should first learn to explode the glottis on whispered vowels, for which purpose the short *u* in *up*, as recommended by Monroe,[3] appears specially adapted.

---

[1] In speaking, however, Helmholtz thinks the vocal bands act as striking reeds—op. cit. p. 155.

[2] The credit of pointing out this fact, which I believe to have verified by laryngoscopic observation, both autoscopic and otherwise, is due to Lunn, op. cit. It appears likely, moreover, that the rough breathing, *i.e.*, the letter H, is in reality formed by an initial puff from the approximated ventricular bands.

[3] Op. cit. pp. 31, 35.

N

Extension of Compass.

The extension of vocal compass may be obtained by specially practising the voice at the extremes of its natural scale. If a gain in the lowest notes is desired, it is necessary to produce an extraordinary relaxation of the vocal reeds. As, however, there is great difficulty in making them vibrate harmoniously, or even at all, when much slackened,[1] one or two notes will usually represent the whole sum of success in this direction, but at the same time the tone of deep notes already existent may be considerably developed.

At the top of the chest register we have seen that a kind of dead-lock occurs when the crico-thyroid chink is closed and the opposing margins of the cartilages come into contact. Hence it is evident that an almost insuperable obstacle exists in the way of pushing the voice upwards in this register. To try to do so is to attempt the compression of the dense cartilaginous material which, if at all practicable, must call forth a hazardous amount of muscular strain. As far as the vocal reeds are concerned they would probably bear more tension than is ever put on them, but since the cartilages interfere it will doubtless be wisest to be content with improving the qualities of the chest notes actually possessed. When this has been done an

---

[1] Müller instances the deep croak of frogs to show what grave tones can be drawn from short membranous reeds when greatly relaxed—op. cit. p. 1038.

upward gain of a semi-tone or two will generally be found within easy reach.

To the upward extension of the falsetto register there would appear to be less opposition, acoustic or physiological, than in either of the instances just noticed. For here, indeed, it seems that the vocal reeds should still be able to vibrate strongly, though excessively shortened by constrictive action, whilst the curtailment of their length is not quickly checked by a mechanical impediment, but is ruled more remotely by power of muscular contractility. And these considerations are practically exemplified by the extraordinary falsetto range for which many celebrated singers, mostly females, have been noted, some of whom could attain to a pitch even an octave above the usual limits of voice.[1] The main obstacle, therefore, to the upward development of the voice in this register must be sought for in the natural constitution of the vocal organs with respect to vigour and tonicity in various individuals. Should the pupil be endowed with perfect soundness and strength of all the parts engaged, an acquisition of two or three tones, or even more, may be the reward of careful and assiduous practice.

[1] *E.g.*, Mara could sing *c'''* ; Catalani *g'''* ; and

Aguiari *c''''* . The last fact rests on the testimony of Mozart. See Fétis, *Biographie universelle des musiciens*, Paris, 1860-65, sub nominibus.

Under the contrary conditions, however, the vocal organs will break down under the strain if the exercise be not kept strictly within the boundary prescribed by the natural gifts.[1]

Vocal Execution.

A rapid execution is probably more frequently a positive acquirement than any other of the qualities displayed in singing, and flexibility of voice may be looked on as the special prize of diligent practice. The laryngeal muscles deserve to be signalized beyond all others for power of making minute movements with extraordinary exactitude—a property which is doubtless derived from their being able to rely on so delicate a guide as the ear. They can determine the amount of their contractions with the utmost precision, and can pass with preconception between degrees furthest apart, either instantly, through a succession of equal intervals, or by the most complicated irregularity of distances. A wide field is

[1] Prof. C. J. Plumptre, of King's College, has called my attention to an interesting observation of his in connection with the management of the larynx by speakers. He has remarked that orators, when producing grave tones, almost invariably incline the head towards the breast, so as to relax the muscles of the throat, and, on the contrary, that during the emission of high sounds, the face is turned upwards, thus putting the neck on the stretch. I believe since to have observed similar actions in the case of professional singers. The explanation is, of course, that the relaxation of the laryngeal muscles required for low notes is favoured by slackening, as far as possible, all the surrounding structures, whilst rigidity of the same parts supports the larynx, and thus assists the steady contraction of all its muscles demanded for the emission of notes in the upper registers.

here open for the ingenuity of the composer or teacher of singing to systematize solfeggi or vocal exercises, which shall contain every possible transition between the various notes in ascending or descending the scale, commencing with the simplest movements, and advancing insensibly to the greatest complexity. An important point to be kept in view during this kind of practice is to facilitate the passage from one register to another by endeavouring to amalgamate the notes in the vicinity of the break, especially those that can be sung in either voice at will. It should, however, be carefully ascertained at what points breaks actually do occur in each voice that comes under notice. It cannot but be injurious to force all voices indiscriminately to make a change of register at one and the same position in the musical scale.[1]

MANAGEMENT OF THE RESONANCE APPARATUS (VOCAL TUBE).

The questions here involved relate mainly to pronunciation of vowels. There are, however, some

[1] On this account, therefore, too much weight should not be attached to the statements found in many treatises on singing, as in these works theory frequently obscures almost completely the actual practice. Singing masters must often, indeed, be sorely perplexed when called on to write a work containing definite rules, suitable to everybody, on matters which really demand in each instance the exercise of the nicest judgment. A competent master should be resorted to, who, under the guidance of both nature and art, can determine what is best for each pupil. If a teacher cannot be obtained, the pupil, as Curwen observes (*Teachers' Manual*, p. 176), should " study his own voice," and note the most " *natural* places of break."

superadded qualities, individual or national, of vocal timbre which may be treated of separately. Thus a *guttural* or *nasal* character may be given to every vowel-sound, though otherwise well defined, by an improper predominance of pharyngeal or nasal resonance.

In the first case the fault lies in the pharynx and mouth not communicating by a sufficiently capacious opening. The causes of such a condition depend either on anatomical conformation or on peculiar and habitual muscular action. The tonsils may be enlarged so as to block up the upper part of the pharynx, or the soft-palate and uvula may be elongated, so as almost to reach the posterior surface of the tongue. Or the individual may be in the habit during speaking of maintaining the tongue in a position arched upwards and backwards, so that it approaches the soft-palate too closely, whilst there may be at the same time an excessive contraction of the muscles of the fauces. Under these circumstances the laryngeal tones will be almost deprived of oral resonance, and, not having a free passage for exit, will have a guttural and muffled sound. In such instances the remedy must be adapted to remove the cause, and if the tonsils or uvula are abnormally large, a part of them may be removed by a simple and momentary surgical operation. And the effect of excision of the tonsils may not only be to render the voice clear and sonorous, but may also allow the compass to be extended one or two notes higher.[1] For the action of the extrinsic muscles of the

---

[1] It is stated that "many of our greatest singers, from Madame Patti downwards, have undergone the operation" with the best results.—Browne, *Medical Hints on the Singing Voice*, 1877, p. 30.

larynx, which is so essential in the production of high notes, is greatly impeded when the pharynx is blocked up by an enormous pair of tonsils. But when the vicious tone of the voice is due to injudicious management of the muscles of the tongue and pharynx, a course of gymnastic training of the parts will soon induce them to the habitual assumption of the proper positions.

With respect to excess of nasal timbre, its causes are also twofold, and it may arise from a deficiency of the soft-palate, which renders the occlusion of the posterior nares impossible, or it may be simply the result of an imperfect action of the same organ. In the former instance the fault will often be irremediable as far as regards purity of tone, but when it is merely a question of muscular control, the pupil should be made to observe the action of the soft-palate, and to practise its elevation before a mirror. If, at the same time, the attention of the ear is thoroughly awakened, the voice may soon be freed from the objectionable timbre.

Another point which deserves notice here relates to a practice by no means uncommon, viz., the keeping the teeth shut during speaking or singing. A considerable loss of resonance is the consequence, because the cavity of the mouth is never placed in the best position for reinforcing the laryngeal tones, and also because the sound-waves cannot issue with sufficient freedom to the external air. It is only necessary to recognize the habit, where existent, in order that the inclination to it may be overcome by the will.

MANAGEMENT OF THE ARTICULATING ORGANS.

Vowel-Timbre.

We have seen that the difference between the various vowel-sounds is not one of kind, but merely of degree, and that they depend on the pitch of the note proper to the resonance cavity formed by the pharynx and mouth. As this cavity can be reduced by infinite gradations from its greatest to its least capacity, whilst the procession of vowels used in any one language advances by steps of about an octave; it follows that the lowest can be made to pass insensibly into the highest through all the other members of the series successively. It is, therefore, possible to produce as many vowels as will correspond to each note, or rather degree of pitch, obtainable from the vowel-cavity. According as our ear recognizes them to approach nearest to one or another of the vowels familiar to us, we class them as varieties of those they most resemble. Hence arises mainly the endless diversity of pronunciation observed in individuals, provincials, and nationalities.

With these facts in view it is easy to understand how many shades of timbre the voice can be made to yield at will. Of these some add sonorousness, some brightness, others softness; whilst others, again, are disagreeable. Thus, in the emission of *a* (as in *father*) the fullest volume of vocal tone can be generated, because the dimensions of the buccal cavity and the size of the oral aperture are most favourable to the formation of strong vibrations. And for the reverse reasons the vowel *e* (*ee* in *feet*) deprives the lower tones of the voice of power, though, on account of its sharpness, it renders high notes penetrating. The choice, however, of vowels or modifications of them, is a complex matter which must be decided by the taste of the pupil or his teacher.[1] It is sufficient to have indicated here the principles on which change of vocal timbre is made. In accordance with these principles, an exercise may be devised for practising the enunciation of all the grades of vowel-timbre. A good understanding of the state of the vocal tube for the different vowels, and the custom of directing the attention to it, will greatly facilitate the accurate imitation of the peculiar vowels found in foreign languages.

Consonants.

A rapid and well-defined pronunciation of the various consonants, either in speaking or singing, requires a considerable amount of lingual and labial dexterity. The tongue or lips may be naturally clumsy and awkward in their movements or the reverse. In order to attain to a good execution in articulating consonants, it is usually only necessary to practise the utterance of numbers of syllables containing every pronounceable combination and succession of them[2] under the empirical guidance of the ear. But, of course, a correct idea

[1] See Ellis, *Pronunciation for Singers*, 1877, or, *Speech in Song*, 1878.
[2] See Hullah, op. cit. appendix, and Bell's *Standard Elocutionist*, p. 29.

of the positions of the parts concerned in the formation of each letter will render the task more easy. In a certain class of persons, however, the action of the vocal organs is specially defective, so that speech, even for ordinary purposes, becomes a matter of great, and occasionally of almost insuperable, difficulty. This leads us to the consideration of defects of speech.

Stammering and Stuttering, or Psellism.

Such affections have been well known from the earliest times, and are often alluded to by Hippocrates[1]; but nevertheless it is only within the present century that systematic endeavours have been made to discover their causes, and to invent suitable modes of treatment. Already, considerable success has been attained with respect to the latter object, although no wholly satisfactory explanation of their intrinsic nature has yet been furnished to us. It is evident, however, that a multiplicity of causes are at work, and that the disability of any of the organs of voice, from the chest to the lips, is sufficient to disturb the consentaneons action of the entire series, and produce the phenomena of psellism.

Stammering may be defined to be indistinctness of pronunciation, arising from the letters of the alphabet not being properly formed by the organs of articulation. It most frequently arises from a muscular defect, giving rise to a clumsiness in getting the tongue round one or more letters, which are, therefore, so imperfectly enunciated as to be unrecognizable; or one letter may even

---

[1] *Præceptiones,* c. 6; *Aphorismi,* s. vi. 32; etc.

be habitually substituted for another; or the difficulty may only be in combining the sounds of certain letters. In some cases stammering may be the result of mere carelessness or too great eagerness in speaking, so that the words are clipped, and successive syllables are allowed to run into one another in a confused manner. In a few instances, however, a decided malformation of the speech organs exists, such as cleft-palate, abnormal enlargement of the tonsils, or shortness of the *frænum linguæ.* A classification of stammering has been attempted according to the character of the defect noticed in different cases. Thus faulty pronunciation of *g* is termed *gammacism;* of *l, lambdacism;* of *r, rhotacism;* of *j, iotacism;* lisping, *sigmatism,* etc.

The *treatment* of stammering is simple and obvious. The pupil should be made to repeat the alphabet slowly, and a note taken of every letter that is ill-formed, and he should also be made to read aloud. From such experience, a series of suitable exercises in pronunciation must be given him to practise. The instructor should be a good practical orthoepist, and should see that the tongue, lips, etc., are put in the proper position for each letter. He should show the pupil, in his own person, the action of the articulating organs and desire him to imitate them. If the stammering arises from hasty and impetuous speech, a slow and distinct delivery must be inculcated. Of course, if there is a malformation, surgical assistance must be sought.

Stuttering [1] is a much more important disorder

---

[1] The distinction between stammering and stuttering is not always accurately drawn, and the terms are often employed interchangeably both in speaking and writing.

and more complicated in its physiological relations. Here we have rapid repetitions of a letter, usually one of the explosive consonants, convulsive stoppages of articulation, and sometimes even contortions of the face and limbs before the utterance of each sentence, or possibly of every word. Nowithstanding the attention that many eminent observers have given to these phenomena, their nature is still in great part obscured, and conflicting theories are held by some of the most exact investigators.

In order to gain an insight into the present state of the question, and the remedial practices employed, a brief review of the different factors in the treatment, as they arose from time to time, with the circumstances which led to their adoption, will be most effective. The methods of treatment are divided into *mechanical, gymnastic,* and *operative* or *surgical,* concerning which in their chronological order :—

1. *Mechanical.*—Demosthenes, as Plutarch [1] informs us, was afflicted with an impediment in his speech, but cured himself by the persevering practice of declamation whilst holding some small pebbles in his mouth. No doubt the idea of the Greek orator was that, by putting an unusual difficulty in the way of fluent speech and surmounting it, he would attain to a specially facile delivery under ordinary circumstances, *i.e.,* that by rendering himself equal to the greater he would obtain a complete mastery over the less.

Subsequent to the age of Demosthenes, his example

---

[1] In *Vita.*

was frequently followed by persons similarly affected, without any special opinion as to the action of the pebbles being put forward, until 1817, when Itard,[1] either from some practical observation or theoretical assumption, conceived the idea that, so far from embarrassing the tongue, they gave it a support that it actually required. He at once proceeded to improve on this view by constructing a small furcated instrument of metal or ivory, which rested against the back of the lower incisor teeth, and received the under and front part of the tongue between its two prongs, so as to steady it during articulation. It is stated that as soon as this fork was introduced the psellism disappeared, and a thickness of speech was the only noticeable defect as long as it was retained in the mouth. It had to be worn until the pupil became accustomed to speak with accuracy and could do without it, a period which in a recorded case amounted to eighteen months. Itard's device does not appear to have ever come into extensive use, and there remains little or no record as to the real extent of its success. Certain mechanical contrivances, however, of much simpler form, such as plates of metal to go under the tongue, or between the teeth, have since been resorted to and may be referred to its parentage. Of these the most remarkable was the *glossanochon*,[2] or tongue-elevator, introduced by Wutzer in 1829, which consisted merely

---

[1] *Journal universel des sciences médicales*, 1817, t. vii. p. 129.

[2] Γλῶσσα *tongue*, ἀνὰ *up*, ἔχω *hold*. Figured and described in *Abhandlungen und Beobachtungen der ärtzlichen Gesellschaft zu Münster*, 1829, Bd. I. pp x. 416.

of a piece of metal, or any suitable substance fitted to fill the space at the back of the incisor teeth below the tongue. The mechanical treatment has now been very generally discarded by those who have paid most attention to the cure of psellism, though some few occasionally have recourse to an inter-dental plate.

2. *Gymnastic.*—The regular practice of speaking or declaiming by reading, reciting, etc., was of course an indispensable part even of the most pronounced mechanical methods. And, moreover, as it had been early remarked that stammerers could generally sing without betraying their defect, they were often directed to adopt a kind of rhythmic delivery, resembling recitative, until they obtained a proper command of their vocal organs. Prior to 1825, however, scarcely any effort had been made to ascertain by observation the precise local nature of the fault which caused the imperfection of utterance, and vague theories only were offered, attributing it to malformation of the hyoid bone,[1] excessive swiftness of cerebral irradiation,[2] etc. But in that year a certain Mrs. Leigh, of New York, in the course of some anxious endeavours to cure a young lady who stuttered, noticed that her pupil when trying to speak always kept her tongue at the bottom of her mouth, instead of raising it to the palate, as is necessary for the formation of all but the labial consonants and lowest vowels. Having made this observation, she

[1] Hahn, *Commercium litterarium ad rei medicæ et scientiæ naturalis incrementum institutum.* Nuremberg, 1736, p. 242.

[2] Rullier, *Dictionnaire de médecine en 21 vol.* art. *Bégaiement.* 1821.

forced her pupil to keep her tongue up, and in a short time, by this simple measure, taught her to speak fluently. Flushed with this success, Mrs. Leigh announced to the public that she had discovered an infallible remedy for psellism, and as a consequence was so much resorted to that in less than three years she was reported to have cured 150 cases. So great, in fact, became her fame that a Frenchman, named Malebouche, repaired to New York, bought the invaluable secret, and imported it into Europe. Of course, in the extended application of the method it was soon found that a large proportion of cases could not be benefited by it; but, nevertheless, Mrs. Leigh may be allowed the merit of being the first to draw general attention to the importance of observing and correcting any faulty action of the tongue.[1]

The next step was made in 1826 by McCormac,[2] an English physician. Having heard of Mrs. Leigh's great secret, and being excited by the accounts of its success, he determined resolutely to try and find it out for himself. He therefore began a careful and practical investigation of the causes of stuttering, which, as might be expected, struck into an entirely different path. He concluded, in fact, that the action of the chest was mainly at fault, and that psellism was the result of habitually attempting to speak when the lungs were exhausted of air. In such case, the

[1] See Magendie, *Archives générale de médecine*, 1828, t. xvi. p. 469.

[2] *A Treatise on the Cause and Cure of Hesitation of Speech.* London, 1828.

emission of a stream of air, to throw the vocal reeds into vibration, being impossible, no voice could come until the chest was replenished. From this point of view, then, the remedy for stammering is at once obvious. See that the patient never commences to speak without taking an inspiration of sufficient length, and that he renews the air at a proper time, and a cure must readily be effected. Such was the discovery made by McCormac, which, though not all-potent as he vaunted, still supplies a valuable indication for treatment.

In 1829 we come to Serres d'Alais,[1] who referred the affection to purely nervous influences, which, as he pointed out, were manifested under a twofold aspect, viz., by spasm and chorea.[2] Thus, in one class of cases, the muscles of articulation were fixed by a kind of cramp, so that the speaker could only move them into the proper position after abnormal exertion, whereas in another the vocal organs, instead of being guided by the will, executed from time to time a number of rapid and aimless automatic motions. In order to conquer such tendencies, Serres recommended the practice of energetic declamation, accompanied by regular movements of the arms. In this manner the whole mind would be directed with a steady and fast determination towards the performance of the vocal organs, and the pupil would gradually secure thereby a complete control over their actions.

[1] *Mémorial des Hôpitaux du Midi*, 1829, p. 371.
[2] That is, a malady of the tongue, etc., akin to St. Vitus' dance in which the person afflicted is agitated at times by all kinds of involuntary movements.

In the same year Arnott[1] suggested that stuttering arose from spasmodic closure of the glottis, which had to be overcome by an extraordinary effort at every moment before the breath could issue and the vocal reeds be thrown into vibration. Such spasmodic closure only occurred as a kind of hyper-compliance with the will of the speaker, as often as he brought the vocal reeds from the separated to the approximated position. But, vibration once established would continue until the glottis had again been thrown open. Hence Arnott proposed to connect all the words spoken by a continuous hum, so that, by keeping up the laryngeal vibrations as long as each expiration could afford, the recurrences of the spasm might be rendered few and distant.

In 1830 one of the most remarkable of orthophonists (the word is his own) came upon the scene. This was Colombat de l'Isère[2] who gained the Monthyon prize from the French Academy for his success in treating psellism. He states that of 452 cases of stuttering that came under his care he cured permanently 354. Colombat did not, however, make any new discoveries with respect to stuttering, but, nevertheless, he deserves considerable credit for being the first to combine the work of his predecessors and to form it into something of a system. Previous to him each investigator rode his own particular hobby and ignored all other methods. But Colombat perceived that what succeeded in one case might readily

[1] *Elements of Physics*, 1829, vol. i. p. 603, et seq.
[2] *Du bégaiement et tous les autres vices de la parole.* Paris, 1831.

o

fail in another, and therefore provided himself with a variety of weapons. He followed Leigh, McCormac, Serres, and used mechanical contrivances. He laid especial stress, however, on the practice of rhythmic speaking, regulated by beating time with the hand or foot. Considering his experience, it is evident from his testimony alone that this expedient must be of great value.

In 1837 Berthold,[1] whilst writing on general physiology, and pointing out that the essence of stuttering lay in an ill-regulated action of the muscles concerned in speech, first drew attention to the fact that the muscles of the lower jaw might be affected as well as any of the other groups.

In 1843 Becquerel,[2] the well-known hygienist, introduced a novel view of the cause of stuttering to the Academy of Sciences. It appears that he himself was a victim to the affection, and had followed Colombat's method for a number of years, but with only a partial success. The theory he propounded was suggested to him by a mechanic named Jourdant, who premised that stuttering resulted from an inability to retain sufficient air in the chest for the production of voice. Thus, as soon as the lungs were properly filled, instead of expiration being graduated according to the needs of speech, the chest-walls rapidly collapsed, and the air rushed out through the wide open glottis before articulation commenced. This may be considered as an elucidation of McCormac's observation,

---

[1] *Lehrbuch der Physiologie.* Göttingen, 1837, p. 430.
[2] *Traité sur le bégaiement et des moyens de la guérir.* Paris, 1848.

and to explain why stutterers should be so prone to attempting to speak with empty lungs. The indication, then, for treatment furnished by Becquerel was that the pupil should practise a suitable retention of his breath, and strive to regulate its emission with slow exactitude. He vouched in person for the advantage he had derived from such an exercise.

From this period up to the present psellism has been dealt with by a crowd of authors, each of whom has classified the subject and modified the treatment in accordance with his own peculiar mental bias. Of these Hunt[1] may be cited as the writer of the most elaborate and systematic treatise. But the most able and important of the recent literary contributions in this field is due to Guillaume,[2] who from having suffered himself has had special practical advantages in studying the affection. The measures in which he places his confidence are, (1) keeping the tongue steadily raised to the palate, (2) taking an ample inspiration at the beginning of each sentence, and (3) careful attention to ensure correct movement of the lips. He further counsels the use, when necessary, of a small wedge to keep the teeth apart, and dwells with considerable weight on the practice of whispering exercises.

3. *Surgical or Operative.*—Another phase in the history of stuttering has still to be noticed, which relates to attempts that have been made to combat the affection summarily by the knife. From time im-

---

[1] *A Treatise on Stammering and Stuttering.* London. 1870.
[2] *Dictionnaire encyclopédique des sciences médicales.* Paris, 1868, art. *Bégaiement.*

memorial the condition called "tongue-tied" has been recognized and treated by incision, for it is described by Aristotle,[1] and Celsus[2] gives directions as to the simple operation required to remedy it. And other obvious malformations of the articulating organs have at all periods been freely submitted to such operative measures as were clearly requisite. But in 1841 a kind of tidal wave swept over the surgical mind of Europe, carrying with it a conviction that, by severing some of the lingual muscles from their attachments, or by excising a portion of the tongue itself, the stutterer might be endowed with immediate and permanent fluency of speech. The source of the movement was Dieffenbach of Berlin,[3] who, thinking he perceived an analogy between the faulty action of the tongue and the awry motions of the eyes in strabismus, concluded that by cutting certain nerves or muscles the one affection might be remedied as readily as the other. His favourite method of procedure was to make a deep transverse division of the back of the tongue and remove a thick wedge-shaped slice. In the wake of Dieffenbach followed many disciples, whilst some other eminent surgeons, such as Velpeau[4] and Amussat,[5] adopted his theory, but modified his practice by executing a section of one or both of the muscles (*genio-glossi*) which join the tongue to the inside of the lower jaw at the

---

[1] *Historia Animalium*, l. i. c. 2.

[2] L. vii. c. xii. 4.

[3] *Berliner medizinische Central-Zeitung*, 1841, p. 163 et passim.

[4] *Annales de la chirurgie française ou étrangère*, 1841, t. i. pp. 355, 378, 439.

[5] *Gazette des hôpitaux*, 1841, t. iii. pp. 93, 105, 141.

chin. At first the success seemed most gratifying, and reports published a day or two after each operation represented the stutterer as receiving the gift of free speech almost instantly in a manner little short of the marvellous. In a brief time, however, the genuineness of the supposed cures began to be doubted, and it very soon appeared that in nearly every instance the patient, after the wounds had healed, found himself in a worse plight than before. It became evident, indeed, that the local shock to the parts only temporarily, and that not invariably, arrested the stuttering, which soon returned as inveterate as ever. And, moreover, the example of one or two cases proved that the operation was not altogether devoid of danger from hæmorrhage or other casualties. After a rage of a few months, therefore, the surgical treatment of stuttering came to be tacitly abandoned by those who were regarded as its originators, whilst not a few of their disciples were so disappointed with their experience that they openly renounced the operation in disgust, and even protested[1] against its further repetition as a barbarity. At present it is so generally repudiated that it might be pronounced obsolete, were it not that a single surgeon[2] is still known who has given in a theoretical adherence to it.

Having examined thus cursorily the chief theories that have been propounded relative to stuttering

---

[1] See Phillips, *De la ténotomie sous-cutanée.* Paris, 1841, p. 393, et seq.

[2] Oré of Bordeaux, *Nouveau dictionnaire de médecine et de chirurgie pratiques.* Paris, 1866, art. *Bégaiement.*

and the modes of treatment that have been adopted, it is manifest that the affection is one of great complexity, and to which, according to circumstances, diverse remedies must be applied with considerable judgment. Thus, to summarize the subject as far as practicable, we see that five principal groups of muscles may be implicated, separately or in various combinations, viz., the muscles (1) of the chest, (2) of the larynx,[1] (3) of the tongue, (4) of the jaw, and (5) of the lips. And the nature of the disorder may be either *spasmodic*, so that the muscles take up a fixed position which can only be overcome by a strong and often prolonged effort of the will; or *choreic*, so that when called on to act they perform a series of eccentric and involuntary movements instead of being instantly subservient to the wish of the speaker. And beyond all this, there is still a mental influence, a nervousness or timidity, which must be banished before the vocal organs can be ruled by the volition into a perfectly concerted action. Hence the first object in treating a case must be to obtain the co-operation of the pupil, and his anxiety must be aroused to conquer the defect.[2] This done, a great step in advance will have been made, as is evidenced by the fact that a marked amelioration of stuttering usually occurs on arrival at adult age, whilst occasionally the affection quite

---

[1] Since the above was written James has actually succeeded in observing laryngoscopically a stammering affection of the vocal bands. See his paper on the case in *The Lancet*, 1879, vol. ii. p. 726, and my comments on the subject, ibid. p. 820.

[2] On this point see further Cox, *The Arts of Writing, Reading, and Speaking*, 1878, p. 330.

disappears about that time of life. This circumstance no doubt arises from the awakening of the reasoning faculties and the confirmation of the powers of the mind, which then assumes a more discretionary control over the impulses of the body. As soon as the pupil has been engaged to assist the teacher with his own endeavours, an attempt to discover the main-spring of the disorder may be made, and such of the exercises above-mentioned as seem most suitable to the case put in practice. The system of Guillaume promises the best results, but every voice-trainer will have to draw largely on his own judgment, and, in the present state of our knowledge, empiricism will sometimes guide most directly to the desired end.

The *originating causes* of stuttering are not well ascertained, and in many cases where it appears to date from infancy it can only be attributed to some accidental organic defect. But sex predisposes very markedly to the affection, and a striking majority of the examples met with occur in males. Thus, of all the instances observed by Colombat[1] and Hunt,[2] only about 10 or 12 per cent. were females. The latter author also endeavoured to discover the origin of 200 cases[3] that he treated, and found that $7\frac{1}{2}$ per cent. dated from convalescence after illness, such as fever, measles, whooping-cough, etc.; 5 per cent. were the result of fright or ill-usage at school; 4 per cent. were caused by voluntary, and 9 per

---

[1] Op. cit. 3ème ed. 1840, p. 268.   [2] Op. cit. p. 342.

[3] Ibid. p. 341.

cent. by involuntary imitation; 10 per cent. were stated to be inherited from the father, and 5 per cent. from the mother; whilst the remainder, $49\frac{1}{2}$ per cent., could not be accounted for.

The numerical relation of stutterers to the whole population is reckoned by Colombat[1] to average about 1 to 5,397. Hunt,[2] however, and some other observers make the proportion much higher, viz., 3 per 1,000.

---

[1] Op. cit. p. 265.   [2] Loc. cit.

CHAPTER V.

THE HYGIENE OF THE VOICE.

SPECIAL HYGIENE OF THE VOCAL ORGANS—GENERAL HYGIENE IN ITS RELATION TO THE VOICE.

Scope of the Subject.—The relations of the voice to the general health of the body are of the most intimate and complete description. The hygiene of the voice in its fullest sense is, therefore, the hygiene of the whole animal economy; and the spirit of the well-known proverb, which sets forth how closely is interwoven the integrity of mind and of body, might with equal propriety be applied to the voice in the form of "*vox sana in corpore sano.*" At the same time, however, the voice, like the mind, has a sphere of its own, within which it may be affected, for good or ill, without immediate reference to the state of the constitution. Hence its sanity may be treated of under the twofold aspects of a general and a special hygiene. The latter, as the more immediate, though less familiar and less investigated, may be first discussed.

SPECIAL HYGIENE OF THE VOCAL ORGANS.

In this section we may consider how far the state of the vocal organs with respect to soundness and vigour may be influenced by their own actions, *i.e.*, by the exercise, moderated or exaggerated, of the voice; whilst at the same time some appropriate rules may be laid down of preservative and remedial hygiene. In the professional use of the voice the parts concerned are urged to perform their functions to a much higher degree than is ever exacted by the ordinary exigencies of social life, and they are, therefore, subjected to a marked intensifying of the conditions, both intrinsic and extrinsic, under which they usually act, whence a signal alteration may be effected in their physical structures.

Voice is generated mainly as the result of two consecutive and specially combined movements, the one primary and vital, namely, activity of muscle, the other secondary and material, viz., motion of air. To these two relations may be traced all the physiological effects of vocal exercise.

Direct Results of Muscular Activity.

The systematized daily use of the various groups of muscles called into action during phonation impels them to gain in size and strength as long as the efforts made do not exceed from time to

time their proper powers. Hence follows increasing
ease in performing the respiratory functions and
extension of the initial faculties of mobility of the
larynx and articulating apparatus. The nutrition
of the local muscles and all the contiguous structures
is carried on with more than ordinary energy; they
glow with health and their growth is accelerated.

Precisely the opposite phenomena are produced by
over-exertion. In this case the muscles become exhausted and diminish in bulk and vigour, because
the waste of their tissues entailed by the excessive
action is pressed beyond the reparative powers of
the vital forces, and fresh material cannot be laid
down in an equal quantity to that which passes
away as effete. At the point when labour becomes
inordinate fatigue is felt and rest becomes a necessity, whilst in the interval of cessation from work
the parts that had suffered from too much wear and
tear are restored to their normal state.

Over-exertion may be of two kinds. Thus it
may consist in sudden and violent effort, or in a
prolongation of ordinary movements until endurance
is completely spent. In the former case the harm
partakes more of the nature of an injury; some of
the tender fibrils of the muscle, and of the minute
blood-vessels or capillaries which traverse it, may be
torn across. Hence there may be soreness, pain,
and swelling, or even inflammation, the results, in
fact, commonly recognized as occurring from a strain
or sprain. Recovery from such a condition is often
protracted. In violent vocal efforts the muscles
engaged may suffer in this way, whence the chest

may for some time after feel sore to the touch and during respiration. But the muscles most likely to be strained are those of the larynx, because they are called on to contract very forcibly in order that the vocal bands may resist by their steady approximation the impetuous rush of air from the lungs. Hence results what is sometimes spoken of as "a strain of the vocal cords."[1] Such an accident is soon betrayed by hoarseness, which, however, generally disappears spontaneously after a few days of rest. But weakness of voice may often be a troublesome symptom for a considerable time.

The consequences of persistent speaking or singing, in spite of great fatigue being felt, are somewhat similar to those just described, but of a less pronounced character. On single occasions, therefore, recovery is usually rapid and complete after a short interval of repose. The evils, however, to be here considered are those attendant on repeated and habitual exertion of the vocal organs beyond the enduring power of the individual. In such instances the fundamental cause at work is generally some vice

---

[1] Positive strains of the voice are now rarely met with, but were common enough in classical times, when the *phonasci* had to force their voice to the utmost in order to fill the enormous theatres. Thus Galen: "Phonasci, qui magno vocis exercitio utuntur, quum contendendo oblæserint vocem. . . . . balneis multis utuntur, et cibos lenes, ac laxantes edunt."—*De Compositione Pharmacorum secundum Locos*, l. vii. c. 1. According to Q. Serenus Sammonicus, Hortensius strained and permanently lost his voice from declaiming intemperately in the Roman forum.—*Præcepta de Medicina*, c. 15. To exerting the voice beyond its natural powers the Greeks applied " nomen (κλασμὸς?) a gallorum immaturo cantu."—Quintilian, l. xi. c. iii. 51.

of voice-production—that is to say, a well-trained voice can seldom suffer from over-fatigue, because the vocalist has learned by precept and experience how to make the best of his natural gifts. Thus, even a feeble voice can be saved, by judicious management, from the consequences of oft-repeated fatigue. Such a result depends mainly on well-regulated respiration and attention to the formation of the laryngeal tones.[1] But when clavicular or other improper modes of breathing are employed, the muscles of the chest-walls soon become tired out. And the evil tends to augment on every subsequent occasion, because the use of the voice, instead of being a tonic exercise for the chest, becomes a debilitating one. Hence the voice loses in fulness and steadiness, and becomes weak and trembling. So far, then, a radical exhaustion of the respiratory muscles sets in, and this is one phase of the convergence of contingencies under which a voice may be worn out.

But the most striking and frequent troubles are those which follow faulty usage of the laryngeal and pharyngeal muscles. When the individual, instead of throwing his vocal bands into even and ample vibration by equable and carefully-moderated expiration, continually resorts to blowing a powerful blast of air through the glottis, both the intrinsic and extrinsic muscles of the larynx must be maintained in an almost constant state of vigorous contraction. Under these circumstances, as in all over-taxed muscles, the over-plus of effete products generated

---

[1] See last Chapter.

by the exertion cannot be removed readily by the
proper channels, but accumulates. As a consequence,
the substance of the muscles becomes turgid, the
capillary vessels traversing it are partially obstructed,
and much of the blood sent to the part, instead of
flowing through measuredly, collects there and increases the intumescence. Such is the condition
generally described as congestion. When occurring
in the laryngeal or pharyngeal muscles, hoarseness
invariably results, because the delicate movements
necessary to regulate the tension and approximation
of the vocal bands are clogged and cannot be
executed with precision. Unequal vibrations are
therefore produced. At the same time, there may
be little or no appearances of disease, because the
mucous membrane which forms the surface and
invests the affected muscles may remain intact.
Such, when induced by fatigue of the voice, appears
to be the incipient stage of the malady, formerly called
Dysphonia clericorum, or clergyman's sore throat,[1]
but now, through a better knowledge of its etiology
and nature, more properly termed "glandular sore
throat."

After repeated congestions, however, the mucous
membrane becomes deeply implicated, and more or
less chronicity then characterizes the disease. In this

[1] Van Swieten first clearly conceived, on physiological grounds, the
separate existence of such an affection.—*Commentaria in Boerhavii
Aphorismos,* Lugduni, t. ii. 1745, p. 632. Guéneau de Mussy was
the first to investigate it scientifically, and to define its place in
medicine.—*Traité d'angine glanduleuse,* Paris, 1857. An obscurity,
however, still hangs over some points relating to its origin, which
forms a subject for continued inquiry.

stage its chief features consist in the swelling of numerous minute glands,[1] which dot the surface of the larynx and pharynx. Their office is to secrete and discharge the lubricating fluid, which is so essential to keep the inside of the throat moist and supple. As soon as they participate in the congestion their orifices become choked and the fluid collects in them. They then appear like granules or small grains of shot, studding the surface of the mucous membrane. Still later on the secretion distends them to such an extent that they re-open or burst, so as to let it exude. It has then become so altered from its natural state, being thickened and of a chalky whiteness, that it remains at the opening, whence it issues as a small white patch, or even projects or hangs down from it like the end of a white thread.

The symptoms of sensation which accompany these phenomena are a feeling of irritation or pricking, heat, and slight soreness in the throat. A short cough is sometimes present.

The effects on the voice are marked, and generally destructive as regards its artistic use. Hoarseness, more or less pronounced, is present, and singers especially complain of a loss of their high notes. This latter consequence arises from the thickening of the mucous membrane, which in the larynx prevents the vocal bands from being properly approximated and tensed, and in the pharynx interferes with the action of the extrinsic muscles, which draw up the

---

[1] Called "racemose" from their resemblance to a miniature cluster of grapes.

larynx and fix and compress the wings of the thyroid cartilage.

A less frequent consequence of abuse of the vocal powers is to provoke the growth of polypi, or warts, on or near the vocal bands. Such new formations are likely to be engendered by tissues which are irritated by being kept in a state of constant congestion. So with the larynx when the voice is frequently over-exerted. The existence of anything of the kind in the larynx is almost immediately felt by the singer, because so slight an alteration in the normal condition of the parts disturbs the formation of the high notes. But the speaker may often go on until the growth attains a considerable size without suffering much inconvenience. If not properly remedied, polypi of the larynx sometimes lead to complete loss of voice.[1]

Influences of Aerial Motion.

We have already seen how a violent effort of the expiratory muscles is transmitted by the body of air in the chest so as to provoke a tantamount action of those of the larynx. Thus, the one set of muscles

[1] Out of 300 cases of laryngeal polypi treated by Fauvel, twenty-one were singers, twenty-nine persons who used the voice professionally, and six appeared to have resulted from straining the voice on single occasions.—*Traité pratique des maladies du larynx*, Paris, 1876. Out of 289 cases tabulated by Mackenzie (100 of his own), thirty-seven were persons who had to make a constant use of the voice.—*Essay on Growths in the Larynx*, 1871.

strives to expel and the other to confine the current of breath.

A further phenomenon of such compression of air in the thoracic cavity has to be considered here, viz., its effect on the lungs themselves. In this connection we find another cause of loss of respiratory power. For the delicate air-cells of the lungs yield suddenly or gradually before the pressure and become dilated. The consequence is immediate laceration and subsequent obliteration of the complex arrangements of fine blood-vessels on their walls which necessarily exist in order to allow of the performance of the essential pulmonary functions. By such an occurrence a portion of the lung is irrecoverably lost as regards respiration, and if the injury is at all extensive a decided dyspnœa, or shortness of breath, results, which, of course, may be translated into an equivalent diminution of vocal power.

The *mode of inspiration* adopted or necessitated in speaking or singing, as already dwelt on in one connection, forms one of the most important hygienic relations of professional voice practice. It has still, however, to be dealt with under another aspect which draws our attention to the distinction between breathing through the nose or mouth. As a rule, we inspire through the nose, and there are cogent reasons why that method of breathing should be regarded as beneficial and protective.

In the first place, the atmosphere is almost always much colder than the blood, and for this reason, if it were allowed to impinge in a direct current on the lining membrane of the air-passages or lung-cells, such

P

a disturbance of function would be likely to ensue as would lead to inflammation of those parts. It is therefore indicated that the air, before arriving in the windpipe and lungs, should be warmed. This requirement is usually fulfilled by the nose. For as the breath is drawn through the several narrow nasal channels, into which each nostril subdivides, its temperature is considerably augmented, and by the time that it has passed down the whole length of the pharynx to the larynx it has arrived nearly at blood-heat.

In the next place, the atmosphere is full of impurities which ought to be eliminated from it before it passes into the interior of the body. As may be seen in a sunbeam, numberless particles of an infinite smallness are continually floating around us, and these being collected and examined by the microscope are found to consist of substances derived from every kingdom of nature. The fine dust of metals and of minerals is mingled with the pollen grains of the highest orders of plants, with the germs of the very simplest forms of vegetation, algæ and fungi, and even with the living bodies of minute animalcules.[1] The air is also contaminated by diverse gaseous emanations, such as the carbonic acid proceeding from animal respiration, putrid effluvia from

[1] See Parkes, *Manual of Practical Hygiene*, p. 93. The air is so crowded with active germs that if a vessel of the purest water be left exposed to it, it will soon swarm with countless growing atoms of animal and plant life; to such an extent, that formerly it was believed that the agency at work could be none other than spontaneous generation. See Tyndall, *On Dust and Disease*, in *Fragments of Science*, 1876, p. 126.

drains, marsh miasmata, etc., and by various subtile essences, incapable of being recognized by scientific tests, generated by diseased processes in the human body. The atmosphere forms, therefore, a rich reservoir whence injurious matters may find their way into the animal economy. In passing through the nose, however, the air becomes very much purified, because almost all dust is arrested in the narrow and tortuous *meatus*, especially so on account of the lining membrane (pituitary) being generally covered with a superabundance of fluid secretion in which the foreign particles may adhere and accumulate, and with which they may afterwards be expelled from the body.

Such facts indicate clearly that nasal inspiration exerts an important protective power, local and general, over the health. Hence we can understand the fervour with which Professor Tyndall exclaims that if he could leave a perpetual legacy to mankind he would embody it in the words, " KEEP YOUR MOUTH SHUT." But in addressing an audience it is difficult, and in singing probably impossible, to avoid inspiring habitually through the open mouth. Because, as before pointed out,[1] in the professional use of the voice, in order that inspiration may be prolonged as much as possible, the lungs must be inflated to a much greater extent than in ordinary breathing. And at each inspiration the replenishment of the chest must be effected by a rapid gush through the mouth, because the nostrils will only permit the passage of a small stream of air. Under these cir-

[1] See p. 162.

cumstances the inside of the throat, and perhaps the lungs, may suffer in three ways, *i.e.*, (1) from the coldness of the air, (2) from its drying influence as it rushes in a large body over the mucous membrane, which in this situation does not, like that of the nose, contain glands sufficiently active and numerous to keep the surface moist if fully exposed to a moving atmosphere, and (3) from lodgment of dust. By such pernicious influences the mucous membrane is irritated and may become congested, whilst the muscles beneath lose their vigour and become relaxed. Hence arises sore and relaxed throat, which interferes with the activity of the vocal organs and deteriorates the qualities of the voice; or troublesome dryness, causing stiffness of the throat, may be produced with equally damaging results as regards voice. And according to some observers[1] breathing through the mouth is a principal exciting cause of glandular sore throat. For the muciparous glands, before mentioned, suffer from the congestion of the mucous membrane in which they are situated, and also because they are stimulated to an abnormal excess of function in order to preserve the rapidly drying surface in a state of moisture. Thus they inflame, swell, become choked, and present all the phenomena described in the last section.

The foregoing observations make it plainly visible that every precaution should be taken in order to reduce to a minimum the evil of inspiring through the mouth. In speaking, the nostrils will usually furnish enough

---

[1] See Krishaber, *Dictionnaire encyclopédique des sciences médicales.* Paris, 1874, art. *Chanteurs.*

air, unless in occasional declamations where great
vehemence is demanded. That the orator will find
assiduous attention to breathing through the nose,
whenever practicable, a most effective agent for the
preservation of his voice, may be considered as proved
by experience on the testimony of numerous eminent
teachers of elocution.[1] We even find that in the
last century the knowledge of this hygienic fact,
then only recognized by experts, was believed to
be, of such value to the professional speaker, that
it was often sold for a large sum under a pledge
of secrecy.[2]

To the singer, nasal breathing is of equal moment, in
order to maintain the sanity of the throat and the
purity of the voice. The exigencies of vocal melody
however, scarcely allow of any exception to the rule
that inspiration must always be performed rapidly
through the mouth. Nevertheless, this disadvantage
of the singer, as contrasted with the orator, is counter-
balanced by the fact that, whereas a speech or lecture
may entail incessant use of the voice for a couple of
hours or more, a song rarely lasts more than a few
minutes, and even the most arduous *rôle* in an opera
is composed of detached songs, between which there
are usually ample intervals of rest. In such intervals, the mucous membrane of the throat has an
opportunity to return to its natural state, if it has
become in any degree irritable or dry during singing.
The vocalist should remember this fact, so that when
off the scene or platform, he may not engage too much

[1] See Plumptre, *King's College Lectures on Elocution*, 1876, p. 59;
also Cox, op. cit. p. 96.   [2] Plumptre, op. cit. p. 62.

in conversation, especially if he has any throat sensa-
tions which indicate irritation of the part. He should
also be on his guard against being led into the habit
of breathing constantly through the mouth, because
compelled to do so while singing his part. Inattention
to these matters has doubtless been the ruin of many
good singers, and it is only those gifted by nature with
excessive strength, constitutional and of the vocal
organs, who can sometimes afford to disregard them
and escape with impunity.[1] Such rare examples, however, should not be allowed to mislead others into
running unnecessary risk.

Singers should generally beware of singing in the
open air, especially in cold or damp weather. Singing
on the water in the evening has sometimes been followed
by disastrous consequences as regards the voice.[2]

Simple Voice Remedies with Local Action.

Almost all persons who use the voice professionally
resort to swallowing from time to time some local

---

[1] It is a well-observèd fact that the greatest singers rarely have
anything the matter with their voice, and it is equally well assured
that this is not always to be attributed to the judicious care which
they take of their health. They owe their pre-eminence chiefly to
great physical strength and soundness of the vocal organs, and to
the same cause may be ascribed this comparative immunity from
disease. The vocalists who suffer most are those of medium rank,
sometimes from carelessness and faulty voice-production, sometimes
from the natural tone of the vocal organs being unequal to the tax
put on them by professional singing.

[2] See Brouc, *Hygiène philosophique des artistes dramatiques*, Paris,
1836, t. i. p. 250.

application, with the view of keeping the throat cool and moist whilst speaking or singing. Such remedies usually partake more of a dietetic than of a medicinal nature, and vary according to the taste and fancy of the individual. It is only certain that the irritation of the throat, caused by its exercise and exposure, can be · relieved and the vocal powers assisted, by bringing some suitable substance in contact with the mucous membrane at proper intervals. Slight throat symptoms, arising from tiring the voice, are also frequently treated in a homely fashion by some popular medicaments or nostrums. A few remarks and recommendations are, therefore, called for here, respecting these classes of remedies.

At the head of the list stands the traditional glass of cold water of the speaker. Notwithstanding its simplicity, I am inclined to believe that sipping of cold water is one of the worst habits that could be contracted with the object of keeping the voice in good order. My reasons for arriving at this decision are two. In the first place, when the throat is dry the wetting power of water is very slight, because it will scarcely adhere to a parched mucous membrane. Secondly, if there is congestion of the throat, as betrayed by a feeling of heat, the effect of a douche of cold water is ultimately to increase that congestion, for the blood is only momentarily driven away, and returns in a few minutes, by reaction, in a larger quantity. The familiar example of the cold bath, which is generally the best of all possible means of making the skin glow, will illustrate this point. In the case of the throat, a temporary relief is of course experienced;

but reactive congestion quickly sets in, and the demand
for a draught of cold water is greater than ever.   For
these considerations, therefore, I think it advisable
that orators should discard the use of cold water
whilst speaking.

Better than plain cold water, is the *eau sucrée*, that is
such a favourite beverage with the French, or gum-water,
rice-water, whey, milk, or thin beef tea, as occasionally
used by some speakers.   Nor can we disapprove of the
tragacanth draughts [1] to which the ancient sophists had
recourse, because all these liquids have a consistency
and adhesive power, so that after they are drunk, the
lining membrane of the throat may be covered and
protected for some little time by a thin moist film.
But, under all circumstances, the coldness should be
got rid of, and whatever is drunk during speaking, or in
the intervals of singing, should have a temperature
near, but below that of the body, viz., 98° Fahr.,
or at least it should not be colder than 60° Fahr.
The proper degree of heat can best be determined
by sensation, and if the drink feels at all chilly whilst
passing down the throat, it may be decided to be too
cold.   At the same time it should not be too warm ; a
neutral temperature, so to speak, should be obtained.
In warm weather, of course, the drink will not require
to be warmed, but a special warning must be entered
against taking iced water, or anything iced, whilst

[1] See p. 30.   The compound tragacanth powder of the British
Pharmacopœia, containing equal parts of tragacanth, starch, and
sugar, may be used to make a lubricating drink for the throat.
About a teaspoonful may be added to a pint of water.   It should
first, however, be well mixed with a little water and then diluted.

the voice is being exercised. The amount of liquid taken should also be limited to a small quantity, so as to avoid any chance of over-charging the stomach. Much difference as to the amount of drink required exists in various persons; some, indeed, have naturally so much moisture in the throat as to want little or none at all. Beer or wines, as containing alcohol, call for consideration in another place.

Another class of remedies for lubricating the throat have more of a solid character. To this division may be relegated eggs beaten up, and all kinds of gelatinous or gummy fruits, and bon-bons. As a rule, such substances should be avoided as likely to clog the throat and stomach. They are particularly unsuited to persons whose mouth and fauces are naturally dry; but those who have a copious flow of saliva may sometimes use them with more advantage than liquids. In such cases, the act of masticating or sucking stimulates the salivary glands, so that the substance is completely dissolved and the throat is well moistened. To persons for whom remedies of this class are suitable, I should recommend lozenges or jujubes of pure glycerine or gum.[1]

---

[1] It may be interesting and not uninstructive to read the following information which the *Pall Mall Gazette* (1869, vol. ii. pp. 676, 714) reproduces from a Vienna paper as to the refreshments taken by some distinguished opera singers to "keep their voices in good order" during the performance. "Each, it appears, has his or her own peculiar specific. The Swedish tenor, Labatt, takes 'two salted cucumbers' for a dose, and declares that this vegetable is the best thing in the world for strengthening the voice and giving it 'the

So far, I have only spoken of adjuvants to the voice in health, while undergoing exertion. In many

true metallic ring.' The other singers, however, do not seem to be of this opinion. Sontheim takes a pinch of snuff and drinks cold lemonade ; Wachtel eats the yolk of an egg beaten up with sugar ; Steger, 'the most corpulent of tenors,' drinks 'the brown juice of the gambrinus' ; Walter, cold black coffee ; Nieman, champagne ; and Tichatchek, mulled claret. Ferenczy, the tenor, smokes one or two cigars, which his colleagues regard as so much poison. Mdlle. Braun-Brini takes after the first act a glass of beer, after the third and fourth a cup of *café au lait*, and before the great duet in the fourth act of 'The Huguenots,' always a bottle of Moët Crêmant Rosé. Nachbaur munches bon-bons during the performance ; Rübsam, the baritone, drinks mead ; Mitterwurzer and Kindermann suck dried plums ; Robinson, another baritone, drinks soda-water ; Formes takes porter, and Arabanek Gumpoldskirchner, wine ! The celebrated baritone Beck, on the other hand, takes nothing at all, and refuses to speak. Draxler smokes Turkish tobacco, and drinks a glass of beer. Another singer, Dr. Schmid, regulates his diet according to the state of his voice at the time. Sometimes he drinks coffee, sometimes tea, and a quarter of an hour afterwards, lemonade, mead, or champagne, taking snuff between whiles, and eating apples, plums, and dry bread." . . . . "Malibran never sang better than when she had drank at least a pot of porter out of the pewter pot—the more difficult the music the larger the quantity. Grisi drank always bottles of Dublin stout between the acts, and if she had to sing a stormy character the dose was strengthened. French singers prefer simply *eau sucrée ;* the Spaniards take strong cups of chocolate, followed by glasses of water sugared and lemoned. The Italians like eggs beaten up simply, or with wine." As a rule, operatic singers are described as very temperate, " they dine early on the day they sing, they take as little as possible, and they receive very few visitors before they have to sing." Mandl (*Hygiène de la voix*, p. 66), from another paper, culls the further information that "Mdme. Sontag takes, in the *entr'actes*, sardines ; Mdme. Desparre, warm water ; Mdme. Cruvelli, Bordeaux mixed with champagne ; Mdme. Ad. Patti, seltzer-water ; Mdme. Nilson, beer ; Mdme. Cabel, pears ; Mdme. Ugalde, prunes ; Mdme. Trebelli, strawberries ; Troy, milk ; Mario smokes ; Mdme. Borghi-Mamo takes snuff ; and Mdme. Dorus-Gras used to eat cold meat behind the scenes."

instances, however, when slight hoarseness or weakness of the vocal organs is present, the sufferers have recourse to remedies with more or less decided medicinal properties. The various voice or cough lozenges that are sold belong to this class. Of these there are about four kinds, viz., those that contain (1) cayenne, (2) cubebs, (3) some expectorant, and (4) opium or morphia. Their applicability may be discussed separately.

1. The effect of cayenne on the throat is to stimulate or irritate the mucous membrane, by which more blood is sent to the part, *i.e.*, some congestion is produced. Such action would be highly injurious if some disorder of voice were present which actually arose from congestion. On the other hand, should there be a weakness of the voice dependent on an anæmic or bloodless state of the throat, cayenne might be a very serviceable application. As, however, it is too much to expect an unskilled observer in disease to distinguish between the two conditions, especially in his own person, I can only advise that lozenges containing cayenne be discarded as a popular voice remedy.

2. Cubebs is often valuable where there is a great deal of expectoration. If the throat be at all dry, it is most likely to do harm. Lozenges manufactured with cubebs may generally be recognized by a biting, bitter taste. It is a weak kind of pepper in fact.

3. Cough lozenges are generally composed of harmless ingredients, unless they contain (4) opium or its active principle, morphia. Opium, in any form, should never be taken without medical advice. It usually has a parching effect on the throat, and throws the diges-

tive system into disorder. In most instances, it is, therefore, likely to exert a deleterious influence over the vocal powers.

From the foregoing observations it may be inferred that popular medicinal remedies should be generally eschewed; not that they are an unalloyed evil in the abstract, but because any drug indiscriminately applied will probably injure as many cases as it benefits.

GENERAL HYGIENE IN ITS RELATIONS TO THE VOICE.

Under this heading we may discuss, in the first place, how far the health of the body may be affected by the systematic exercise of the voice; and secondly, to what extent the voice may derive benefit or suffer from the general habits and surroundings of the individual.

Effects of Regular Vocal Exercise on the Animal Economy.

It has already been observed[1] that the ancient physicians believed from experience, that a vigorous course of declamation was one of the most salutary and health-preserving exercises that could be practised, and that they therefore prescribed it systematically as an important curative agent in many debilitating

[1] See p. 22.

diseases. Although modern practitioners have not exactly followed their example, the principle that increased respiratory movements are highly beneficial in the treatment of invalids from pulmonary maladies is fully recognized. Some efforts have also been made, and are still in course of maturation, to inflate the lungs in certain affections beyond their ordinary capacity, by means of artificial instruments, such as the compressed-air apparatus of Waldenburg,[1] and promising results have already been obtained.

There is, indeed, considerable statistical evidence to prove that the professional use of the voice exercises an important prophylactic influence against the development of consumption, and several investigators have shown that a remarkably small relative percentage of singers, orators, public criers, etc., fall a victim to that disease.[2]

---

[1] See Josephson, *Ueber Waldenburg's Vergleichung der pneumatischen Cabinette.* Hamburg, 1875.

[2] *E.g.*, according to Benoiston de Châteauneuf, out of 1,554 fatal cases of phthisis occurring in the Paris hospitals in the course of ten years, not one was a professional speaker or singer. Most of the cases were persons who were compelled by their occupation to inhale dust constantly, and those who followed sedentary employment with the body in a curved position, such as writers, shoemakers, tailors, etc.—*De l'influence de certaines professions sur le développement de la phthisie pulmonaire*, Paris, 1831, pp. 37, 45. After a still more extended statistical inquiry, Lombard, of Geneva, obtained results almost equally favourable as regards constant vocal exercise. Thus he found that the mean number of cases of illness due to phthisis occurring in sick persons of general occupations was 114 per 1,000; amongst voice-using professions it was, however, only 75 per 1,000, whilst in workpeople who had to inhale varnishes, turpentine, etc., it rose to 369 per 1,000.—*Annales d'hygiène publique*, Paris, 1834, t. xi. p. 35.

The general well-being of the constitution is promoted by voice-practice, because the wider chest-movements accelerate the circulation of the blood, at the same time that they cause a more ample flow of fresh air into the lungs. The obstacle to expiration offered by the contraction of the glottis during phonation, confers a greater penetrating power on the pulmonary air, which therefore permeates the minute bronchi, and distends the air-vesicles of the lungs more effectively.[1] Thus the blood attains a higher oxygenation and greater purity, by which qualities it gains in power of stimulating the vital activities of the various tissues of the body as it courses through them. Effete matters are freely cast off, and new wholesome material is assimilated in increased amount. The appetite, so to speak, of the various corporeal structures becomes more keen, and they are thus subjected to an exalted nutrition. And, moreover, these effects have a certain permanency on account of the gains to the thoracic

[1] Such is the principle which some physicians, postulating that consumption was chiefly caused by incomplete respiration, have sought to apply to its cure by directing the patient to practise breathing for a certain period daily through a tube constructed so as to present an obstacle to expiration.—See Ramadge, *The Curability of Consumption*, 1861, p. 54. This penetrating power is also possessed by compressed air. Cuvier, according to Combe (*Physiology applied to Health*, pp. 121, 206), believed that he was saved from incipient consumption by receiving a professorship which obliged him to lecture for some hours daily. Playing on wind instruments appears to have a beneficial effect on the lungs in the same way. Sax, the celebrated maker of brass musical instruments (quoted by Mandl, op. nuper cit., p. 241), states that the men in his employ, whose business it is to test the tone of all the instruments produced, enjoy a complete immunity from phthisis.

capacity derived from the habitual increase of lung expansion necessitated by constant vocal exercise.[1]

The mode in which the voice is used alters, of course, considerably the sanitary aspects of the exercise, and a proper method of voice-production, according to the indications already given, must be pursued. A division of another kind may also, however, be regarded here, and the four degrees of voice-practice, viz., conversing, reading aloud, declaiming, and singing, may be alluded to in relation to their gymnastic efficiency. Thus, in ordinary conversation, the vital activities are stimulated least of all; in reading aloud, fatigue is apt to supervene rapidly, because the posture, especially if the person be seated, is somewhat constrained, and freedom of action is limited by the attention being concentrated on the text; in declamation and singing, on the other hand, there is ample scope for respiratory play and appropriate gesture or carriage of the body.

---

[1] Almost innumerable sanitary advantages have been claimed by various writers for the exercise of singing. Thus Colombat de l'Isère states that it has a great protective influence against epidemic diseases, such as cholera, etc.—*Traité médico-chirurgicale des maladies des organs de la voix*, Paris, 1836, p. 96. Diemerbroek also thinks that the plague may be warded off by song and music.—*Tractatus de Peste*, Amstelodami, 1665, p. 150. Pigray holds a similar opinion.—*Épitome des precrptes de médecine*, Rouen, 1615, p. 532. The conception of these authors is mainly that joy is a potent prophylactic against all disease, and that such a state of mind is best promoted by song. In this connection see further, Broquin, *Considerations sur l'utilité que la médecine peut retirer du chant*, Montpellier, 1807; Colombat de l'Isère, *De la musique dans ses rapports avec la santé publique*, Paris, 1871; and Burette's essay on the medicinal powers attributed to music by the ancients, epitomized in Burney, *History of Music*, vol. i. p. 173.

The ill effects of exaggerated vocal labour on the health are, generally, those of any kind of over-work, *i.e.*, lassitude, depression, loss of appetite, and sluggish performance of the various vital functions. Specially, they are the result of any particular accident that may occur, such as emphysema, by which a portion of the lung is lost to respiration, and a permanent diminution of thoracic capacity. with consequent impairment of the constitution, results. Or a vein in the lungs may be ruptured, and loss of blood occasion a long illness, with subsequent obstinate debility. Or an overflow of blood to the head, inducing congestion of the brain, apoplexy, etc., may arise from a violent vocal, as from any other inordinate effort.[1] Lastly, the forcible compression of the abdominal organs may cause some of the viscera of that cavity to protrude beyond the limits assigned to them by nature, forming the condition known as *hernia.*[2]

[1] Antigonus Doson, King of Macedonia (Plutarch, *in Vita Cleomenis*), and Valentinian I., Roman Emperor (Suidas, sub Λεἰας), are reported to have died in giving vent to an excited exclamation. In the former case a blood-vessel burst, and blood issued from the mouth; and in the latter some kind of a fit supervened. Seneca seems to allude to accidents of this class as if they were of frequent occurrence.—*De Brevitate Vitæ*, c. 2. See also Brouc, op. cit. t. i. p. 225. Blowing a violent blast on a wind-instrument has also caused sudden death in a similar manner. For instances, see Lucian, *Harmonides*, and Ramazzini, *De Morbis Artificum*, Ultrajecti, 1703, c. xl.

[2] Several authors observe that speakers and singers are remarkably liable to suffer from herniæ. Thus, Fallopius states that "there are few of those brothers who shout and sing much, but suffer from hernia."—*De Tumoribus præter Naturam*, c. xxxi. See also Salmuth, *De Morbis Concionatorum*, Ienæ, 1699, p. 13; and Becquerel, *Traité élémentaire d'hygiène privée et publique*, Paris, 1876, pp. 736, 725.

Influences of Mode of Life on the Voice.

Man, in order to live and preserve health, must conform to certain natural laws, which impel him to take food, to sleep, to take exercise, etc. He is also subjected to various external influences derived from diverse conditions of earth and air, which affect him potently with respect to his health. Such esoteric and exoteric forces do not, however, hold him in fast servitude, but, whilst allowing him a considerable freedom of choice, merely instigate him gently towards the course he should select. He is called on, therefore, constantly to exert his judgment, and he enjoys extensive powers of avoiding evil, and of taking refuge in good. To such contingencies hygiene owes its existence, and it may thus be defined as the science which teaches the recognition and practice of what is best for health. Amidst the many ramifications of this wide subject we may notice here, with brevity, the bearing of the principal factors that make up life on the function under examination.

I. *Alimentation.*—Every action of the animal body, whether mental or muscular, is accomplished at the expense, and accompanied by the destruction, of a portion of the fabric of which it is composed. That which is destroyed is at once carried away and cast

Q

off from the body, and in its place fresh material supplied by the blood is laid down.[1] Hence the desire for aliment, which is received into the stomach and, if solid, is there digested until brought to such a state of fluidity that the suitable part of it may be conveyed into the blood, as the whole mass passes through the long tract of intestine. Thus the stomach and intestines feed the blood, and the blood feeds the tissues. The material primarily introduced into the stomach may be of two kinds, viz., food and drink, which may be considered separately.

1. *Food.*—About two-thirds of the body of man

[1] The wear of the tissues is in proportion to the amount of exercise taken, and also, of course, the quantity of food required for repair. The following table has been calculated by Playfair (*On the Food of Man in Relation to his Useful Work*, 1865, p. 19) of the daily quantity of the different classes of food required by the male adult under varying circumstances (in ounces avoirdupois).

CLASSES OF FOOD.	Subsistence diet—i.e., sufficient for the mechemical force necessary to carry on the internal work of the body.	Diet in quietude.	Adults in full health, but with easy work.	Adults in active work.	Adults in laborious work.
Nitrogenous substances	2·	2·5	4·2	5·5	6·5
Fat	0·5	1·	1·4	2·5	2·5
Starch	12·	12·	18·7	20·	20·
Salts	..	..	·71	·9	..
Carbon (total)	6·7	7·4	11·9	13·7	14·3

is composed of water, and the remaining one-third consists of substances supplied by the solids of the food naturally taken by him. These latter may be conveniently distributed into four classes, *i.e.*, into (1) nitrogenous substances, richest in flesh or meat, (2) fatty or oleaginous matters, (3) starchy or saccharine (sugar) compounds, and (4) mineral matters, or salts. A supply of all these different kinds of food is necessary to maintain the body in health, and they are, therefore, found in proper proportion in the natural provision of milk. Thus, cheese is a nitrogenous substance, butter a fatty matter, lactose, or sugar of milk, represents the starchy or saccharine class, and there are also abundant salts, the whole being dissolved in water.

Although meat or animal food is richest in nitrogen, there exists an abundant quantity of that element in many vegetables, such as wheat, beans, peas, etc. It is consequently practicable to live in health without eating any meat, and on this account some persons advocate a purely vegetable diet. As far as the comparative nutritiveness of meat and vegetables is concerned, there appears to be little distinction, if we may judge by contrasting carnivorous animals with those who are entirely herbivorous. Thus the lion and tiger, though fiercer, more combative, and more agile, because of the actions they have to perform in order to supply themselves with food, are not in reality stronger or more enduring than the more docile horse, ox, or elephant. The inference to be drawn from such observations is that each animal should have the kind of food to which its mode of life has accustomed it, because its digestive organs obtain by habit facilities for disposing of certain substances, whilst their healthy action is likely to be disturbed by strange sorts of aliment.

European races have mostly used a mixed diet of flesh and vegetables for as long as there are any records to prove the fact, and it seems, therefore, inadvisable to attempt any change in this respect. Another point, however, which deserves consideration, is that a mixed diet is more economical, because it affords most nearly a due proportion of the various classes of solid aliment mentioned above. Thus, in order to obtain a proper amount of each of these, a man, if restricted to meat, would have to eat about seven pounds daily. On the other hand, he could subsist on a less quantity of bread, viz., about four pounds in the twenty-four hours. But when taking both combined a much smaller aggregate weight would suffice, namely, about one pound of meat and a pound and a half of bread.[1] Hence the duty of the stomach would be lightened, and the abdominal viscera would not be loaded

[1] The statements in the text are deduced from the calculation that a man of average build should consume about 300 grains nitrogen and 5,000 grains carbon (contained in the second and third kinds of food elements) daily. Meat is comparatively rich in nitrogen and poor in carbon, the proportions being about as 30 parts of nitrogen to 100 parts of carbon in 1,000 grains. In bread, *vice versâ*, there is little nitrogen and plenty of carbon, the relations being as 10 to 300 in 1,000 grains. In both cases the quantity of nitrogen is small contrasted with the whole bulk, or even with the carbon, but nevertheless considerable from a dietetic point of view.

with a large quantity of refuse matters. If, however, eggs and milk be added to a diet otherwise of vegetable products, meat may be almost superseded as far as bulk is concerned.

An important question in dietetics relates to the digestibility of the various substances used as food. Some kinds of food only require to be acted on for an hour or two before they are brought to a state to yield up their nutrition to the blood, whilst others remain as long as four or five hours in the stomach, or pass out of the body unchanged, being indigestible. Tender meat, well masticated, is soon digested, whereas tough meat, swallowed without being well divided by the teeth, remains several hours in the stomach. The digestibility of meat also varies according to the manner of cooking. When boiled or stewed it is, as a rule, more easily digested than when roasted or baked. According to their aptness for digestion, some of the ordinary articles of diet may be conveniently arranged into three classes, as follows :—

1. *Substances easily Digested.*—From various experiments that have been made it has been ascertained that rice, tripe, whipped eggs, brains, sago, tapioca, barley, broiled liver, boiled milk, raw eggs, salmon trout, white fish, venison, turkey, goose, lamb, beans, parsnips, mashed and baked potatoes, cabbage, raw apples, and fricassed chicken, in the order given, are the most easily digested substances. Thus rice disappears from the stomach in one hour, and fricassed chicken in about two hours and three quarters.

2. *Substances not so readily Digestible.*—Beef, stewed pork, mutton, oysters, carrots, sausages, butter, bread, cheese, veal, boiled potatoes, eggs (fried and hard boiled), and boiled and roasted fowls are less easily digested. Beef passes out of the stomach in three, and roast fowl in four hours.

3. *Substances difficult of Digestion, or Indigestible.*— Fried veal, roast wild duck, boiled, fried, and roast pork, salt beef and salt pork require more than four hours to be digested, whilst fungi, such as truffles and mushrooms, are in great part indigestible.[1]

Nutritious soups, such as beef tea, mutton broth, chicken broth, etc., are often valuable when the digestive system is delicate.[2]

As regards the precautions in alimentation, to be observed with a view to preserving the integrity of the voice, it is obvious, in the first place, that a choice should be made of those articles of diet which do not tax excessively the powers of the stomach to get rid of them. Should the stomach be habitually subjected to digestive over-exertion, it will soon become inefficient in the performance of its functions, and the condition termed dyspepsia, or imperfect digestion, will be brought on. In such case, the direct consequence is that the blood does not receive a proper amount of nutrition, and the body is badly nourished. Loss of

[1] Most of this information was obtained by the observations of Beaumont on Alexis St. Martin, who had a permanent and direct opening into his stomach as the result of an injury. The statements, however, cannot be regarded as conclusive, but only as approximate. See Combe, *The Physiology of Digestion*, 1860, p. 123.

[2] Some doubt exists as to the facility with which soups are digested. Ibid. p. 126.

flesh ensues, the muscles diminish in tone and vigour, and the strength is impaired. Amongst the rest, the muscles of the vocal organs suffer, and lose the faculty of firm and ready contractibility. The respiratory apparatus cannot expel the air with steadiness and force, and the laryngeal muscles act defectively. Hence the voice becomes wanting in tone and timbre, and sounds weak and wavering. More or less enervation is also produced, and therefore the manner lacks energy. Thus the individual appears apathetic, whilst his speech is irresolute and his delivery shows indecision.

Such are the evils, variable in degree according to circumstances, of dyspepsia, which may arise in several other ways, such as irregularity of meal times, taking cold, excesses of all kinds, etc.

Another point to be observed, is to avoid exerting the voice when the stomach is full. When the process of digestion has reached its height, about an hour after eating a substantial meal, the stomach is not only distended with food, but is also swollen through the determination to it of a large quantity of blood. This state of congestion is necessary, in order to enable it to pour out the gastric juice, which is an indispensable agent in bringing the food to a proper fluidity. At this time, therefore, the proximity of the firm and bulky stomach to the under-surface of the diaphragm, greatly impedes the contractions of that muscle, and thus reduces the abdominal type of respiration within narrow limits. A further effect of the distended stomach is to compress the aorta or main trunk of the blood vessels, which are distributed to the lower

Such *condiments* as contain irritating principles, *i.e.*, pepper, mustard, curry, the many hot sauces, etc., are open to the same objections as have already been urged against cayenne in "voice lozenges." They are likely to produce congestion, which may ultimately lead to thickening of the lining membrane of the throat, and thus damage temporarily or permanently the purity of the voice. Pale and delicate persons, however, often find that they afford a valuable stimulus to digestion, and in such instances, as the opposite condition to congestion mostly prevails, they may often be taken without harm, or even with some benefit to the vocal powers.

A few remarks may here be made as to the effects of *tobacco*. The action of this herb on the animal fabric is constitutional and local. Thus nicotine, the name given to its active principle, exerts a powerful depressant influence over the nervous system, being, in fact, a virulent poison, a very small quantity of which, when pure, would suffice to cause death by prostration. Persons, therefore, who indulge to excess in smoking are likely to become nervous, so that their hand trembles, and the command of the brain over the muscles generally is lessened, whilst there is a tendency to palpitation of the heart and oppressed breathing. As a natural consequence, there is a failure to some extent of the vocal powers, and a hesitation in delivery, the results, on the one hand, of the lack of respiratory

brandy, without sugar), or a glass or two of claret or sherry." For a fuller discussion of the dieting of corpulence, see Pavy, *Food and Dietetics*, 1875, p. 459.

vigour, and, on the other, of enervation. Habit, however, usually produces such a tolerance of tobacco, that the constitutional effects of moderate smoking are most frequently imperceptible, unless in delicate individuals.

As regards the local injury that may be sustained from tobacco, it consists in dryness and congestion of the mucous membrane of the mouth and pharynx from their coming in contact with the hot and often acrid smoke. Should the membrane be naturally very active in furnishing the necessary lubricating secretions, it will probably escape unscathed, unless subjected to an incessant play of smoke from full-flavoured cigars. But in the opposite case it is likely to become soon parched, whence some hoarseness and roughness of voice may arise. In taking snuff the voice may suffer similarly if the particles of tobacco pass backward from the nostrils, and become lodged continually on the pharyngeal mucous membrane.

A further disadvantage of smoking is waste of saliva, of which the fumes of tobacco provoke in some persons a profuse flow into the mouth. Under these circumstances the salivary glands become exhausted from time to time, and do not supply the proper amount of fluid during mastication of food. Hence some disorder of digestion may arise with a chronic dyspeptic tendency, which may tell indirectly on the voice in the way already noticed. Persons, therefore, who are obliged to expectorate much during smoking should be on their guard against the abuse of the habit.[1]

[1] For detailed information respecting the use and abuse of tobacco, see Richardson, *For and Against Tobacco*, 1865.

2. *Drink.*—Tea, coffee, and cocoa or chocolate contain active principles, termed respectively thein, caffein, and theobromin, which have identical properties as dietetic substances. In small quantities they stimulate the nerves, and are refreshing after fatigue; but if taken to excess they often produce nervousness and tremor. Over indulgence in strong tea is a frequent cause of palpitation of the heart and oppressed breathing. Those who make a professional use of the voice should remember, therefore, that moderation, even in these apparently harmless beverages, is required in order to preserve the integrity of the vocal organs.

We now come to the all-important class of *alcoholic drinks*, the evil effects of the abuse of which are so familiar to almost every one, that they call for very little comment, except from the point of view of scientific inquiry. Taken in moderation by a healthy person, spirituous liquors may be considered as a kind of agreeable stimulus of the nature of a luxury, which, if seldom beneficial, is still not absolutely harmful. It is difficult, however, to determine the precise amount that may be consumed habitually without injury, especially as it doubtless varies according to the fundamental constitutional strength of each individual. From some careful scientific observations Parkes[1] has concluded that the average male adult may take from one to one-and-a-half fluid ounces of pure alcohol daily without any resultant injury to health. In order to apply this calculation

[1] Op. cit. p. 277.

practically, it is necessary to estimate the percentage of alcohol contained in the different classes of liquors commonly used. Thus, beer and the weaker wines (clarets) contain about 6 per cent., the stronger wines (port, sherry, etc.) about 15 per cent., and spirituous liquors (brandy, whisky, etc.) 50 or 60 per cent., or even more, of alcohol. Hence we may decide that a man desiring strictly to avoid excess may drink in the twenty-four hours—

Of brandy ...   .   2½ ounces.[1]
Of sherry or port (strong wines) 5   „
Of claret or hock (weak wines) 10   „
Of beer   20   „

For females the above amounts should be reduced to half or two-thirds, on account of the lessened power of resistance of their physical economy. In addition to alcohol, wines and beer contain a small quantity of certain nutritive and tonic principles, which have an invigorating effect on the constitution. For general consumption or for invalids they possess, therefore, an important advantage over the various kinds of spirits.

Considered specially with reference to the voice, too much stress cannot be laid on the warning against making too free a use of alcoholic drinks. "The voice," as Brouc[2] judiciously observes, "is the hygrometer of sobriety." Alcohol exerts a degenerative influence over every organ and tissue of the

[1] An ordinary wine glass holds about 2½ ounces, a beer glass about 10 ounces.
[2] Op. cit. t. ii. p. 109.

body,[1] and nowhere more markedly than on the mucous lining of the cavities. Here it produces constant congestion, which soon leads to thickening of the membrane. In the throat such a condition is betrayed sooner than elsewhere, because so slight a physical alteration is sufficient to induce a perceptible modification in the delicate tones of the voice. Thus hoarseness, at first slight, but always steadily progressive, is one of the earliest symptoms that over-indulgence in alcoholic beverages has commenced to undermine the constitution. And when once unsoundness has been induced in any of the organs of the body, they lack the vigorous vitality necessary to protect them against the exciting causes of disease, or to promote a facile recovery, should they be actually attacked. Thus a mild malady, of properly ephemeral character, may gain a firm footing and deepen into a serious affection, through the insufficient potency of the recuperative forces of the body. A slight sore throat, instead of getting well in a day or two, is likely to be the precursor of inflammatory or ulcerative ravages that may permanently injure the voice, or an ordinary cough, which seldom calls for other than domestic treatment, may be the premonitory sign of an intense lung mischief, prostrating in its attack, protracted in its course towards convalescence, and the parent of shattered health ever afterwards.

It is especially important to observe that the ill effects of intemperance are not necessarily confined to those cases in which there is frequent and positive

[1] For some striking exemplifications of this fact, see Dickinson, *The Lancet*, 1872, vol. ii. pp. 633, 855.

excess. Oft repeated, though small, draughts of alcohol are in proportion as pernicious as large quantities taken at longer intervals, whilst in the former case, as the psychical influence of the spirit may be scarcely, if at all, felt, the individual may be wholly unconscious of running any risk. Hence the practice of drinking many separate glasses of beer, stout, or wine, as a support against fatigue and a stimulant to further exertion, must be strongly con-demned. Such a habit once contracted soon becomes a necessity, because every period of briskness arising from artificial stimulation is followed by a correspond-ing interval of depression, which can only be banished by resorting again to the alcoholic spring. Thus a state of decided, but almost imperceptible, inebriation is perpetually kept up, which, like an insidious disease, incessantly preys upon the life-holds of the body, and presses on a premature decay and death.[1]

II. *Exercise.*—Whilst the greater portion of the substance of our body, the muscular system, exists ·for the direct purpose of conferring the power of volun-tary motion, it is evident that exercise must form an

---

[1] The fact that Grisi and Malibran had recourse to draughts of stout whilst sustaining their part has often, I have no doubt, been regarded by other singers as a precedent for doing likewise. The first-named *artiste* by keeping to a strict moderation appears to have escaped without harm, but the circumstance should be recorded with emphasis that the career of Malibran was unusually short, and that she died at the early age of twenty-eight. See Fétis, op. cit. s. n. The presumption is too immediate to be passed over that her consti-tution succumbed to inconsiderate efforts to maintain an artificial excitement.

integral and irremovable part of the phenomena that make up our life. For, in accordance with a well-ascertained law, no organs of the animal body can possess qualities which are absolutely purposeless, but they must perform the functions for which, by their structure, they are designed, or else lose their distinctive characters, or dwindle to a rudimentary state. Thus our muscles, through disuse, become at first soft and flaccid, and subsequently diminish progressively in bulk, until partially or completely atrophied. Concomitantly, most of the other organs of the body, including the brain and nerves, undergo, by a parallel process, a similar change, because their activity is, in great part, the result, on the one side, of the demand of the working and thriving muscular system for a regular supply of nutrition and nervous energy, and, on the other, of the office of removing effete matters generated by exertion. Hence a sedentary life induces feebleness of body and may also give rise to apathy of mind.

A moderate amount of exercise is, therefore, a vital necessity. To the beneficial effects of systematically sustained muscular movements already some reference has more than once been made. We have seen the value of vocal exercise directly on the organs of voice and generally on the constitution. Exercise should not, however, be confined to any particular part, if it is desired to preserve a full integrity of wind and limb. Free action of all the members should be encouraged, and in no way can this object be better attained than by walking daily in the open air. The motions called forth in walking are sufficiently forcible and general, without requiring anything like effort—an error on the side of excess—for their performance. A daily walk of at least four or five miles should be taken by every person in health. This would be about equivalent to walking for two hours, not necessarily consecutive, at a rather slow pace. And the fact must not be lost sight of that a supply of air as fresh and pure as can be obtained, is essential during exercise, in order that the full advantage may be gained. For thus the blood, stimulated by the exercise to a swifter course through its vessels, attains its highest qualities, and is enabled to nourish the tissues most energetically.

With reference to special exercises, such as running, rowing, swimming, and the system of operations that make up "training," they are useful within carefully defined limits, both to develop the vital forces of those that are naturally delicate, and to maintain the muscular activity of the more robust, at the same time that they counteract the tendency to corpulence.

A well-regulated course of training, which includes a carefully-ordered diet, generally effects an increase of breathing power, with a strengthening of the circulatory system, an enlargement of the muscles, and altogether a state of more vigorous health.[1] If carried to excess, however, such a course may be injurious, and it is moreover uncertain whether in any case the advantages derived are permanent. For if the exercise is not kept up, the body soon readapts itself to the ordinary

[1] See Maclaren, *Training in Theory and Practice*, 1874; or Lee, *Exercise and Training*, 1873.

R

mode of life, and returns to its former condition. The best rule to be adopted, is that each person should take as much exercise as appears best suited to his normal physical development. Thus the delicate may restrict themselves to exertion, gentle, but sufficiently prolonged, such as walking, whilst the vigorous should have recourse to more decided muscular efforts, such as feats of a gymnastic character.[1]

It is worth while to notice here a peculiar bearing of general bodily motion on the artistic use of the voice. This relates to the familiar circumstance of being out of breath after making any unusual exertion, a condition which is the direct consequence of the quickened flow of blood through the lungs, and the increased respiratory action thereby occasioned. At such

[1] In order to estimate and compare different amounts of exercise for scientific purposes it has been found convenient to consider the force put forth in the aggregate and to express it in so many tons lifted one foot. Thus it has been estimated that walking on a level surface is equivalent to raising about one-twentieth of the weight of the body through the distance traversed. Hence a man weighing 150 lbs. would raise 7½ lbs. to a height of 1760 yards whilst walking a mile, the sum of which force is equal to what would be required to lift 17·67 tons one foot high. From instituting a comparison between walking and the work done by labouring men, both being reduced to the standard of foot-tons, to walk twenty miles, 353·4 tons lifted a foot, is judged to be a good day's work; to walk thirty miles, 530·1 tons raised a foot, a hard day's work. Hence we may see that a five-mile walk daily, 88·35 tons lifted a foot, must come under the head of gentle exercise. Yet comparatively few professional people take this amount of exercise every day. In estimating exercise an allowance must be made for the rapidity with which the work is done. Thus to run a mile briskly would probably be equal to covering three or four miles at an easy pace. As a rule, however, the moderate but sustained exercise appears to be most beneficial. On the estimation of work by foot-tons, see Haughton, *Principles of Animal Mechanics*, 1873, p. 54.

a time singing, or speaking with the measured delivery of rhetoric, would, of course, be impossible. On this account, care should be taken to avoid all superfluous movement whilst it is necessary to make a sustained use of the voice; for, otherwise, fatigue of the vocal organs is likely to arrive rapidly through interference of hurried breathing with phonation. This remark applies particularly to the orator, as, during histrionic singing or dramatic declamation, there are always intervals of rest sufficiently long and frequent. The speaker should, therefore, as Becquerel[1] observes, avoid energetic contractions of the muscles of the lower limbs and trunk, and make free use only of the arms and shoulders, in order to confer the requisite animation and expression on his utterances.

III. *Care of the Skin.*—The skin does not form merely a covering for the body, but it also has important functions to perform, which afford an indispensable aid in maintaining the health of the organization. For this purpose it contains in its thickness an almost countless number of minute glands, each of which opens by a microscopic orifice on its surface for the purpose of discharging their proper secretion.[2] These glands are of

---

[1] Op. cit. p. 734.

[2] Each gland consists of a fine convoluted tube about $\frac{1}{4}$ inch long, and the average number of pores marking their openings in a square inch of skin is computed at 2,800. The area of the surface of the body in a man of ordinary stature is about 2,500 square inches, and hence the total number of pores may be reckoned at 7,000,000. As to each pore corresponds a gland, we should thus have 1,750,000 inches of tubing, equal to 145,833 feet, or 48,611 yards, or nearly twenty-eight miles. See Wilson, *Healthy Skin*, 1876, p. 43.

two kinds, termed respectively *sudoriparous*, or perspiratory, and *sebaceous*, or oil-elaborating. The perspiratory glands purify the blood by removing from it effete matters, which they discharge, dissolved in water, on the surface of the skin. The water evaporates at a rapidity proportionate to the degree of heat of the external air, and thus regulates the temperature of the body, keeping it cool in warm weather or during exercise, when it exudes in greatest quantity. The solid portion of the perspiration, consisting of organic and mineral matters, remains and collects on the skin, and if not removed by some means, interferes with the continuance of its action.[1] The sebaceous glands lubricate the skin, so as to prevent its becoming dry and cracked, and on this account they are especially numerous in natives of tropical climates. A further function of the skin, of the highest moment, is the oxygenation of, and removal of carbonic acid from the blood, as it circulates through the capillary vessels near the exterior of the body.

Thus, it may be seen that the office of the skin is, to a great extent, similar to that of the lungs, and, therefore, there exists a *cutaneous* as well as a *pulmonary* respiration. And should the eliminative action of the skin be interrupted, it follows that the lungs would be called on to perform an increased amount of duty, which would be likely to provoke hurried and difficult breathing. At the same time, the accumulation of

---

[1] According to Krause the usual amount of perspiration in twenty-four hours is 25 fluid ounces, in which are contained 120 grains of organic matter and volatile salts, and nearly 40 grains of mineral salts.—Ibid. p. 50.

the solid effete matters in the blood would necessitate an inordinate activity of other internal organs, especially the kidneys, and a general constitutional disturbance would arise. Should the function of the skin be completely suspended, as would occur if it were coated with some impermeable substance, such as varnish, death would supervene in a few hours, with symptoms resembling those of suffocation ; a fact which has been ascertained by some experiments that have been made on animals.[1]

From the above observations it is easy to perceive the general importance of keeping the skin in a healthy state, as well as the direct influence that its derangement may exert over the soundness of the vocal powers. Attention to the health of the skin comprises the judicious employment of *clothing, ablutions,* and *cosmetics.*

1. *Clothing.*—The variable temperature of the atmosphere, arising from circumstances of climate, season, and habitation, necessitates the use of apparel, in order to obtain an equilibrium of the external influences which tend at one time to overheat, and at another to chill injuriously the surface of the body. In order to carry out this indication most economically, regard must be paid to the quantity, the quality, and the colour of the clothing employed. Thus the

[1] See a *résumé* of them in Flint, *The Physiology of Man,* vol. iii. p. 131, New York, 1874. In some reptiles, such as frogs, the function of the skin is so active that the lungs may be removed without causing death. See Carpenter, *Principles of Human Physiology,* 1876, p. 406.

heat of the body is better preserved in proportion to the thickness of the garments worn; but their power in this way also depends very much on the material of which they are made. The principal substances used in the manufacture of clothes are linen, silk, cotton, and wool.

Linen is composed of fine, hard fibres, which conduct heat with comparative rapidity. Clothes made of linen are, therefore, cool, and suitable for warm weather.

Silken fabrics are also cool, but still form a warmer covering than linen.

Cotton materials are much warmer, and softer to the touch, than either linen or silk.

Wool conducts heat most slowly of all the substances which enter into the composition of clothing, and, as a covering to the skin, thus causes, to a maximum degree, the retention of the animal heat evolved by the vital activities. Woollen garments are, therefore, the most suitable for cold climates. They are also especially valuable and protective against taking cold when persons are obliged to experience sudden transitions of temperature, either through dwelling in changeable climates, such as our own, or by reason of their occupation compelling them to emerge frequently from heated rooms or halls into a comparatively colder external air. Under these circumstances, flannel should be worn habitually as underclothing. This rule applies very forcibly to dramatic artists, who are often obliged to wear light or heavy clothing on the stage, irrespective of the actual exigencies of temperature. A further important property of wool is to condense and absorb perspiration. For this reason it is valuable as a covering, when rest is taken immediately after exercise, as it prevents the body cooling too rapidly by continued evaporation. The application of this fact would, of course, not need to be observed in hot and calm weather.

As regards colour, it need only be mentioned that white fabrics resist much longer than dark materials the passage through them of heat rays' from refulgent bodies. They should generally, therefore, form the outer attire of persons when exposed to the glare of the sun in hot seasons or climates.

The evils of insufficient clothing to maintain the skin at a normal temperature are very marked, and are manifested by enervation, depression, and general sluggishness of the vital functions. Such a condition is the result of impoverishment and defective nutrition of the various structures near the surface of the body, owing to the proper supply of blood being kept out of them by the constringent action on the peripheral capillaries of the persistent cold. At the same time the internal organs also suffer from being passively congested by an excess of blood, which is driven inwards instead of being distributed equally throughout the whole circulatory system. In such case, if disease is not directly produced, the constitution is enfeebled, and laid unusually open to the numerous exciting causes of maladies to which we are perpetually exposed. Hence the fallacy becomes palpable of wearing insufficient clothing, under the impression that the constitution can thereby be ren-

dered more hardy and vigorous. The dress should
be carefully adapted to every variation of indoor and
outdoor temperature, and also to periods of exercise
and repose. The skin should be invariably kept
comfortably warm, but at the same the error of
excessive wrapping up should be avoided. In the
latter case, indeed, a delicacy or exaggerated sus-
ceptibility of the surface to slight thermometrical
changes may be engendered, which may be a constant
source of mild catarrhal affections, the forerunners,
possibly, of serious inflammatory attacks in the throat
or lungs.

As a protection against sharp winds, the best
clothing is something wholly impervious, such as
waterproof cloth, or leather in the form of strong
skins with or without fur. The objection to this class
of garments is that they prevent the evaporation of
the perspiration, and the body thus remains in a state
of continual dampness. For this reason they should
generally be dispensed with during exercise, unless
required to keep out rain.

With respect to the *corset,* enough has already
been said in order to show how detrimental its improper use may be to the free play of the chest, and
consequently to the artistic employment of the voice.[1]
As a covering for the skin, its place could easily be
supplied by any looser vestment of similar substance.[2]

Whilst alluding to tight articles of female apparel,

[1] See p. 167.
[2] For a complete exposition of all that concerns the corset, see
Bouvier, *Études historiques et médicales sur l'usage des corsets,* in
Bulletin de l'Académie de médecine, t. xviii. 1853, pp. 355, 389.

a word of warning may be spoken against the wearing of rigid and narrow cravats amongst the male sex. A dangerous compression of the superficial blood-vessels of the neck, causing congestion of the brain or even fatal apoplexy, has not unfrequently been laid to the charge of a neckerchief drawn so tight as to become an unintentional instrument of strangulation.[1]

2. *Ablutions (Baths).*—The systematic cleansing of the skin, which is carried out even by many of the lower animals through an impulse of instinct, is in man both a social and a sanitary necessity. The products of perspiration, as well as any foreign matters derived from the dust of the atmosphere, which tend to accumulate on the skin, are thereby removed, and the pores are opened so as to allow the various sets of glandules to carry on unhindered their office of excretion. The universal detergent is water, which is applied most effectively to the surface of the body in the form of a bath. Water baths are of various kinds, and differ either in temperature or by holding in solution some mineral substance, wherefore they may have other hygienic actions besides their cleansing properties.

Pure water baths may be cold, tepid, or warm.

The cold bath, generally at about 60° Fahr., has a tonic and stimulating effect on the skin and constitution of persons in ordinary health. It causes the blood to rush inwards momentarily, whence, however, it is soon again driven outwards if the circulatory apparatus is moderately vigorous. A

---

[1] See Percy, *Dictionnaire des sciences médicales*, t. vii. 1813, art. *Cravates.*

comfortable glow of the surface is then felt, which is termed "reaction." This reaction is the index to the benefit derived from the bath, and the skin is thereby stimulated to a more energetic performance of its functions. On the contrary, should it not occur, the skin remains pale and cold, whilst the internal organs are injuriously congested, especially the lungs, and there is evidence that the cold bath is harmful. On such an event the reaction should be encouraged by friction of the surface with a rough towel or with flesh gloves, but the bather should in future refrain from the use of a decidedly cold bath. It must also be observed that in no case should the cold bath be taken when the skin is cold, as there is then hardly any possibility of provoking a reaction, and injury may even result from increasing the already existing congestion of internal organs. Moreover, it is a standard rule not to bathe after a meal, as a disturbance of the circulation is then inadmissible.

The tepid bath, at about 90° Fahr., has no particular effect on the circulation, and is, therefore, suitable for delicate persons who merely desire to fulfil the duty of washing.

The warm bath, 100° to 120° Fahr., determines a flow of blood to the surface of the body and increases the cutaneous action. At the same time it relaxes all the muscular structures and renders the flow of the blood through its channels more laboured, a tendency which is met by greater contractile efforts of the heart, whence arises a quickened respiration. The warm bath, when short, supplies a salutary stimulus and alterative to the vital activities, but if indulged in too long or too often has a debilitating influence on the system, which loses in tone on account of the excessive or repeated relaxations. After a warm bath the bather should remain at rest and well covered for a short time until the circulation has regained its normal course.

Of mineral baths, cold sea-water need only be mentioned here. Sea-bathing has always been considered tonic and invigorating ; the motion of the water, the exercise taken whilst immersed in it, the stimulating atmosphere, and possibly the absorption by the skin of some of the mineral salts held in solution, combine to exert a peculiarly beneficial action on the system. Most persons can generally, therefore, bathe in the sea with marked advantage, except the very delicate and timid.

Another class of baths deserves a short notice, viz., the dry hot-air bath and the Turkish bath, of which it is the chief part. By the dry and hot air the glands of the skin are solicited to a very energetic action, and they respond by a copious flow of perspiration. A purifying effect on the blood is thus obtained, which is often highly salutary in the robust, especially if there be an inclination to corpulence. In the Turkish bath the perspiration is checked by a cold-water douche, and a reaction is then brought about by friction, shampooing, etc. These baths should, however, be taken with caution, as they are too powerful to be advisable in all cases. As a rule, they should never be persevered in without a medical recommendation.

3. *Cosmetics.*—The chief of cosmetics is soap, a combination of oil and alkali, which is indispensable to every toilet on account of its solvent power over all foreign matters that may coat the skin. It may be made more agreeable to the senses of sight and smell by clarification and admixture with various odoriferous oils or balsams, but beyond this there is usually but little choice to be exerted in the selection of so universal a commodity. The simplicity and cheapness of the articles that enter into its composition generally ensure a sufficient purity. Certain medicated soaps, containing tar, carbolic acid, sulphur, etc., are sometimes used, but are unnecessary unless when there is some structural disease of the skin, for the relief of which the special ingredient is intrinsically suited.

This term also includes the various applications used for the skin, such as violet-powder, rouge, hair-oils, various lotions for the complexion, eau-de-Cologne, etc., which are employed mostly about the face only for the sake of appearance. Such substances should always be used guardedly, unless their precise composition is known, as they are sometimes compounded with poisonous drugs, notably lead and arsenic, which may act perniciously both locally and generally.[1]

IV. *Climatic Influences.*—The hygienic estimation of climate resolves itself almost entirely into a con-

---

[1] See Ménière's essay, *Les vêtements et les cosmetiques*, Thèse de Paris, 1838. Very many scattered papers, too numerous to be referred to here, have been published giving instances of dangerous symptoms and even fatal poisoning produced by cosmetics.

sideration of the state of the atmosphere in different parts of the earth and at various seasons, as to temperature, humidity, density, movement, and any foreign element that may permeate it, such as marsh miasma. The action of the air on the health of the body is determined by the degree in which it possesses these qualities, which spring from terrestrial and solar influences.[1]

1. *Hot Climates.*—In excessively hot weather (80° to 90° Fahr., or higher), if the air is dry, the skin is stimulated to provide a large quantity of perspiration and the body is kept cool by rapid evaporation. At the same time respiration is quickened because the rarefied air contains less oxygen, and a larger supply of it is therefore required for breathing purposes. The increased rush of the dry air through the vocal channels tends to parch the mucous membrane, an effect which may deteriorate the quality of the voice.

[1] Méliot conceives that climate exerts a peculiar influence over voice. He states that in hot countries there are finer voices than in cold regions, and that high voices are also more common there than deep voices. Thus in Italy more tenors than basses are found, and in Germany more basses than tenors. In France, Picardy furnishes most bass voices. Languedoc and especially Toulouse and its environs are celebrated for tenor voices. Burgundy and Franche-Comté (Jura, Doubs, and Haute-Saône) supply most female voices.—*La musique expliquée aux gens du monde*, Paris, 1867 (quoted by Mandl, *Traité pratique*, etc., 1872, p. 294). History, however, appears to indicate that musical gifts of voice are rather ethnogenetic in their origin. Thus Italy, so prolific in our own times with fine singers, was not remarkable in the same manner in the age of the Romans; seemingly, indeed, the reverse (see p. 38). And in the classical period Greece and Asia Minor, which do not now produce singers of note, must have furnished the most esteemed vocalists.

Moreover, the heat relaxes the muscular system, so as to reduce the aptitude for exertion. Under these conditions, therefore, the voice may lose in power and purity.

Should the air be unusually moist, although the parching effect is not present, the heat is more than ever depressing, because the normal temperature of the body cannot be preserved by perspiratory evaporation.

When wind is present it facilitates evaporation. It therefore increases the molestation if the air be already too hot and dry, but lessens the evil of humidity with elevation of temperature.

It is only in hot weather that marsh miasmata are potent for harm. They arise from low-lying tracts of land covered with decaying vegetable matter, but cannot emanate so as to pervade the general atmosphere, unless aided by a temperature above 60° Fahr. They engender the class of fevers called intermittent or agues, and in thus disturbing the animal economy interfere, of course, with the artistic exercise of the voice. These noisome exhalations consist of heavy gases which hug the ground, being unable to ascend into the higher regions of the air. On this account they can be avoided by living on the hills,[1] should there be any, in the infected districts.

In hot climates the vicinity of the *sea-coast* is generally more healthful than the inland districts. The marine air has stimulating and tonic properties owing to its being impregnated with iodine, bromine, and various saline principles. It contains the largest,

---

[1] The height, however, at which safety is obtained varies in different parts of the world: 400 feet may suffice, but it may be necessary to ascend 2,000 feet. See Parkes, op. cit. p. 411.

amount of oxygen, because, allowing for temperature, it has the greatest density; for, the sea level being the lowest, atmospheric pressure is there at its maximum. Its humidity is generally of an average measure according to the temperature, whilst miasmata, in infected localities, are lessened on the shore and absent on the water at a short distance from it. The seaside is, therefore, a valuable and ready refuge against many of the evils encountered in tropical climates.

2. *Cold Climates.*—Very cold weather (25° to 40° Fahr.), if the air is dry, is invigorating. It renders the function of the lungs more active, in order that a greater amount of animal heat may be evolved, with the object of preserving the normal degree of temperature. But the breathing is not consequently hurried or oppressed, because the cold air, being condensed, contains a comparatively large quantity of oxygen. The dryness of the atmosphere creates little tendency to parching of the air-passages, because it is counterbalanced by the cold, which checks evaporation. On the whole, therefore, a cold, dry climate is favourable to vocal exercise, or at least is not injurious to the integrity of the voice.

The combination of cold and damp is notorious for its pernicious influence on health, though why it should act so injuriously is not quite certain. It may be taken for granted, however, that the exhalation of watery vapour, by the skin or lungs, or by both, is a vital necessity; probably because the water holds in solution certain fœtid organic matters which exert a poisonous effect on the system, and which cannot be otherwise removed.[1]   In cold and damp air we have the conjunction of the two atmospheric conditions most potent in their antagonism to evaporation. In such case little or no aqueous vapour can be given off by the cutaneous or pulmonary surfaces, and the fœtid organic matters, therefore, accumulate in the blood and tissues, tending to originate disease, mostly of a rheumatic character.   But cold and damp also greatly exaggerate the liability to congestion of internal organs, and are prolific generators of inflammatory affections of the air-passages, such as quinsy, laryngitis, bronchitis, etc.

Fogs generally occur in cold, often in frosty weather.   They consist of molecules of water, which float about, suspended in the air.   They are evidence of excessive dampness, and they are also particularly noxious in cities, as they there entangle and fix fuliginous or sooty particles in the stratum of air near the earth.   The effect is that persons involved in such fogs are obliged to inhale damp smoke, which has an irritating action on the air-passages.   In foggy weather it will generally be found that the nasal discharges and expectorated matters have a blackened appearance.

It has been asserted that the gravity of the voice is increased in a cold and humid atmosphere,[2] but the statement needs proof.   Retention

---

[1] See Parkes, op. cit. p. 98; Carpenter, op. cit. p. 412.

[2] The following incident would appear scarcely credible did it not rest on a high authority.   When Grassini came to England the hygrometric influence of the climate caused her voice to descend in

of moisture in or about the vibrating portion of the vocal apparatus might, indeed, by increasing the density of the vocal bands, lower their tones. Singers certainly feel the effect of chill and damp weather, and are then seldom in good voice.

Persons who are obliged to be out of doors in chilly and moist weather should be especially careful to breathe through the nose, as the air, being thus considerably warmed, will be enabled to carry off more watery vapour from the lungs. The mucous lining of the throat is also thus guarded from the ill effects of the cold. Should breathing through the nose be difficult from any cause, a *respirator* should be worn. This instrument is worn over the mouth, in order to warm the air and catch any particles of dust during inspiration. It supplies, in fact, the place of the nasal channels for those who are obliged to breathe through the mouth.

The action of wind in dry, cold weather is to cause the cold to be disagreeably felt. A cold, but dry climate is usually, indeed, well tolerated or even pleasant, when an uniform calmness of the air is the prevailing condition. In chilly, damp weather a brisk movement of the air increases the evaporation, but, in doing so, also augments the cold, which is then most painfully felt. Although winds are often

pitch by an octave. Its quality was not, however, deteriorated by this curious change; on the contrary, she had a great success in her lyric achievements until, by her becoming accustomed to the climate, her voice regained its normal compass. She then actually lost her popularity here, though her vocal powers had returned to the condition to which she previously owed her fame.—Bishop, op. cit. p. 1481.

favourable in maintaining atmospheric purity, and will dispel fogs, it seems that, on the whole, in decidedly cold weather, their influence is not precisely hygienic.

The *sea-air*, even in cold climates, retains its tonic properties. Its humidity on or near the shore is generally uniform, as far as terrestrial influences are concerned, because the soil in the vicinity of the ocean is usually of a sandy nature.

3. *Temperate Climates.*—The characteristic of most temperate climates is their variability, for, whilst their summer may be almost tropical, their winter is not unfrequently of polar severity. And the junction of these two extremes is not effected by insensible gradation, so as to amalgamate the seasons imperceptibly, but sudden changes of temperature to the extent of 20° or 30° Fahr. may occur in the course of a single day. At one time dryness, and at another humidity of the air may be present to a marked degree. This mutability is chiefly due to the action of winds, which, if they come from the north, have no opportunity to become heated, or, if from the south, are not exposed to any cooling influences before reaching the temperate zone.

The hygienic qualities of temperate climates are in direct relation with their variability, and the rapid transitions from heat to cold are especially inducive of catarrhal and inflammatory maladies, such as usually result from taking cold. Diseases of the throat are, therefore, frequent, and the inhabitants have some difficulty in preserving the purity of voice required for its professional use. On this account they are obliged to be particularly careful in adapting their clothing to the manifold emergencies of weather.

Notwithstanding these circumstances, it is in the temperate zone that some of the most agreeable and salubrious districts for dwelling in may be found. For, as the solar influences, if undisturbed, would generally confer a well-poised mean of temperature, it is only necessary to neutralize the action of the winds in order to obtain a stable climate free from hurtful extremes. This requirement is effected in many localities on the south coasts of temperate lands, such as Torquay, the Riviera, etc., where a mountainous chain intercepts the northern blasts, whilst the marine evaporation cools the sultry air blowing from the south. Such are the localities which are best adapted for the residence of invalids, as the constitution is not disturbed by the necessity of perpetually re-adapting itself to altered conditions of climate, whilst the weather is so equable as seldom or never to debar the taking of out-door exercise. Life in the open air is, indeed, the most potent re-invigorator of those afflicted with consumptive tendencies.

4. *Mountain Air.*—The air of mountains or elevated plateaus has a favourable effect on the health of the animal economy, either from its purity or from its lightness. As the atmosphere is considerably attenuated on account of the altitude, it contains less oxygen, and consequently the breathing

is hastened and the circulation of the blood accelerated. This change is salutary, and not attended with any sensation of pulmonary oppression, because the diminution of the atmospheric pressure on the surface of the body and the lessened force of gravitation facilitate exercise and increase the activity of the limbs. In hot climates the mountain air has also the advantage of being cool,[1] whilst in cold regions it is beneficial on account of its dryness. Life on the slopes of a mountain, at a height of from 3,000 to 7,000 feet, is now considered as an eminently curative agent in the treatment of many debilitating diseases, especially scrofula and consumption.[2] In cases of mild constitutional depression, such as continued fatigue from overwork, when a change of air is required, no better choice could be made than of residence for a few weeks in a temperate and elevated situation amongst the hills.

[1] The decline of temperature, according as we ascend, may be roughly estimated at 1° Fahr. for every 300 feet of elevation.
[2] See Weber, *Climate of the Swiss Alps*, 1864.

APPENDIX.

I.

GALEN ON THE ACTION OF THE LARYNGEAL VENTRICLES.[1]

THE views of Galen on this point illustrate well the remarkable scientific acumen of that indefatigable observer, and are interesting on account of having been recently revived by Wyllie[2] quite independently from experimental considerations. And that an important function of the ventricles of the larynx has been indicated by both authors cannot, I think, be doubted by anyone who has paid full attention to the question.

Οὐ μόνον δὲ εἰς τὸ τῆς φωνῆς ὄργανον ἀναγκαῖον τῷ λάρυγγι τουτὶ τὸ σῶμα τῆς γλωττίδος, ἀλλὰ καὶ τῇ καλουμένῃ καταλήψει τοῦ πνεύματος . . . . εἰς ὅπερ ἔργον οὐ σμικρὰ συντελεῖ τῆς προειρημένης γλωττίδος ἡ φύσις· εἰς ταὐτὸν γὰρ αὐτῆς ἔρχεται τὰ μόρια τῶν ἀριστερῶν καὶ τῶν δεξιῶν, ὡς συμπεσεῖν ἀλλήλοις ἀκριβῶς, καὶ κλεῖσαι τὸν πόρον. Εἰ δέ τι σμικρὸν ἄκλειστον ὑπολειφθείη, οὐδὲ τοῦτο ἀπρονόητον παρῶπται τῇ φύσει, τρῆμα κατὰ ἑκάτερον μέρος τῆς γλωττίδος ἐν ἐργασαμένη ὑποθείσῃ τε τῷ τρήματι κοιλίαν ἔνδον οὐ σμικράν. Ἐπειδὰν μὲν οὖν εὐρείαις ὁδοῖς ὁ ἀὴρ χρώμενος εἰσείη τε εἰς τὸ ζῷον, ἐξίῃ τε αὖθις, οὐδὲν εἰς τὴν κοιλίαν παρωθεῖται· φραχθείσης δὲ τῆς διεξόδου, στενοχωρούμενος ὠθεῖταί τε βιαίως πρὸς τὰ πλάγια, καὶ τὸ τοῦ τρήματος τῆς γλωττίδος ἀνοίγνυσι στόμιον, ὃ τέως ἐκέκλειστο τῶν χειλῶν ἐπεπτυγμένων· πληρωθεισῶν δὲ πνεύματος τῶν ἐν τῇ γλάττῃ τοῦ λάρυγγος κοιλιῶν, ἀποχεῖσθαι μὲν δήπου τὸν ὄγκον ἀναγκαῖον εἰς αὐτὸν τοῦ πνεύματος τὸν πόρον, ἀκριβῶς δὲ στενοῦσθαι, κἂν εἰ σμικρόν τι πρόσθεν ἀνέῳκτο.

"But this body[3] of the glottis is not only necessary to the organ of

[1] From Oribasius, l. xxiv. c. 9, see page 102.

[2] Op. cit.

[3] Galen considers the "body," which he calls glottis, to consist of the vocal and ventricular bands of both sides with the ventricles between them.

voice, but also to what is called holding the breath . . . . to which action the nature of the aforesaid glottis contributes not a little; for to effect the said purpose the parts of it of the right and of the left approach, so as to fall together accurately and close the passage. But should a small portion be left unclosed, not even this, as being unforeseen, has been disregarded by nature, who has worked an opening on each side of the glottis, and placed in continuity with the aperture a cavity within by no means small. When, therefore, the air, making use of a wide channel, goes into the animal, and passes out again, none of it is turned aside into the cavity. When, however, the passage out is blocked, the air, being confined in a narrow space, is diverted forcibly towards the sides and opens the mouth of the aperture of the glottis, which hitherto had been closed by the folding together of the lips. The cavities in the glottis of the larynx being thus filled with wind, it is, of course, necessary that the swelling so produced should bulge towards the passage of the breath and shut it with exactitude, even if a small part had previously been left open."

II.

TALKING MACHINES.

The instrument of Kratzenstein [1] was only designed to imitate the five vowels (*a, e, i, o, u*), and the object was to some extent attained by the application of various modifications of conical tubes to reed pipes like those of an organ. The attempt was, however, purely empirical, and the author believed erroneously that his success was due to the peculiar shapes he had given his tubes. Almost at the same time Baron von Kempelen, of Vienna, was occupied independently with the construction of a speaking machine, and he has left us a full history [2] of the progress of his invention through a number of years, as well as a minute description of the instrument itself, with the view of instructing others how to manufacture a similar one. He began his task with a set of pipes adapted for the *vox humana* stop of an organ, thinking it would be easiest to have a separate tube for each letter; but he soon abandoned this method in favour of one by which the human vocal organs were more closely imitated. The apparatus, when completed, consisted of a bellows which sent a blast of air through a reed pipe, or artificial larynx, opening into a cavity representing that of the mouth. The front outlet of the mouth was

[1] See page 142.   [2] Op. cit.

formed by a bell-shaped cylinder of india-rubber of such a size as to let its orifice be easily closed with the palm of the hand. From the upper part of the oral cavity led two small tubes to imitate the nostrils, whilst two side openings, governed by keys, were shaped so as to give S and Sh. A third key caused a kind of tongue to vibrate for R. In using the machine the principal part was played by one of the hands acting on the orifice of the india-rubber bell. Thus, for P it was first completely stopped and then suddenly opened; for B the same motions were executed, but a few vibrations of the reed were allowed to squeeze out at one part where the hand was held rather loosely to the edge of the bell. F and V were obtained somewhat similarly. The vowels were imitated by covering the bell to a greater or lesser amount by the hand. When quite open the sound resembled Ah; when nearly closed, U. By graduating the area of the aperture in a manner to be learned practically by the performer, the rest of the vowels could be obtained. The keys were acted on by the other hand, and also the nostril holes, one of which was left open for N, and both for M, the front being blocked in the meantime. D, T, G, and K were wanting to the instrument.[1] Kempelen's own account of the efficiency of his speaking machine is as follows:—"In the space of three weeks a surprising dexterity can be acquired in playing on the talking machine, especially if the learner applies himself to the Latin, French, or Italian languages, for the German tongue is much more difficult on account of the consonants which meet so frequently. . . . I can pronounce immediately on request any French or Italian word, but a German word costs me much more trouble, and it is rare that I can succeed perfectly. As to entire phrases, I can produce but few, and they must also be short, because the bellows is not large enough to furnish the necessary amount of air. For example: *vous êtes mon ami ; je vous aime de tout mon cœur ;* or in Latin *Leopoldus secundus ; Romanorum imperator ; semper Augustus.* In fine, I am convinced that the machine could easily be arranged with keys, like those of the harpsichord or organ, so as to be played on much more easily. But this is a step towards perfection which I leave to those of my readers who may pay attention to this new invention still in its infancy." From a scientific stand-point Kempelen deserves the credit of deducing and indicating from his experiments that varying capacity of the mouth is the most important factor in the emission of vowels.

[1] Sir C. Wheatstone made such an instrument after Kempelen's directions, which is in the philosophical collection of King's College. Another, somewhat similar in principle, has lately been exhibited in London by Herr Faber, see *The Times*, Feb. 12, 1880.

It is strange that a third inventor should have busied himself about the artificial production of speech contemporaneously with Kratzenstein and Kempelen. This was the Abbé Mical, who made two speaking heads of colossal dimensions, and exhibited them in Paris in 1783. The means he adopted are, however, unknown, and it only appears that he had a number of pipes and reeds, each of which corresponded to one or two letters. Rivarol, who saw these heads, was delighted with their performance, and has left his opinion of them in the following passage [1] :—" M. Mical applies two key-boards to his speaking heads, one cylindrical, by which a determinate number of phrases only is obtained, but by which the intonation of the words and their prosody are correctly marked. The other contains in a row all the syllables of the French language, reduced to a small number by an ingenious method of the author's own. With a little skill and practice one can speak with the fingers as with the tongue, and can give the language of the heads the rapidity, repetition, and in fact all the expression that speech can have when not animated by the passions. The stranger can take the *Henriade* or *Telemachus* and cause them to be recited from one end to the other by placing them on the vocal key-board, like the parts of an opera on the ordinary key-board." The Abbé wished to sell his heads to the French government, but the person who was appointed to inspect them appears to have given an unfavourable report, in consequence of which they refused the purchase. The inventor, in the pangs of disappointment, immediately broke the heads to pieces and destroyed them. The greatest use which Rivarol could foresee for such machines was to fix and perpetuate the pronunciation of languages. For such a purpose, however, all talking instruments of the kind are now superseded by the phonograph.

III.

The Vocal Powers of the Lower Animals.

A few remarks on this subject will probably be read with interest here. Amongst the ancients there was, indeed, a wide-spread belief that brutes had a regular language of their own, which enabled them to converse with each other on passing events with as much freedom as human beings. Even so late as the beginning of the seventeenth century, Fabricius of Acquapendente,[2] after consider-

---

[1] Op. cit.   [2] *De Brutorum Loquela*, Padua, 1604.

ing the evidence systematically, concludes that "it is clear a language of brutes must be conceded, and that an articulate voice." The most ingenious upholder of this notion, however, was Porphyry,[1] who argues out the subject with great earnestness. Amidst much else to the same effect he says :—"For men, indeed, speak by the law of humanity, but other animals by that law which has been conceded to each kind by the gods and by nature. If we do not understand them, what does that prove? For the Greeks educated in Attica are unable to apprehend the language of the Indians, Scythians, Thracians, or Syrians. Not otherwise than the clangor of cranes do the vocal sounds of the one race strike the other. The voice of the Persians seems to us illiterate and inarticulate, as does that of other animals to all men. . . . But, if the ancients can be credited, as well as some who have lived in our own times and those of our fathers, there are those who have perceived and understood the language of other animals. For example, in the memory of the ancients, Melampus and Tiresias, and not long ago Apollonius Tyaneus. Of the latter it is said that once in the company of his friends, when a swallow flew close to them and sang some indefinite notes, he stated that she was announcing to other swallows that they should hasten to a place outside the city where an ass loaded with grain had fallen and strewed the corn all over the ground. And a friend used to tell us that he happened to have had a servant, a boy, who thoroughly understood the language of birds of omen, such as are aware of events that are on the point of taking place. The mother of the boy, however, fearing lest he should be sent as a present to the king, deprived him of the faculty by doing an injury to his ears (εἰς τὰ ὦτα ἐνουρησάσης). . . . For every one knows that there are nations who recognize the language of some brutes. Thus, the Arabs understand the chattering of crows, the Tyrrhenians that of eagles. . . . Now crows, magpies, and parrots imitate men. And the Indian hyæna, which the indigenes call *corocotta*, so speaks after the human fashion, even without a master, that he is accustomed to frequent dwelling-places and call out those whom he knows he can easily conquer. He mimics the voices of those most dear to his victims, so that they, being deceived by the similitude, come out and follow the voice until they are destroyed and perish. But if all animals do not imitate and are not apt to learn our language, what does it argue? For neither have all men the faculty of imitating the speech of other animals, or even of mastering any five of the dialects used amongst men," etc.

[1] *De Abstinentia ab Esu Carnium*, l. iii. ; about A.D., 300.

To return, however, to the scientific view of the question; the descriptions given of the human larynx may be applied generally with but slight change to that of other mammals. Whether the lion roar or the mouse squeal the sound is alike produced, on the same acoustic principle, by the approximation and vibration of their vocal bands. Some mammals, indeed, such as the rabbit and giraffe, have little or no voice, and are deficient in the development of the vocal bands. Amongst these must also be reckoned the curious order of marsupials (kangaroo, etc.) and the cetaceans (whale, etc.), who emit little or no sound. But even those mammals who are well endowed with voice, as far as loudness is concerned, have a very limited power of varying their tones; and the dog who barks, growls, whines, etc., is as versatile in respect of voice as almost any of his class. An exception, however, must be made to this rule in the case of the gibbons or long-armed apes. "They alone," says Professor Owen,[1] "of brute animals may be said to sing. I heard, with astonishment, the Wouwou, captive at the Zoological Gardens, emit the rising and falling scale of semitones throughout the octave." Mr. Darwin[2] also reminds us that mice can be taught to sing, and have been made an exhibition of for this quality.

Regarding next the class of birds, we are surprised to find them, in respect of voice, differing almost in every way from, and at the same time much in advance of, the other denizens of the fields and forests. We find no longer a vocal larynx situated below the tongue, but a lower larynx, or syrinx, at the bottom of the windpipe, where it divides into the bronchial tubes. Nor are there here well-developed bands that can be drawn together and separated at will, but a comparatively smooth passage, the most noticeable structure in song-birds being a membrane (*membrana semilunaris*) projecting upwards for a fraction of an inch from the apex of the bronchi.[3] Several muscular bands not possessed by mammals in this vicinity indicate the importance of the part in relation to voice. The acoustic method of voice production in birds is by no means well ascertained. To me it appears most likely that by the aid of the syrinx sonorous vibrations of the column of air in the windpipe are created, after the manner of the flute, and that the principal factor in effecting change of pitch is variation in the size of the upper orifice of the trachea, where it opens into the pharynx or back of the mouth. Be this as it may, every one is

---

[1] *Anatomy of the Vertebrates*, vol. iii. p. 600.
[2] *Descent of Man*, ed. 1874, p. 567.
[3] A concise, but very clear, description of this organ will be found in Huxley's *Anatomy of the Vertebrates*, 1871, p. 313.

acquainted with the wonderful vocal versatility in the sphere of music of most birds, and cannot fail to be struck with the remarkable contrast they offer in this domain to the lower mammals with their more apparent advantages of mental evolution. But the vocal superiority of the feathered tribe does not cease here, for it also extends into the far higher region of articulate sound. Be he ever so intelligent we cannot teach a dog to speak, nor yet an ape, who in his morphological elements is so nearly akin to humanity.[1] Yet we can teach the seemingly more stupid bird; and the talking achievements of the starling, raven, parrot, etc., need only be alluded to in this connection. It is the same if we observe them in their state of nature; they still exhibit a marked faculty for articulation. The cries of birds are singularly syllabic; they are the "airy tongues" which counterfeit man's speech. The goldfinch may be heard to twitter his *stiglit, picklenit, ki-kleia* (whence his German name of *stieglitz*) as he flits from shrub to shrub; *mai* is his note of alarm, and *ra-ra-ra-ra-ra* indicates anger. Some warblers (*sylviadæ*) pronounce *judith, brief,* and *tack-tack* with great distinctness. The American nightjar, or whip-poor-will, not only repeats his popular name, but is said, when intruded upon, to exclaim *ha-ha-ha-ha, who-are-you, who-who-who-are-you;* and also at other times *work-away, work-work-work-away.*[2] The Scotch peasants are said to have a rooted antipathy to the yellow bunting, because its usual phrase of notes is so suggestive to their ears of *de'il-de'il-de'il-*TAKE*-you.* Such are a few examples out of many, and we may now abandon further investigation here of the vocal powers of the lower animals in favour of the poetical description of Ovid[3]:—

> Dum turdus trutilat, sturnus tunc pisitat ore,
>   Sed quod mane canunt, vespere non recolunt.
> Cuccabat hinc perdix, hinc gratilat improbus anser,
>   Et castus turtur, atque columba gemunt.
> Plausitat arborea clamans de fronde palumbes,
>   In pluviis natans forte tatrinat anas.
> Grus gruit, inque glomis cygni prope plumina drensant.
>   Accipiter pipat, milvus hiansque jugit.
> Cucurrire solet gallus, gallina gracillat,
>   Pupillat pavo, trinsat hirundo vaga.

* * * * * * * * * * * *

---

[1] Mr. Darwin thinks deficient intelligence the only obstacle in the way of the higher apes speaking, op. cit. p. 90.

[2] See Brehm's *Thierleben*, vol. iii. Hildburghausen, 1869.

[3] *Philomela*, ascribed to Ovid.

Tigrides indomitæ raucant, rugiuntque leones,
　　Panther caurit amans, pardus hiando felit,
Dum lynces oreando fremunt, ursus ferus uncat.
　　Ast lupus ipse ululat, frendet agrestis aper.
Et barrus barrit, cervi glocitant et onagri.
　　Ast taurus mugit, et celer hinnit equus.[1]

---

[1] This extract is interesting as containing a number of words not to be found in any Latin dictionary.

INDEX OF AUTHORS REFERRED TO.

A.

Ægineta, Paulus, 21
Aitken, W., 161
Amussat, J. Z., 196
Annales, etc., *Francorum*, 46
Antiphon, 30
Antyllus, 22
Aphrodisiensis, Alexander, 22
Apollinaris, Sidonius, 21
Aristophanes, 19, 21, 25
Aristotle, 10, 22, 24, 26, 27, 28, 31, 101, 196
Arnott, N., 193
Athenæus, 31, 32, 33
Aurelianus, Cælius, 22, 172

B.

Banting, W., 233
Battaille, C., 121
Béclard, J., 92, 127, 130
Becquerel, A., 194, 224, 243
Bede, the Venerable, 44, 45
Bell, A. M., 185
Benoiston de Châteauneuf, L. F., 221
Beroaldus, P., 31
Berthold, A. A., 194
Bingham, C., 40

Biographia Britannica, 143
Bishop, J., 127, 257
Borgnis, J. A., 143
Bouvier, —, 248
Brehm, A. E., 267
Broquin, L. P., 223
Brouc, M. M., 214, 224, 237
Browne, L., 182
Bunsen, C. C. J., 11
Burette, J. P., 223
Burney, C., 14, 27, 28, 45, 47, 50, 223

C.

Camden, W., 45
Capella, Martianus, 19, 33
Carpenter, W. B., 245, 256
Celsus, A. Cornelius, 196
Chappell, W., 28, 71
Cicero, M. Tullius, 17, 19, 20, 27, 33, 35, 36, 37, 39, 51
Clemens Alexandrinus, 12
Colombat de l'Isère, 113, 193, 199, 200, 223
Combe, A., 222, 230, 232
Condillac, B. de, 3
Cox, E. W., 198, 213
Cresollius, L., 33, 42
Cruveilhier, J., 131
Curwen, J., 123, 141, 181

Cuvier, G., 108
Czermak, J., 113

D.

Darwin, C., 5, 8, 266, 267
Demosthenes, 21, 26
Despinay de Bourg, F., 111
Dibdin, C., 43
Dickinson, W. H., 238
Dieffenbach, J. F., 196
Diemerbroek, I. de, 223
Diodorus Siculus, 11, 13, 16
Diogenes Laertius, 22, 23
Dionysius of Halicarnassus, 15, 20, 34, 38
Dodart, C. J. B., 105
Donaldson, J. W., 24, 25, 33
Donders, F. C., 143, 153
Dutrochet, R. H. J., 108

E.

Ellis, A. J., 56, 68, 148, 185

F.

Fabricius ab Acquapendente, 103, 264
Fallopius, G., 224
Fauvel, C., 208
Ferrein, A., 107
Fétis, F. J., 14, 47, 130, 179, 239
Flint, A., 245
Fournié, E., 123, 125, 135
Frobisher, J. E., 173

G.

Galen, Claudius, 21, 32, 102, 172, 204, 261

Garcia, M., 113
Geoffroy St. Hilaire, I., 109
Gibbon, E., 34, 41
Gladstone, W. E., 16
Grote, G., 15, 18
Gueneau de Mussy, A., 206
Guillaume, A., 195, 199
Guttmann, O., 173

H.

Hahn, J. G. von, 190
Haughton, S., 242
Hawkins, Sir J., 44, 47, 50
Helmholtz, H., 56, 59, 61, 63, 66, 70, 71, 74, 76, 123, 132, 144, 147, 177
Henle, J., 88, 124, 129
Herder, J. G. von, 5
Hermann, L., 97
Hermolaus Barbarus, 31
Herodotus, 4, 14, 15, 16, 17
Herschel, Sir J., 53, 66
Hieronymus (Jerome), 30
Hippocrates, 100, 186
Hollingshed, R., 44, 45
Homer, 15, 16, 17, 26
Hopkins, E. J., 130
Horatius Flaccus, 2, 38
Hullah, J., 78, 185
Humboldt, W. von, 1
Hunt, J., 195, 199, 200
Huxley, T. H., 266

I.

Illingworth, C. R., 113, 118
Isidorus of Seville, 31, 41
Itard, J. M. G., 189

J.

James, P., 198
John Diaconus, 46
Josephson, J., 221

K.

Kavanagh, M., 4
Kayser, C. L., 18
Kempelen, W. von, 143, 262
Kircher, A., 25, 143
Kratzenstein, C. T., 142, 262
Krishaber, M., 118, 212

L.

Largus, Scribonius, 32
Lee, R. J., 241
Lehfeldt, C., 111
Leibniz, G. W., 7
Leigh, Mrs., 191
Lepsius, C. R., 11, 33
Liscovius, C. F. S. (1), 109, 130
Liscovius, C. F. S. (2), 112
Littré, E., 68
Livy, T., 38
Lombard, H. C., 221
Longinus, 20
Lubbock, Sir J., 4, 5, 6
Lucian, 19, 21, 224
Lucretius Carus, T., 4, 8
Lunn, C., 137, 141, 177
Luschka, H. von, 85, 88, 90, 91, 121, 128

M.

McCormac, H., 191
Mackenzie, M., 89, 208
Maclaren, A., 241
Macrobius, A. A. T., 37

Magendie, F., 110, 121, 130, 191
Malgaigne, J. F., 110, 133
Mandl, L., 117, 125, 126, 141, 163, 170, 218, 222, 253
Martial, M. V., 30
Méliot, J., 253
Ménière, P., 252
Mercurialis, Hieronymus, 22, 172
Merkel, C. L., 97, 117, 123
Mersenne, M., 104
Mical, Abbé, 264
Mommsen, T., 35
Monroe, L. B., 173, 177
Müller, F. Max, 2, 6, 7, 8
Müller, J., 76, 110, 111, 130, 178
Myrepsus, Nicolaus, 32

O.

Oertel, M. J., 124
Oré, J. R., 197
Oribasius, 22, 102, 261
Ovidius Naso, P., 267
Owen, R., 127, 129, 134, 266

P.

Pall Mall Gazette, 217
Parkes, E. A., 210, 236, 254, 256
Pausanias, 15
Pavy, F. W., 234
Percy, —, 249
Percy, T., 48
Perrault, C., 105
Persius Flaccus, A., 30
Phillips, C., 197
Philostratus, 18, 19
Pigray, P., 223
Plato, 11, 13, 18, 23, 24, 27
Playfair, L., 226
Plinius Secundus, C., 31, 39

Plumptre, C. J., 180, 213
Plutarch, 9, 10, 18, 20, 23, 27, 34, 35, 188, 224
Porphyry, 265

Q.

Quanten, E. von, 148
Quintilian, M. Fabius, 21, 27, 36, 37, 204

R.

Rabanus Maurus, 31, 41
Ramadge, F., 222
Ramazzini, B., 224
Richard, P., 114
Richardson, B. W., 235
Rivarol, A., 143, 264
Romer, F., 113
Root, G. F., 172
Rousseau, J. J., 34, 44
Rullier, P., 190
Rush, J., 42, 135, 176
Rymer, T., 45

S.

Salmuth, J. H., 224
Sammonicus, Q. Serenus, 204
Savart, F., 109
Schech, P., 120, 121
Schlieman, H., 16
Ségond, L. A., 135, 138, 140
Seiler, E., 88, 124, 140
Seneca, L. Annæus, 224
Serres d'Alais, —, 192
Shakespeare, W., 232
Smith, A., 3

Spencer, H., 3, 8
Steinthal, H., 5
Stephanus, H., 21, 84
Strabo, 14, 15
Suetonius Tranquillus, C., 21, 32, 39
Suidas, 224
Swieten, G. van, 206
Synesius, 30

T.

Tacitus, C. Cornelius, 9
Taylor, S., 54, 71
Tyndall, J., 53, 55, 59, 66, 68, 210, 211

V.

Velpeau, A. A. L. M., 196
Vesalius, A., 103
Virgilius Maro, P., 37
Vitruvius Pollio, M., 25, 31

W.

Waldenburg, L., 221
Walton, G. L., 129
Warton, T., 48
Weber, H., 260
Wheatstone, Sir C., 143
Wilkinson, Sir G., 11, 13, 14, 15
Willis, R., 143
Wilson, E., 88, 243, 244
Woiliez, —, 127
Wutzer, P., 189
Wyllie, J., 111, 125, 130, 261

Z.

Ziemssen, H. W. von, 121

INDEX OF SUBJECTS.

———◆◇◆———

A.

Abdominal breathing, 82, 97, 167
Ablutions, 249
Abuse of voice, maladies from, 204, 212
Age, relations of, with voice, 91
Air, damp, 214, 255
    foggy, 256
    impurities in, 210
    marsh or miasmatic, 254
    mountain, 259
    sea, 254, 258
    where most dense, 255
Alcohol, ill effects of, on voice, 237
Alimentation, 225
Altitudes, air in high, 53, 260
Alto voice, 118, 138
Animals, lower, their vocal powers, 264
Articulation, 80, 142, 157, 184
    of consonants, 148, 185
    of vowels, 142, 184
Arytænoid cartilages, 85, 89, 115, 120

B.

Bands, vocal, 77, 86, 114, 116, 173
    breadth of, 156
    ventricular, 88, 126

Banting's system for the reduction of corpulence, 233
Baritone voice, 136
Bass voice, 136
Baths, 249
    cold, 249
    hot, 250
    hot-air, or Turkish, 251
    medicated, 251
    sea, 251
Beer, 237
Birds, voice in, 266
Break of voice at age of puberty, 91
Breath, holding the, 172
Breathing, abdominal or diaphragmatic, 82, 97, 167
    by the skin, 243
    clavicular, 82, 98, 168
    costal or rib, 82, 97, 168
    exercises for development of, 170
    management of, during vocal exercise, 162
Bronchial tubes, 83

C.

Cartilages of the larynx, 83
    arytænoid, 85, 89, 115, 120
    cricoid, 85, 121

T

Cartilages of the epiglottis, 85, 127
    of Santorini, 86
    of Wrisberg, 86
    sesamoid, 86, 118, 138
    thyroid, 85, 125
Cayenne, 214, 234
Chest, action of, 96, 162
    anatomy of, 81
    development of, 170
Chest-voice, laryngoscopic appear-
    ances in, 114, 116
    muscular mechanism of,
    120
Circulation, influence of vocal ex-
    ercise on, 222
Clavicular breathing, 83, 98, 168
Clergyman's sore throat, 206, 212
Climates, 252
    cold, 255
    hot, 253
    relations of, with voice, 253,
    255, 256
    temperate, 258
Clothing, different kinds of, 245
    insufficient, 247
Cocoa, 236
Coffee, 236
Cold climates, 255
Colour in clothing, 247
Compass of voices, 136
Composer, separate office of musi-
    cal, 49
Compound sounds, 63
    vibrations, 58
Condiments, 234
Conduction of heat in clothing, 246
Consonants, mechanism of the pro-
    duction of, 148
    classification of, 151
    formation of, 148
Contralto voice, 136
Cords, vocal, 77, 86, 114, 116, 173
    true and false, 86, 88, 108

Corpulence, ill-effects of, on voice,
    232
    remedy for, 233
Corset, injurious effects of, 168
Cosmetics, 252
Corti's organ, 63
Cotton as clothing, 246
Coup de glotte, 176
Cricoid cartilage, 85, 121
Cubebs, 219

D.

Damp air, 214, 255
Declamation among the ancients,
    17, 35
Defects of speech, 186
Diaphragm, breathing by, 82, 97,
    167
Differences, individual and sexual,
    of voice, 91, 136
Digestibility of food, 229
Digestion, vocal exercise during,
    21, 231
Diseases from abuse of voice, 204,
    212
Drama, Greek, 24
    Roman, 36
    mediæval, 42
Duration of vocal tones, 156, 157,
    159
Dust, ill-effects of inhalation of,
    210
Dyspepsia, deleterious influence of,
    on voice, 231
Dysphonia clericorum, 206, 212

E.

Echo, nature of, 57
Efforts, excessive vocal, 204, 224
Egyptians, 11
    their music, 13

Egyptians, their ideas of oratory, 12
Elements in the formation of voice, 80
  motor, 80, 96, 162
  resounding, 92, 126, 181
  vibrating, 86, 99, 114, 173
Epiglottis, description of, 85
  functions of, 127
Eustachian tube, 95
Evaporation from the skin, 244
Evolution of language, 2
  of singing, 8
Exercise in general, 239
  vocal, general effects of, 220
    local effects of, 202
Expiration, act of, 98
  in singing or speaking, 157
  muscles of, 83
Extension of vocal compass, 178
Extent, musical, of voice, 136

F.

Faculties of voice, 50
Falsetto-voice, laryngoscopic appearances in, 119
  muscular mechanism of, 122
Fatigue, effects of vocal, 204
Flannel as clothing, 246
Foggy air, 256
Food, animal, 226
  digestibility of, 229
  vegetable, 226
Foot-tons, calculation of exercise by, 242
Force or intensity of sound, 64
  of voice, 156
Fundamental tone, 69

G.

Germans, ancient, 9
Glandular sore throat, 206, 212

Glottis, 87, 115, 117
Glycerine for the voice, 217
Greeks, 15
  relations of, with Egypt, 15
  their drama, 24
  their medicine and hygiene of the voice, 29
  their music, 26
  their oratory and voice-training, 17
Growths in the larynx, 208
Gymnastics, general, 241
  vocal, 170, 176, 178, 184

H.

Hard-palate, 93, 130, 132
Harmonics, 68, 132, 133
Health, beneficial effects of vocal exercise on, 220
Holding the breath, 172
Hot climates, 253
Humidity of air, 255
Hydrogen, effects of, when respired, 53
Hygiene, definition of, 225
  general, in relation to voice, 220
  special, of vocal organs, 202

I.

Inspiration, act of, 82, 96
  in singing or speaking, 162
  muscles of, 82
Instruments, reed, 73
Intensity of sound, 64
  of voice, 156
Interjectional theory of the origin of words, 6
Intermittent illumination of larynx, 124

L.

Language, origin of, 2

Laryngoscope, 112

Larynx, anatomy of, 83
>> as viewed with the laryngoscope, 114, 116, 119, 124, 156
>> >> by intermittent light, 124

Larynx, cartilages of, 83
>> muscles of, 89
>> physiology of, 99, 114
>> variations of, in age and sex, 91

Laws, custom of singing, 10

Linen as clothing, 246

Lips, action of, in articulation, 94, 150, 185

Lower-jaw, in articulation, 94
>> in stuttering, 194

Lozenges, voice, 219

Lyric stage, invention of, 48

M.

Maladies from abuse of voice, 203, 206, 212

Management of articulating organs, 184
>> of breath, 162
>> of vocal reeds, 173

Marsh miasma, 254

Medicine of the voice, 214
>> among the ancients, 29

Membrane, mucous, 86

Mezzo-soprano voice, 136

Mountain air, 259

Mouth, breathing by the, 209, 211
>> resonance in, 132, 144, 184

Muscles of expiration, 83
>> of inspiration, 82
>> of larynx, 89

Music, Egyptian, 13
>> Greek, 26
>> Roman, 38
>> mediæval, 43

N.

Nasal timbre in instruments, 73
>> in voice, 133, 183

Nodal elevations on vocal bands, 175

Noise, as distinguished from music, 61

Nose, anatomy of, 93
>> breathing by the, 209, 213, 257
>> sounds of, 133, 183

Nostrums of eminent singers, 217

O.

Obesity, *see* Corpulence

Occupation, statistics of, in relation to health, 221

Ohm's law of hearing, 63

Onomatopœia, 6

Opera, invention of, 48

Opium or morphia, 219

Oratorio, 49

Organ, construction of pipes of, 74, 77, 130

Overtones, 68, 133

Oxygen, increased respiration of, during vocal exercise, 222
>> amount of, in air relative to climate, 255, 259

P.

Palate, hard, 93, 132
>> soft, 93, 134, 183

Partial tones, upper, 68, 133

Perspiration, 243, 247, 248

Pharynx, anatomy of, 92
>> resonance in, 131, 182

Pitch of sounds, 64

Preaching in the Primitive Church, 40

Pre-laryngoscopic theories of voice, 100

Prime tone, 68

Professional use of voice, statistics of, relative to health, 221

Pronunciation, 142, 184

Psellism, 186

R.

Reeds, production of sound by, 73

Register, chest, 117, 120, 139
  falsetto, 119, 122, 139

Registers of voice, limits of, 139

Resonance apparatus, 80
  action of, 126
  anatomy of, 92
  management of, 181

Resonators of Helmholtz, 70

Respiration, *see* Breathing

Respirator, use of, 257

Respiratory exercises, 170

Ribs, arrangement of, 81
  movements of, in breathing, 97

Romans, 33
  relations of, with Greece, 33
  their drama, 36
  their music, 38
  their oratory, 35

S.

Santorini, cartilages of, 86

Silk as clothing, 246

Singing, origin of, 8
  in the early Church, 43
  utility of, in rude ages, 9

Siren, the, 64

Skin, care of the, 243
  functions of the, 243

Smoking, effects of, 234

Soft-palate, 93, 134, 183

Sophists, extravagancies of, 18
  studies of, 18

Soprano voice, 136

Sound, definition of, 52
  intensity of, 64
  in tubes or pipes, 71
  pitch of, 64
  timbre of, 68
  transmission of, 52

Sound-waves, 54

Speaking machines, 262

Stammering and stuttering, 186
  gymnastic treatment of, 190
  mechanical treatment of, 188
  surgical treatment of, 195

Statistics (health) of professional use of the voice, 221

Stroke of the glottis, 176

Sustaining power of voice, 156, 157, 159

Syrinx or larynx of birds, 266

T.

Talking machines, 262

Teeth, use of, in articulation, 94, 150, 183

Temperate climates, 258

Tenor voice, 118, 136

Thorax, 81

Thyroid cartilage, 85, 125

Timbre, acoustic nature of, 68
  guttural, 131, 182
  nasal, 133, 183
  vowel, 142

Tobacco, effects of, on the system, 234

Tongue, action of, in articulation, 94, 145, 150, 185

Trachea, or wind-pipe, 83, 110

Tremolo, surmise as to formation of, 130

Tube, Eustachian, 95
    vocal, 72, 92, 126
Tubes, laws of sonorous vibrations
    in, 71

U.

Uvula, 93, 153

V.

Vegetarianism, 227
Veil of the palate, 93, 134, 183
Ventricles of larynx, 88, 126, 261
Ventricular bands, 88, 126
Vestibule of larynx, 80, 131
Vibration, sonorous, 58

Vocal bands or cords, 77, 86, 114,
    116, 156, 173
Voice in the lower animals, 264
Voice remedies, simple, 214
Volume of voice, 156
Vowels, formation of, 142
    pronunciation of, 184

W.

Water-waves and air-waves, 54,
    56
Whispering, nature of, 153
Wool as clothing, 246
Words, first sources of, 5
Wrisberg, cartilages of, 86

London : Pardon & Sons, Printers, Paternoster Row.

OPINIONS OF THE PRESS

ON THE

FIRST EDITION OF THIS WORK.

The Lancet, NOVEMBER 1, 1879.

"This book is well written, and gives evidence of great industry and considerable and varied learning on the part of the author. . . . The chapters on vocal culture will be appreciated by professional speakers and singers. . . . Contains many valuable hygienic hints. . . . The work is in every sense a creditable one."

The Saturday Review, NOVEMBER 8, 1879.

"He has evidently qualified himself for the study by researches. . . . . He has brought together much curious learning. . . . The copious and varied sources to which he has turned for his authorities sufficiently attest the pains he has taken. . . . Admirably illustrated. . . . The work is marked by sound sense throughout, and can be read with pleasure no less than profit."

Nature, JANUARY 22, 1880.

"We welcome with pleasure the appearance of a work which. . . . cannot fail to be largely useful. . . . Admirably given. . . . The value, therefore, of such information as is contained in this work, both to teachers and learners, can scarcely be overrated. . . . The advice the author gives, coming as it does from one having authority, is most valuable."—Dr. W. POLE, Mus. D., F.R.S.

Dublin Medical Journal, MARCH, 1880.

"Of great excellence. . . . The perusal of which will well repay any person interested in the art of singing, or in the physiology of the voice."

The Westminster Review, APRIL, 1880.

"A valuable book on the voice. . . . The various ways in which the voice may be injured and preserved, and its injuries remedied, are all carefully set forth, and the author's experience is here given in such a form as to be easily appreciated by all who have occasion to maintain the voice in a state of health."

The Athenæum, APRIL 24, 1880.

"Will be most useful. . . . The historical portion is highly interesting, and abstruse theories of the vocal mechanism are recapitulated, not in a dry and tedious manner. . . . The most original part of the treatise is the chapter on the hygiene of the voice, which treats of the influence of exercise on the vocal organs and the effect of different diet and modes of living on the powers of vocalization in a truly scientific spirit."

New York Medical Record, NOVEMBER 22, 1879.

"The elementary principles of sound are given in a very satisfactory manner. . . . The descriptions are much more clear and satisfactory than in ordinary books of physiology."

Philadelphia Medical Times, DECEMBER 6, 1879.

"We do not remember having ever read a book on this subject with more pleasure and profit to ourselves than this treatise. . . . We have no doubt but that both classes will derive great benefit from studying it and following its precepts. . . . The chapters on vocal culture and on hygiene of the voice. . . . are fully equal in excellence to the first chapters. . . . The woodcuts. . . . are very good."

Lightning Source UK Ltd.
Milton Keynes UK
UKOW06f2154131113

221059UK00006B/51/P